THE WILDS OF LONDON • JAMES GREENW(

Publisher's Note

The book descriptions we ask booksellers to display prominently warn that this is an historic book with numerous typos, missing text or index and is not illustrated.

We scanned this book using character recognition software that includes an automated spell check. Our software is 99 percent accurate if the book is in good condition. However, we do understand that even one percent can be a very annoying number of typos! And sometimes all or part of a page is missing from our copy of a book. Or the paper may be so discolored from age that you can no longer read the type. Please accept our sincere apologies.

After we re-typeset and design a book, the page numbers change so the old index and table of contents no longer work. Therefore, we usually remove them.

Our books sell so few copies that you would have to pay hundreds of dollars to cover the cost of proof reading and fixing the typos, missing text and index. Therefore, whenever possible, we let our customers download a free copy of the original typo-free scanned book. Simply enter the barcode number from the back cover of the paperback in the Free Book form at www.general-books.net. You may also qualify for a free trial membership in our book club to download up to four books for free. Simply enter the barcode number from the back cover onto the membership form on the same page. The book club entitles you to select from more than a million books at no additional charge. Simply enter the title or subject onto the search form to find the books.

If you have any questions, could you please be so kind as to consult our Frequently Asked Questions page at www.general-books.net/faqs.cfm? You are also welcome to contact us there. General Books LLC™, Memphis, USA, 2012. ISBN: 9781150791260.

⁕ ⁕ ⁕ ⁕ ⁕ ⁕ ⁕ ⁕

is the time for a fellow to take a walk through Brunswick. Street." "Why one in the morning, policeman?"

"Because they've hooked their fish and carried it home by that time, and the public-houses being shut up, are as drunk as they are likely to be for that night. That's when the hello begins, not before; when they've choused the flats of every rap they've got about 'em, and would rather have their room than their company. Why, you might walk through David's Lane, or Palmer's Folly, or White Hart Street this time o' night with a dimond pin in your shirt, as the saying is, and not so much as get it once snatched at. The tigers, as you call 'em, are all out hunting."

I expressed my sense of the obligation Mr. Policeman had conferred on me in terms that not only touched his heart but moved the forefinger of his right hand as high as the peak of his helmet, and then ventured further to inquire as to the favourite hunting grounds of the she-tigers. He was good enough to specify several. "There's the Globe and Pigeons," said he, "and the Gunboat, and the Malt Shovel, and the White Swan. However, if you want to find the last mentioned you mustn't ask after it by the name I've give it, which is the proper name; you must ask after it as ' Paddy's Goose;' that's what they call it in these parts."

I took leave of my friend, and walked up the Highway not a little perplexed as to what was to be done. I had come on purpose to view Tiger Bay—to witness what the constable graphically described as the "hello" when at its fullest blast.

That, however, could not be; it was not yet nine o'clock, and the "hello" did not commence until one. Besides, I was bound to confess to my dissatisfied self that I had been a little out in my calculations as to the nature of the said "hello." I Since this paper was written, Brunswick Street has been swept away by railway improvements.

...usive individual might spend an hour or so taking mental notes, nobody troubling his head about the matter; now, however, I had learned that it was a mere stronghold of dens to which were carried for picking and plucking the game after it had been run down and tethered, and I did not see my way quite so clearly. And in this unsettled condition of mind I went along, when suddenly the enlivening strains of music greeted my ear, and, looking towards the spot from whence it proceeded, beheld the " Globe and Pigeons" inscribed on a lamp. This was one of the camps of the "hunters " Mr. Policeman had mentioned.

Without further reflection on the matter, I crossed over, and, pushing open the swinging door, found myself in view of a dingy bar (still adorned with the garlands and mistletoe of Christmas), before which an old tigress, aged about sixty, and two young ones (one quite a cub—you could see, when she opened her mouth to swear, that her baby teeth were yet serrated and ungrown) were drinking gin. A mariner had "stood " the gin, and there leant against the counter with his face on his folded arms, his cap on the back of his head, and his favourite fore-lock dabbling in the glass of liquor that had been generously allotted him out of the half-pint he had paid for. I don't know whether he was crying, but he spoke as though he was, and with gin in his heart, gin in his head, gin in his hair, he was murmuring complaints against the eldest cub of the two on the score of her infidelity. The young tigress was for growling and showing her claws, but the gray old one wagged her head against any such premature proceeding, and poured out the cub some more gin, doubtless to assist her in bearing up against the mariner's unjust aspersions.

Passing this party, I spied a passage, and across the end of it hanging curtains of dirty chintz, through the chinks of which shone the glare of gas beyond; likewise there was to be heard the scraping of feet against the floor, and the twanging of a harp, and the shrill piping of a cornopean. No one hindering me or requiring to know where I was going, I approached the calico barrier to the realms of bliss, raised it, and entered.

If the spectacle revealed was not enchanting, it was at least highly curious. It was like being "behind the scenes " at a theatre during the pantomime season. A barn-like, long, narrow building with whitewashed walls, on which in flaming colours were a series of hideous pictures illustrative of the domestic habits and customs of the Chinese. There was a big fire-grate in the place, with a broad mantelpiece, on which reposed short pipes and splints, and a quart pot with beer in it, and with one of her naked arms resting lovingly against the pot, and a foot on the fender, stood the most magnificent female it was ever my lot to behold. Her hair was economized in its ornamentation of her fair head by a coronet of green leaves and pearls, and her maiden blushes were modestly screened from public gaze by a substantial coating of some ruddy pigment; her bodice was low, as were *not* her skirts, and she wore scarlet shoes with brass heels. Yet for all these fairy-like attributes she was not proud, for with *his* foot on the fender, and his elbow on the shelf, and a particularly short and dirty pipe in his mouth, stood a dirty-faced, unpleasant-looking person (the potman of the establishment), and she was talking quite familiarly with him.

The dance was just finished as I entered, and the mob, composed of tigresses and mariners (sailors of colliers as far as I could make out), mingled freely and partook of each other's beer. As for me, I took a seat in a corner, but had scarcely settled myself when up came a second fairy, *he facsimile* of the first, but shorter and somewhat thicker, and said she to me,

"Did you say 'bacca?"

"I did not say 'bacca, miss; what made you suppose that I did?" I replied. "Cause I've got it—screws and arf ounces, as well; an' cigars; and if you wants any you may as well have it of me."

And as she spoke she revealed a tumbler with the goods she mentioned in it. I did say," 'bacca " now, seeing that she had rather I would, and I gave her twopence for "arf a ounce" of ifc Discovering this second one, I looked about me for other fairies, but no more were discoverable. These were the only two, and they were the regularly engaged "dancing girls" of the establishment. This was evident, for on the musician stamping with his foot to notify that he was ready when his customers were, and no one being in a hurry to respond, the potman before mentioned called out to one of the fairies, "D'ye hear, Loo? Keep the game alive;" on which Loo seized on a mariner and danced him to the middle of the barn.

Her sister was likewise adjured by the authority before mentioned to keep the "pot bilin'," and though she still held the glass with the screws and arf ounces in it, and somebody had presented her with a ham sandwich, which occupied her other hand, she responded to the call with alacrity, tripping it before her partner, and supping on the bread and bacon the while. As for the tigresses assembled (a poor lot, by the way, and looking very shabby contrasted with the fairies), they didn't care a fig for dancing, preferring to purr and paw their victims to good humour at their ease; but the victims had come there to dance, and dance they would, so the tigresses were compelled to rise on their able legs, and stump through a polka or two with them.

Having my misgivings whether the Globe and Pigeons hunting ground was a fair representation of its kind, I by-and-by finished my beer, and slipped out. As I passed the bar I heard one mariner whisper to another that he had " had enough of this," and was going up to the Gunboat, so, keeping in his wake, I presently found myself at the hunting ground so named.

Along a passage exactly similar to that pertaining to the Globe and Pigeons (screened by exactly similar curtains), and except that it was somewhat larger, and had a sort of raised platform at the end, I found myself in an exactly similar barn, just as dirty as to its walls, and bespattered with saliva as to its floor, just as uncomfortable in every possible respect, and as suggestive of the wonder how it could prove attractive to any class of men possessed of the least degree of sense or decencyHere the tigresses assembled in greater numbers than at the Globe and Pigeons, and were of a different class, being better dressed, and ten times bolder and more foul-mouthed. From what stock they originally sprang is a mystery. It seems that they must have been from one and the same. Take fifty of them, and, setting aside trifling variations as regards complexion and colour of hair and eyes, they would pass as children of the same parents. The same short, bull-like throats, the same high cheek-bones and deep-set eyes, the same low retreating foreheads and straight wide mouths, and capacious nostrils, the same tremendous muscular development stamps one and all.

The sailors, too, were different from those met at the Globe and Pigeons, being, as could easily be seen, men in the merchant service. I am glad that I could make out no man-o'-war's men amongst them, since truth compels me to declare that a more spoony or weak-minded crew it was never my misfortune to fall in with. There was not a spark of dash or devil-maycare hilarity amongst them. There they sat (when they were not engaged in mooning through a dance), swilling beer, and gin, and rum, and shelling out their hard-earned money like melancholy idiots as frequently as the muscular tigresses chose to demand it of them, and submitting to abuse and insolence, and not unfrequently slaps on the face, tamely as henpecked husbands. Matters in this respect must have sadly altered; since Mr. Dibdin lived and wrote. Once upon a time, as we have reason to believe, there was truth in the maritime stave in which occur the lines—

"If we've peril on the seas, my boys, We've pleasure on the shore."

Pleasure! Perilous indeed must be the ordinary occupation of the man who can find delight and relaxation in being bullied and contemptuously treated by a brawny-armed, big-knuckled,. wretch, whose breath is pestilence and her language poison. Where amongst all these petticoated creatures was to be met the kind-hearted "Molly," who studied to an atom of sugar the flavour of her Thomas's grog, and was so sedulous as to the spotlessness of his unmentionables? It is scarcely saying too much that not one woman in ten getting drunk at that Wapping Gunboat would have scrupled to doctor her Thomas's grog with a dose of laudanum, while her only care as to the clean or dirty condition of the before-mentioned unmentionables would be the difference it would make in the price they would fetch at the "Dolly Shop," after she had stolen them from him.

She is an arrant thief, the modern Molly of Wapping, as it. was my painful lot to witness in the same Gunboat dancingroom. There was a young man there, not a common sailor I should judge from the cut of his clothes, and, being a fool like the rest, he went on melting his money in a rum measure until he came to the last of it. But he was youthful and gallant. So when a siren, with an arm which, delivered straight from the shoulder, might have floored a prize-fighter, tweaked him imperiously by his budding beard, and demanded "another jorum," he told her that he "hadn't another shot in the locker," but she might take his jacket, and sell it if she liked. "If I like!" replied the tigress, with a laugh louder than the dance music; "why, I'd sell your life if I had the chance."

So he took off his heavy pilot jacket, and while her companions yelled at the fun, she ran off, and in less than two minutes returned without the jacket, and with what might have been a shilling's worth of rum and water. That this was all the poor young man got for his property I am certain, for presently he made the unwelcome discovery that he had run out of tobacco. "Damme, Eva! (Heaver, it should have been) I've got no baccy!" "Then you're lucky in havin' a wesket as is as good as money," responded the gentle Eva, and instantly acting on the hint the gallant young fellow divested himself of this article of apparel, as well as the other (I was glad to perceive that he wore a coloured woollen shirt beneath), and, stepping fleetly off with it, his sweetheart promptly returned with half an ounce of tobacco as its equivalent. There was an old tigress of the Jewish persuasion who witnessed this little stroke of business, and even she called "shame;" but on being threatened with a " oner in the mouth" if she did not confine her attention to her own affairs, she prudently had no more to say about it.

I may as well mention that the amusements provided at this establishment differed materially from that offered at the Globe and Pigeons. Besides dancing, at the Gunboat there was clog-hornpiping and comic singing. For some time I had noticed a wretched-looking little boy with a monstrously big head, attired in a tight-fitting dress of some light-coloured material and with wooden shoes on his feet. He crept close to the fire, looking very unhappy and sleepy and surly, and I very much pitied the child (he could not have been more than eight years old) and wished it had been in my power to send him to bed, as a poor little drudge who had been hard at it all day cleaning pots and kettles and running about with beer. But lo! he presently turned out to be one of the "talented company." "Master Whatyercallem will oblige with a clog dance," cried the landlord (who was likewise M. C. and evidently on the best terms with the tigresses), and at once the young gentleman, whose name I couldn't catch, shuffled to the platform end of the room and commenced wearily footing it to the soul-stirring music emitted from the piano. "Chuck it out, Bill! chuck it out," the M.C. called in a sharp reproving tone, and Bill "chucked it out" spitefully, as though it was his malicious design to split his clogs and put his proprietor to the expense of buying him a new pair. However, he made a tremendous clatter, and appeared to give general satisfaction.

The comic singing was performed by the waiter, a poor object in shabby black, lame of a leg, and with a wen on his forehead. "Mr. Sidney Barry will be the next entertainment" was announced, and, limping to the stage and hunting out an old white hat from amongst some lumber that happened to be there, Mr. Barry put it on, and with a stick in his hand proceeded to make an entertainment of himself. His song was an Irish song entitled "Paddy don't care," and its success with the audience seemed to depend entirely on the singer's ability to deliver himself of a roaring devil-may-care laugh and dealing a terrific whack to the floor boards at the close of each verse. The waiter had no voice for singing, but long practice had made his drunken laugh perfection itself, and he was tolerably strong in the arm, so that the applause was universal, and quite a brisk shower of copper money fell on the platform as the reward of his exertions.

Quitting the Gunboat, I discovered and looked in at the other hunting grounds Mr. Policeman had mentioned, but in the main they were all alike. There was the spoony sailor, and there was the tigress of the Bay. At some of the larger houses, such as Paddy's Goose, and the Angel and Crown, and the Sailors' Saloon, her coat was sleeker and glossier—she sported amber and satin and blue and ermine (very favourite with the well-to-do, middle-aged, and corpulent tigresses), but she was still the same heartless, cold-blooded animal, with a mouth brimming with blasphemy, and claws concealed beneath her dainty kid glove ready for rending and pillage. I don't see what is to be done with her, but decidedly she is a person to be put down—or at least checked in her depredations on the kind-hearted donkey in the blue-jacket, who, knowing woman in no other shape (for your tigress in brown serge or blue satin infests every port), is content to pay homage to her in this, and wag his head good humouredly while she bullies him, and call it a " spree" when she robs him, and goes to sea again and again, filling his glass to her amongst his foc'sall mates a thousand miles at sea, and toasts her as "Faithful Poll of Wapping." *AN EVENING AT A WHITECHAPEL "GAFF.* TIT APPENING to pass that way in the morning, I was just in time to witness a gentleman belonging to the establishment (a lank, dirty-bearded gentleman he was, who smoked a dirty pipe, and wore the sleeves of his dirty shirt rolled above his dirty elbows) engaged in affixing to a great board that hung against the "gaff" door an announcement of a new piece to be produced that evening.

It was an announcement calculated to arrest the attention of the passers-by, being inscribed in bold and flourishing red and blue letters on orange-coloured cardboard, and that it was the work of the gentleman who published it was evident from the fact that his face and hands and the sides of his trousers were smudged with the same brilliant colours. "Astounding!" (in blue); "Startling!!" (in red); "Don't miss it!!!" (in red and blue artistically blended) were the head-lines of the placard, which further went on to inform the public that that evening "your old favourites," Mr. and Mrs. Douglas Fitzbruce, would appear, with the rest of the talented company, in a new and original equestrian spectacle entitled "Gentleman Jack, or the Game of High Toby," with real horses and a real carriage. By the time the person with the short pipe had finished tacking up the placard, and had added a few additional touches by means of a small paint-brush to the most telling lines, several young men and women of the neighbourhood had congregated to spell and discuss its contents. Their criticism was highly favourable. They prognosticated that it would be a "clippin'" piece, not only on account of the real horses, but because Mrs. Douglas Fitzbruce was a "reg'lar stunner" in the highwayman line. The majority of the critics vowed "strike them blind" if they wouldn't come and cee it, while the rest promised themselves the treat provided they could raise the ha'pence. As for me, I made up my mind on the spot.

"First performance at half-past six," the bill stated, and, desirous of obtaining a front seat, I was at the "gaff" door at least twenty minutes earlier. Not early enough, however. The "pit" and "box" passages leading to the inner doors were already densely thronged, and that by individuals who would not submit to elbowing. I did not attempt it. No one is so tenacious of his rights to recognition as a fellow-man as the budding costermonger aged fifteen or sixteen, and no one is readier to uphold his dignity than the female of his bosom, who, although a year or two younger, comes of a stock that will stand no nonsense. The mob pressing about the gaff were nearly all of the sort indicated; the exception being a few old men and a few children.

In a few minutes the doors were opened, and we were admitted—the box customers on payment of twopence, and the pit customers at the rate of a penny each. It was not a commodious building, nor particularly handsome, the only attempt at embellishment appearing at the stage end, where for the space of a few feet the plaster wall was covered with ordinary wall paper of a grape-vine pattern, and further ornamented by coloured and spangled portraits of Mrs. Douglas Fitzbruce In her celebrated characters of "Cupid" and "Lady Godiva." There were many copies of these portraits, and they were ticketed for sale—the former at sixpence, and the latter at ninepence; though why the difference is hard to say, since in the matter of spangling, or, indeed, any other kind of covering, the cost of producing Lady Godiva must have been even less than that incurred in perfecting the print of the "God of Love." The stage itself was a mere platform of rough boards; the seats in the pit were of the same material. The boards that were the box seats, however, were planed, and, further to insure the comfort of the gentility patronizing that part of the theatre, there were written bills posted up to the effect that "smoking and spitting was objected to on account of fire," but as the audience treated this vague and contradictory notice with well-merited con-

tempt, I was not sorry that I could advance no closer than the back seat of all.

The performance was commenced by a black man,—a brawny ruffian, naked to the waist, and with broad rings of red round his ankles and wrists, illustrative, as presently appeared, of his suffering from the chafing of the manacles he had worn in a state of slavery. It was a very long descriptive ballad, set to the not over lively tune of "Mary Blane," and the audience—who had possibly heard it on a few previous occasions—at the termination of the fifth verse expressed a desire that the singer should "cut it short," and on the oppressed negro taking no notice of the intimation, but beginning the sixth verse in all coolness, somebody threw a largish crust of bread at him, which narrowly missed his head, and somebody else threw a fish-bone with more certain aim, so that it was lodged in the unfortunate African's wool, and there instantly followed an explosion of mirth that by no means tended to solace the indignity cast on him. He glared to the right and the left of him, and, apparently marking the delinquent in the pit, jumped off the stage and rushed towards him. What then transpired I cannot say, not being in a position to see, but after a minute of uproar, and cursing, and swearing, and yelling laughter, the black man scrambled on to the stage again with a good deal of the blacking rubbed off his face, and with his wool wig in his hand, exposing his proper short crop of carroty hair. "Now look/ here!" exclaimed he, with a desperate, but not entirely successful, effort to deliver himself in a calm and impassionate manner, "Looky' here, if you thinks by a-choking me off to get at the new piece a bit the sooner you're just wrong. When I've done a-singin' my song then the piece'll be ready and not a oat before, and the more you hinterrupts why the longer you'll be kept a-waitin', that's all." And having expressed these manly and British sentiments in genuine Whitechapel English, he readjusted his wig and became once more an afflicted African bewailing how

"Cruel massa stole him wife and lily

piccaninny," and continued without further interruption till he had accomplished the eighth verse, and was about to commence the ninth when some one behind the scenes audibly whispered, " Off, Ginger," and off he went, and the star of the evening, Gentleman Jack, came in with a bound and a bow that elicited even a louder roar from the company than had greeted the lodgment of the fish-bone in Ginger's wool.

It was Mrs. Douglas Fitzbruce fully equipped for the "High Toby game." She wore buckskin shorts, and boots of brilliant polish knee high and higher, and with spurs to them; her coat was of green velvet slashed with crimson, with a neat little breast pocket, from which peepedacambrichandkerchief; herraven curls hung about her shoulders, and on her head was a three-cornered hat, crimson edged with gold; under her arm she carried a riding whip, and in each hand a pistol of large size. By way of thanking her friends in the boxes and pit for their generous greeting (it is against the law for the actors to utter so much as a single word during the performance of a "gaff" piece), she uttered a saucy laugh (she could not have been more than forty-five), and, cocking her firearms, "let fly" at them point blank as it seemed; however, the whistling and stamping of feet that immediately ensued showed that nobody was wounded—indeed, that the audience rather enjoyed being shot at than otherwise.

Being debarred the use of speech, the bold highwayman was driven to the exercise of his vocal talent, in order to explain his own game in general, and the High Toby game in particular. The highwayman sang a song all about another highwayman, who, "mounted on his mare, with his barkers at his belt," boldly faced an old miller "jogging home from market," and appropriated his bag of gold after blowing his brains out. Also how the same thief and murderer was pursued by Bow Street runners—one a blue-eyed man. But the " High Toby" boy, turning about in his saddle, took aim with his pistol at the runner and fired, and—

"His eyes of a colour a minute ago, Were now one of 'em *red* and the t'other one blue"—

a jocular result which the company assembled seemed keenly to appreciate. It terminated the song, and besides shouts of "Hencore!" and stamping and whistling, there was a cry of "Chuck 'em on!" followed by a casting of halfpence on to the stage. Not many, however; not more than amounted to sixpence; but the dashing highwayman seemed very grateful, and looked after the rolling coins with an avidity that showed how ill he could afford to forego the smallest of them.

Presently in rushed another highwayman, seedier than Gentleman Jack. This was Mr. Douglas Fitzbruce, and, from his being pitted with small-pox, and having a slight squint in his right eye, I at once recognized in him the gentleman who had nailed up the outside poster in the morning. He came in for some applause, but chiefly from the female portion of the audience, the males appearing to entertain feelings of envy and jealousy against him as the lawful proprietor of the lady in the long boots.

The second highwayman, who was greeted as Tom King, seemed in a tremendous hurry about something. He slapped his breast energetically, and pointed repeatedly and determinedly in a certain direction; on which Gentleman Jack started violently and commenced to load his pistols to their muzzles with powder and ball, the other highwayman following his example. Then Gentleman Jack straddled his legs and bobbed up and down, working his arms "as though he held reins in his hands, as an intimation to the second highwayman that he wanted his horse; then, waving their hats in the most daring and gallant manner, they both rushed off.

After a lapse of about a minute a hurricane of applause welcomed the approaching sound of horse's hoofs, and presently appeared Gentleman Jack, with a bit of black crape concealing the upper part of his features, on horseback. It was a remarkably docile horse, not to say a subdued one, and hung its big head down to its thick and heavy legs in a decidedly sleepy manner. Properly, I believe, he should have showed his high mettle by rearing and plunging a bit when Gentleman Jack spurred him, but though the bold rider sawed at its bit until the animal's toothless gums were visible, and spurred it until the rowels were completely clogged with the yielding hair of its flanks, it only wagged its tail languidly and snorted. Again was the sound of approaching hoofs heard, this time accompanied by the rumbling of wheels, and Gentleman Jack, rising in his stirrups, detected the sound and gave a low whistle, which was responded to, and Tom King promptly made his appearance with black crape on his face, and a naked sword in one hand and a horse pistol in the other. Then the highwaymen clasped hands, and looked upwards, as though calling on the gods to witness the compact they had made to stick to each other till the death.

Now all was ready for the robbery, but it couldn't come off for some unknown reason. The rumbling of wheels had stopped suddenly, though the sound of hoofs had not, and there were heard as well strange muffled "clucking" noises, as of men urging on a horse disinclined to move. This rather spoilt the scene, for the gentlemen of the audience having a practical knowledge of donkeys and horses, and of the obstinate fits that occasionally seize on those animals, instantly guessed the difficulty, and gleefully shouted suggestions as to the proper mode of treatment to be applied to the quadruped that was stopping the play. "Hit him on the 'ock!" "Twist the warmint's tail!" "Shove him up behind!" Which —if either—of these suggestions was adopted I cannot say, but suddenly the vehicle that contained the highwaymen's booty bolted on to the stage, amid the uproarious plaudits of the spectators.

It was not a very magnificent turn-out, being nothing else indeed than an old street cab drawn by a vicious brother of the animal Gentleman Jack rode, and made to look slightly like a chariot by the driver's seat being set round with coloured chintz, hammer-cloth wise. A driver in a cocked hat sat on the box, and a footman with a cocked hat stood

card in his hand. It was blackbordered, and as he offered it to me he remarked,

"Did yer know him?"

As he spoke he laid his finger on the name of "Jemmy Baldwin," printed on the black-bordered ticket. I replied that I wasn't quite sure that I did know him, but at the same time inquired what was the matter with Jemmy.

"Snuffed it," replied the gruff man impressively—" snuffed it, and left the missus and the kids—eight on 'em—in Queer Street. Howsomever, take a ticket; it's only threepence, and then you'll know all about it."

I took the ticket, which informed a sympathetic public that "Jemmy Baldwin had died sudden, leaving nothing to bury him," and "that a few friends would meet that (Sunday) night at the Tinkers' Arms, Spicer Street, for the benefit of the widow and orphans. P.S.—Mr. Cullum will show his celebrated battling finch." The last line decided me as to my line of conduct.

Between seven and eight that evening I once more found my way to the Tinkers' Arms, and on producing my ticket was directed to the "parlour," which was at the end of a passage and down a flight of steps, giving rise to the supposition that the chamber now so called was at one time a kitchen or beercellar. Early in the night as it was, the aspect of the parlour was significant of the esteem in which the late Jemmy Baldwin was held. Capable of accommodating about twenty-five persons comfortably, the parlour was made to hold at least seventy, and as there was a tremendous fire in the grate, and at least half the seventy were tobacco smokers, the terrible fog that came lazily belching out on one as the door was opened may be easily imagined. At first glance I thought that there could not possibly be room for another individual, but my friend with the gruff voice was there, and, recognizing me, rose and beckoned me with the stem of his pipe to come and sit beside him, an invitation I at once availed myself of.

"Rather crowded," I remarked.

"Will be bimeby," replied the gruff man. "Cullum ain't come yet, but he's sent his finch. That's Cullum's finch over agin the chimbley. That there back cage with the black crape on it is Jemmy's goldfinch, poor feller."

Whether the gruff man's expression of compassion was intended for the deceased Jemmy or the goldfinch was not clear, but certainly the bird, whose cage was in mourning, was not SUNDAY EVENING WITH THE "FANCY." unworthy of pity. There it hung, poor little creature, and there, as I could contrive to make out through the dense fog of tobacco smoke, now that my attention was specially called to the matter, hung thirty or forty small birdcages, each with an occupant. On every table in the room, further sweltered and stifled by having its habitation enveloped in a handkerchief, were at least half-a-dozen similar cages, and the birds within could be heard hopping about and chirping as merry as crickets. Will any learned ornithologist kindly unravel the mystery? How is it that my goldfinch would die before morning if I were guilty of the barbarity of hanging him on retiring to bed beneath my bed-curtains, and that the "muffin man's" goldfinch retains its sprightliness in an atmosphere foul enough to poison a well-sinker? How is it that any dicky-bird of mine will pine and die if the smallest quantity of tainted matter is allowed to remain in his house, while cat's-meat sellers with impunity combine the bird-dealing business with their proper one, and perch their "store cages," containing songsters of every kind—including that ethereal creature, the skylark—on mounds of feculent horseflesh in their shop-windows?

To return, however, to the parlour of the Tinkers' Arms. Not for the sake of anything that remains to be said concerning poor Mr. Baldwin's benefit, or the show of birds that graced it. The " show" meant nothing at all, and why on earth the gentlemen who met to smoke their pipes could not have left their finches at home was altogether a puzzle. In nine cases out of ten the cages that were brought in tied in a handkerchief remained so standing on the table by the side of the owner's pint-pot during the hour or so that I remained in the room, nobody inquiring after the sweet-throated tenants, or making, as far as I could see, the slightest allusion to them. I inquired of my gruff-voiced friend (who, by-the-by, turned out to be a very decent fellow) where was the use of bringing the birds if they didn't uncover them for people to see. "Oh, I don't know," he replied. "It's their fancy, don't yer know) that and flash ness," an explanation which I submit to the reader without a word of comment.

By nine o'clock the room became at least thirty per cent, more crowded than when I entered it, and I was not sorry to. hear my gruff friend presently remark that he had had almost enough of it. "Besides," said he, "I promised to look in at the Ship in Hunt Street; there's a dawg-show there to-night; Lemike's in the chair. Lemike's a-goin' to show his white bulldawg, and King's dawg Prince 'H be there."

"I'll take a turn there with you if you like," said I, and away we went there and then.

Hunt Street is a rather dark street, and the Ship Tavern not so brilliantly illuminated as it might be; but there was no difficulty in discovering it, knowing beforehand that dogs were there assembled. The deep-mouthed barking of bulldogs, the sharp challenging bark of the English terrier, the pettish, snappish bark of the spaniels and "toys" blended to make an uproar not commonly heard. The gruff-voiced man led the way past the bar, before which a dozen or so of doggy men, with their canine property in their arms, or between their legs, were carousing, and into a room beyond.

In all respects it was an inferior spectacle to that presented by the lively room at the Tinkers' Arms. The room itself was filthy in the extreme; its walls and ceiling black with tobacco smoke, and the atmosphere of the place simply pestilential. As for the company—dogs and men—the former, though possibly in a minority, formed by far the most respectable portion —indeed, it was quite saddening to see some of the well-bred dogs in such detestable company.

The chairman was not at his post, a circumstance that seemed to puzzle the company generally not a little, as Mr. Lemike was known to be the most punctual of men, and always proud and happy to bring his pets to a show. But, alas for poor Mr. Lemike! his absence was presently accounted for. It was sorrow and deep distress that kept him away from the Ship that night. Himself a publican, the police had most provokingly paid an untimely visit to his house a day or two before, and there discovered *fifty-three* young thieves and their sweethearts engaged in a raffle in Mr. Lemike's tap-room; jQ$ was the penalty in which the unfortunate publican was mulct, with the magisterial intimation that it would be wasting his time to apply next March for a renewal of his licence. No wonder that Mr. Lemike had no heart for dog-shows that Sunday night.

The place was crowded, and there was scarcely standing room, so that, until you took courage from the indifference displayed by the company generally, one could not help feeling slightly nervous at the close proximity of furious bull-dogs, with glaring eyes and lolling tongues, savage at sight of each other, and not improbably hard-pressed by thirst in that hot, close den, and panting for the blood of the first creature they could plant their teeth in. True, their masters, not caring to trust to their leash, held them each by the collar as a policeman holds a thief; but this seemed only to increase their fury, and they strained and strove, as only a bull-dog can, to break away, and then, with one's calf within a foot of the monsters' jaws, and not even the protection of a Wellington boot, came the thrilling reflection, " If it should!"

Different, too, from the bird-show was the present exhibition in the matter of passive enjoyments of the " fancy" involved. Louder even than the barking of the bigger dogs was the uproar of shock-headed, loud-mouthed ruffians extolling the qualities of their canine pets, and staking the security of their eyes and limbs—of their lives even— on the truth of the barefaced lies that came so freely from their blasphemous mouths. Matches for dog to fight dog, for dogs to kill rats against time, and against each other, and for dogs to "show for points," were yelled out with many oaths, and with a horrible din that made one shudder. And in this precious amusement, in this one foul pot-house, were engaged at least sixty men, all on a Sunday evening.

There is always to be met an exception to the prevailing rule, and it was not wanting on the present occasion. This was a man with a bull-dog pup, who sat in a corner nursing his pet, and speaking not until he was spoken to. He was a middleaged man this, with long, well-oiled hair, the ends of which were trained to turn under, and, as was plain to be seen, his hair and his pup were that man's chief treasures on earth. It was almost melancholy to reflect that human hair *will* decay as age creeps on— that puppies will grow and assume the stature of mature dogs. It was a white puppy, and he nursed it like a baby, with its hideous head resting against his greasy bosom. Alternately he sleeked his hair and coaxed it to remain turned under at the ends, and fondled the bull-dog, and tenderly rubbed its gums with his forefinger. "That's a pooty thing," remarked a connoisseur; "what might be the age on it?"—" Seven months and a week," replied the oily man, looking up with almost maternal pride in his eyes; "it's pooty, as you say, now, but what will it be bimeby?" THREE YEARS QF PENAL SER VITUDE. TT is not necessary for me to tell my name, the exact nature of the offence of which I was convicted, or the precise date of the conviction. I may say, however, and the reader may take it as truth—as indeed he may every line that is here printed —that up to the time when I was arrested I never before in my life knew what that sort of trouble was—never was locked up for so long as a single night, or saw the inside of a stationhouse cell.

How my misfortune came about is easy enough to explain. I was a young man, and I lodged away from home; and I liked to do as other young men, go about a bit of evenings to see a play, or hear a song along with two or three mates employed at our firm, and young fellows like myself. That led to my picking up a sweetheart—a thorough good girl—and we kept company. She worked in the day, and had her evenings, and of course I took her out. Then the game that cost me three years' liberty began. My wages were only eighteen shillings a week, and out of that I paid twelve for board and lodging and washing, so that there was only six left for clothes, going out, tobacco, and everything. I won't state the nature of the goods our firm dealt in, but half a crown's worth might easily be stowed in the waistcoat-pocket, and in a manner of speaking you were free to help yourself out of thousands of pounds' worth.

The young woman just mentioned was very respectable, and dressed well; and so was I well-dressed, and, as she thought, respectable too. I went on courting her honourable, and from the first meaning to marry her, but I didn't have the pluck to tell her how small my wages were. If I had it would have opened her eyes at once, so I kept it dark, and by-and-by we got married, and still I didn't tell her how much I got a week. I asked her what she thought she could do comfortably with, and she said she thought she could do with a guinea if I bought my own tobacco and beer. "Very well," I says, "then it shall be a guinea a week, my dear."

That was three shillings more than I was earning, and of course it had to be made up, and I needn't again mention how, and things went on pretty comfortable (barring the thought that would at times come across me of the kick-up there would if I should be found out) for a year. We had two rooms nicely furnished (for Jenny was a beautiful little manager) and come the time a baby was born—a boy it was. That seemed the beginning of the down-hill. Everything was more expensive, she was ill a longish time, and the firm suffered. I was wretched for weeks and weeks before the blow-up came, and in my own mind was not at all surprised when on leaving the warehouse one evening a man whom I knew in an instant, in spite

ed work, if the red end, that your wants were of a personal nature.

In the course of the day the barber came and shaved off what little whiskers I had, and cut my hair close. If a Millbank prisoner is any trade that can be made useful in the prison he is set at it, but men of no trade are put to mat-making and tailoring (and they know all about that without asking, since a record of your trade, crime, and conviction, together with every antecedent that may affect you as a prisoner, attends you to every prison after leaving Newgate). I was no trade, and by-and-by the master tailor brought me a pair of blue serge trousers, already cut out, and some needles and thread, and showed me how to stitch the seams; and I was kept to work at tailoring all the time I was there, which, I am happy to say, was not long, the batch of which I was one remaining at Millbank only until some men were drafted off from Pentonville to Portland to make room. The horrible gloom of the place made it so terrible. The victuals was neither bad nor scanty. At breakfast you got a pint of cocoa and what I should think was fully three-quarters of a pound of bread; at dinner a pint of soup, five ounces of meat, and a pound of potatoes; and at supper a pint of gruel and a slice of bread. The knife allowed at dinner was a tin knife and no fork. You can neither stab a warder with a tin knife nor use it as a picklock, though it is quite sharp enough to sever the meat, boiled to, rags as it is at Millbank. The work was not particularly hard. You might almost take your own time at the tailoring, and all else you had to do was to exercise for an hour about the crank that raises the water to the upper cisterns of the prison; a quarter of an hour at pumping, and a quarter at marching up and down, off and on. But, as I said before, it is such a terribly gloomy place—gloomy walls, gloomy faces, gloomy silence, nothing but gloom from bell-ring in the morning till bell-ring at night. It was almost like escaping to actual liberty when one evening, after three weeks at Millbank, I got a hint that in the morning I formed one of a gang going to Pentonville.

The first step towards my transfer from Millbank was not of a sort to impress me favourably with my prospects. After an early breakfast we were brought out of the cells and each fitted with a " bracelet," the lock of which was a sort of cap through which was a hole. As we stood in rows of ten, with the handcuff on, a chain was threaded through the hollow caps and secured at the ends—not a very stout chain, but quite strong enough for the purpose.

As though to make amends, however, for this degradation, our conveyance was not the prison van, but a genteel private omnibus, with covered seats. Being chained together, we could not enter and take our seats like ordinary omnibus passengers, but the leading man entering the 'bus on the righthand walked right round it and finally took his seat next the door on the left-hand side, the rest of course following, and taking their seats in order. A warder sat inside with us, and there was another outside as conductor; it was a beautiful sunny morning, and quite a treat to look out through the windows, and see all the life and bustle of the streets, people going where they liked, and laughing and talking, and smoking comfortable pipes some of them, which last, to a man who has never missed his half an ounce of tobacco a day until two months ago he was shut out from it, is a much more tantalizing sight to witness than might be imagined.

Soon as we reached Pentonville we were again stripped and bathed, a suit of clothes lying ready for each bather. The clothes were as nearly as possible like those of Millbank, but the cell in which I presently found myself was more cheerful looking than the one at Millbank, and more resembled that at Newgate, with the additional convenience of a drawer fixed under one of the shelves. By-the-way, I should have mentioned that after bathing, and before dressing, the doctor made his appearance and thoroughly examined me, and asked me just the same sort of questions as I have heard that they ask people who go to insure their lives. Nor are they at Pentonville more careless about your education than your bodily health. The very first visitor that came to my cell was the schoolmaster, who sounded me as to the extent of my scholastic knowledge, and shortly afterwards supplied me with two books of arithmetic, a geography, a dictionary, an atlas, and a slate and pencil; which, with the Bible, and Prayer-book, and Hymn-book brought with me from Millbank, made quite a show, ranged on my shelf. Beside these books, if you behave as you ought, you are allowed to borrow one from the school library, the library books being of the "Leisure Hour" and "Sunday at Home" kind. I had but one half-day at school in a week, but there were some—the most ignorant—who had two half-days. The prison chapel is used as the school-room, and the same rule as regards keeping silence towards each other is observed as rigidly there as in every other part of the prison. There are two warders on duty in the school-room, perched in something like pulpits, so that they can see all about them. But they cannot stop talking entirely either in the school or in chapel; at the latter place especially it is indulged in. The prisoners sit in gangs all in a row of a dozen or so, every prisoner having a space of about six feet between himself and his neighbour, a warder being attached to each gang to see that order is kept. Some of the old hands, however, are too knowing for him. Long practice has taught them how to talk without moving their lips, and it is not uncommon to see the warder in command staring his hardest along the row and scrutinizing the face of every man with a most perplexed face of his own. He is certain that talking in an undertone is going on. He can hear the mysterious sounds, but every face is to the right and every eye devoutly fixed on the parson. There was one warder, however, who was particularly acute in detecting the talkers, instantly pouncing on them and conducting them back to their cell for punishment. It was understood amongst us that the warder in question had made the discovery that although it was possible to utter sounds more or less intelligi-

ed work, if the red end, that your wants were of a personal nature.

In the course of the day the barber came and shaved off what little whiskers I had, and cut my hair close. If a Millbank prisoner is any trade that can be made useful in the prison he is set at it, but men of no trade are put to matmaking and tailoring (and they know all about that without asking, since a record of your trade, crime, and conviction, together with every antecedent that may affect you as a prisoner, attends you to every prison after leaving Newgate). I was no trade, and by-and-by the master tailor brought me a pair of blue serge trousers, already cut out, and some needles and thread, and showed me how to stitch the seams; and I was kept to work at tailoring all the time I was there, which, I am happy to say, was not long, the batch of which I was one remaining at Millbank only until some men were drafted off from Pentonville to Portland to make room. The horrible gloom of the place made it so terrible. The victuals was neither bad nor scanty. At breakfast you got a pint of cocoa and what I should think was fully three-quarters of a pound of bread; at dinner a pint of soup, five ounces of meat, and a pound of potatoes; and at supper a pint of gruel and a slice of bread. The knife allowed at dinner was a tin knife and no fork. You can neither stab a warder with a tin knife nor use it as a picklock, though it is quite sharp enough to sever the meat, boiled to, rags as it is at Millbank. The work was not particularly hard. You might almost take your own time at the tailoring, and all else you had to do was to exercise for an hour about the crank that raises the water to the upper cisterns of the prison; a quarter of an hour at pumping, and a quarter at marching up and down, off and on. But, as I said before, it is such a terribly gloomy place— gloomy walls, gloomy faces, gloomy silence, nothing but gloom from bell-ring in the morning till bell-ring at night. It was almost like escaping to actual liberty when one evening, after three weeks at Millbank, I got a hint that in the morning I formed one of a gang going to Pentonville.

The first step towards my transfer from Millbank was not of a sort to impress me favourably with my prospects. After an early breakfast we were brought out of the cells and each fitted with a " bracelet," the lock of which was a sort of cap through which was a hole. As we stood in rows of ten, with the handcuff on, a chain was threaded through the hollow caps and secured at the ends—not a very stout chain, but quite strong enough for the purpose.

As though to make amends, however, for this degradation, our conveyance was not the prison van, but a genteel private omnibus, with covered seats. Being chained together, we could not enter and take our seats like ordinary omnibus passengers, but the leading man entering the 'bus on the righthand walked right round it and finally took his seat next the door on the left-hand side, the rest of course following, and taking their seats in order. A warder sat inside with us, and there was another outside as conductor; it was a beautiful sunny morning, and quite a treat to look out through the windows, and see all the life and bustle of the streets, people going where they liked, and laughing and talking, and smoking comfortable pipes some of them, which last, to a man who has never missed his half an ounce of tobacco a day until two months ago he was shut out from it, is a much more tantalizing sight to witness than might be imagined.

Soon as we reached Pentonville we were again stripped and bathed, a suit of clothes lying ready for each bather. The clothes were as nearly as possible like those of Millbank, but the cell in which I presently found myself was more cheerful looking than the one at Millbank, and more resembled that at Newgate, with the additional convenience of a drawer fixed under one of the shelves. By-the-way, I should have mentioned that after bathing, and before dressing, the doctor made his appearance and thoroughly examined me, and asked me just the same sort of questions as I have heard that they ask people who go to insure their lives. Nor are they at Pentonville more careless about your education than your bodily health. The very first visitor that came to my cell was the schoolmaster, who sounded me as to the extent of my scholastic knowledge, and shortly afterwards supplied me with two books of arithmetic, a geography, a dictionary, an atlas, and a slate and pencil; which, with the Bible, and Prayer-book, and Hymn-book brought with me from Millbank, made quite a show, ranged on my shelf. Beside these books, if you behave as you ought, you are allowed to borrow one from the school library, the library books being of the "Leisure Hour" and "Sunday at Home" kind. I had but one half-day at school in a week, but there were some—the most ignorant—who had two half-days. The prison chapel is used as the schoolroom, and the same rule as regards keeping silence towards each other is observed as rigidly there as in every other part of the prison. There are two warders on duty in the school-room, perched in something like pulpits, so that they can see all about them. But they cannot stop talking entirely either in the school or in chapel; at the latter place especially it is indulged in. The prisoners sit in gangs all in a row of a dozen or so, every prisoner having a space of about six feet between himself and his neighbour, a warder being attached to each gang to see that order is kept. Some of the old hands, however, are too knowing for him. Long practice has taught them how to talk without moving their lips, and it is not uncommon to see the warder in command staring his hardest along the row and scrutinizing the face of every man with a most perplexed face of his own. He is certain that talking in an undertone is going on. He can hear the mysterious sounds, but every face is to the right and every eye devoutly fixed on the parson. There was one warder, however, who was particularly acute in detecting the talkers, instantly pouncing on them and conducting them back to their cell for punishment. It was understood amongst us that the warder in question had made the discovery that although it was possible to utter sounds more or less intelligi-

catgut. A pound and a quarter does not seem much, and it doesn't look much—a piece as thick as a man's wrist and as long as his hand would weigh a pound I should say—but a pound and a quarter of it to a man whose fingers are as soft as a woman's, and who hasn't the least idea how to go about it, is a tremendous day's work. I knew that for the first four or five days I was at work on it from morning till night, with my nails broken andfmy fingers bleeding, and even then it was not done so well as it should have been —at least, so the warder said when he came to "weigh it away." The oakum is weighed after picking as well as before, a slight allowance being made for dust and waste—a precaution that seems unnecessary, only that (and I don't think I before mentioned it) there is a water-closet in the cell, and it would be easy to stow some of it there.

For breakfast I got one pint of gruel and a half-pound of bread—both very good. Then a bit of work till ten o'clock, when the chapel bell rang, and we were filed out and marched to chapel, where we heard a chapter read out of the Bible and a hymn sung, and then marched back to the cells again. At twelve o'clock dinner was brought, which I may as well here mention consisted, three days out of the seven, of a pint of meat soup and half-pound of bread, and the other four days of four ounces of meat and a pound of potatoes. During the day one hour's exercise in the yard is allowed—that is, you walk round and round with the rest unceasingly for an hour. At five o'clock, supper, as before mentioned.

After a man's conviction one visitor is allowed, and, if necessary, you may write a letter to the friend you wish to come and see you. The prison authorities find you in note-paper and an envelope, though if a man wanted to write to a relation who moved in respectable society he would much rather be allowed to find his own writing materials, since those that are provided for you are stamped "Gaol of Newgate" in black printed letters both on the paper and the envelope. I of course had a friend come to see me—poor little woman! She had found out all about it by this time, all about the small wages I had always had, and the rest of it; and p'r'aps being fond of each other, she found more excuse for me than I deserved. She would have given something considerable, I'll wager, to have got close enough to shake hands. But there is no shaking hands between Newgate prisoners and their friends. There is a grated door and a cross-passage about six or eight feet from it, and in this passage your visitor stands along with a warder. That's how I saw my wife that day, looking through the iron grating, and that's how she saw me. For her sake, I was sorry that she came at all, and for my sake, too, for that matter, though I suppose it all went to make up the punishment I deserved, but never till it was my good luck to see it again could I get her woful face out of my sight, as I saw it that afternoon. It was worse to me than the oakum-picking, the knowledge that I was a convict—everything.

One day is so much like another in a gaol that I need not describe day by day the time I spent at Newgate. I was a month in that prison, and began to wonder if they meant keeping me there altogether, when one morning I was made aware that something unusual was about to take place, for they brought me no oakum to pick, and the breakfast made its appearance at least twenty minutes earlier than was common. But I was not kept long in suspense. Immediately after breakfast I was led from my cell to a great room, where were a goodish number of prisoners already, and a warder was busy taking handcuffs and anklets out of a canvas bag, and fitting them on to the prisoners wrists and ankles. Then I heard it whispered that we were going to Millbank. At first I wondered why some men were coupled two and two by the leg, a chain about as thick as a trace chain connecting them; but I think I found the reason in the fact that we were taken away in the ordinary police van, which has a passage up its middle and a range of boxes on each side, each one big enough to hold a man; but there were too many of us for the boxes, and some were crowded into the passage as well. We in the passage were leg-ironed, my companion having been a clerk to the secretary to a public company, as he himself told us.

Our clothes (the private ones that were taken from us and bundled and ticketed, when we were convicted I mean) were taken in the van with us, and as soon as we got to Millbank (which of all prisons it has been my misfortune to enter is by far the most appalling), we were stripped of our Newgate clothes and our irons, which the Newgate warders took back with them. Then we were bathed, and a Millbank suit was provided for each. It is a rather peculiar suit, consisting of a striped shirt, a snuff-coloured jacket and trousers, broadly striped with red, and a pair of red-ribbed woollen stockings, a pair of shoes, a cotton neckerchief, and ditto pocket. Nothing about the clothes, however, was so peculiar as their smell. They were new clothes, or very nearly, and were made of common coarse cloth, but the smell that arose from them was one that I never before or since have met with. It was pungent at the same time that it was sickening, and it seemed to fly off in a sort of dust, and lay on your lips and nostrils. If at any time — which the Lord forbid—I should be fool enough to think of jeopardizing my liberty again, just a sniff of those prison clothes would bring me to my senses sooner than anything.

The cell in which I was placed was smaller than the Newgate cell, but not half so comfortable-looking. The floor was bare flagstones, and against the wall was suspended the rules of the prison. Furniture—a small four-legged table, slop tub, with lid to it, that serves as a seat, hammock, as at Newgate, with an addition to bed-clothes in the shape of a rug, a new Bible, Prayer-book, and Hymn-book, and a stick painted one end red and the other end black. This last was a puzzler, imtil I was told its use. In the wall, at the corridor side, was a narrow slit, and when you wanted anything you thrust your stick through the slit and kept it there till it happened to catch the eye of the warder on duty. If he saw the black end out, he knew that you want-of his private clothes, taps me on the shoulder and says, "I want a word with you, young man. Just step in here."

Into the counting-house that was, and when I got in who should be there but two of my mates, looking as white as death, and sitting on two of the office-stools with handcuffs on. "Shall I search you, or will you hand over all that doesn't belong to you that you have in your pockets?" said the detective. So where was the use of having a word to say for myself? I pulled out what I had in my waistcoat-pocket, and something else that I had folded up in my neck-handkerchief, and laid them on the table. "Is that all?" said the young governor, who was there all the time. "That is all, sir," answered the plain-clothes man (who, it afterwards came out, had been watching us since the morning, and knew what goods we had taken and how we had disposed of them). "Very well; take them away, and I will be at the station presently to make the charge," said the young governor, who naturally was very savage and spiteful.

Well, the charge was entered, we were locked up, and next morning taken before the magistrate and committed for trial— all of which I will pass over, as well as the trial itself, and "the evidence of the prosecutor" and his witnesses, and the address of the lawyers in their wigs to the judge (for Jane's father was kind enough to find me a lawyer), and the finding of a verdict of guilty by the jurymen. I had quite made up my mind to be brought in guilty, and to be sent to prison for some time. Six months was the term that had somehow got into my head, and all the time the jury were making up their minds I was reckoning what time o' year it would be six months to come, and found that it wouldn't be far off of Christmas. "I'll begin the new year by turning over a new leaf, I'm blessed if I don't," I thought.

But there was something of a surprise in store for me and for the missus, too, poor thing (for she was in the court with the boy in her arms). I'm as certain as certain can be that of the three who were being tried there wasn't a pin's point to choose between us; we were much of an age, our wages the same, our opportunities for pilfering the same, and our inclination to avail ourselves of them as like as peas in a pod. But somehow the judge had got a notion that I was the worst of the lot, chiefly, I believe, because I had been longest in the employ of the firm. His sentence showed it. One of my mates nine months' hard labour, the other twelve months, and me *three years' penal* servitude. P'r'aps it might be easy enough to make out that I deserved it, but I do think if the judge had said I was to be hanged by the neck till I was dead, I shouldn't have been more thunderstruck. There was some sort of noise and bustle just about where the missus was standing with the boy when the judge named my term, but I had no time to see what it was.

Just outside the dock there was a gaoler, and he instantly let us out, and separating me from the other two, marched me through some passages, and when he got to some steps that led down to the cells, he called out my name and the length of my sentence, and handed me over to another gaoler. Mine wasn't at all dirty work, and I always wore a decent suit of black clothes. Now, however, I had to take them off. "Strip," said the warder, and when I had taken off everything he gave me a gray suit, consisting of a jacket, waistcoat, and trousers, and a sort of Glengarry cap, and a pair of woollen stockings; but he allowed me to keep my boots, and as soon as I had put on the gray suit, he made a bundle of the clothes I had taken off, pinned a ticket to them, and threw them into a cupboard; then he led the way to a cell, unlocked the door of it, and pushed me in. And all so quickly, that from the time when my wife saw me in my own clothes till when I was in a prison suit and in a Newgate cell, if she walked home, she could hardly have got as far as Blackfriars Bridge.

Knowing nothing about prison cells, I thought the one I found myself in the most wretched place that could be imagined. It was a very little place, with a window with an iron grate before it, and lime-washed walls, and a floor of asphalte. There were two shelves in the cell, one to stow the hammock away in the daytime, and the other to accommodate a tin pannikin, a copper bowl, a wooden spoon, and a wooden salt-cellar, a piece of soap, and a brush— the soap, though I don't know for what reason, being carried away at night and returned the next morning. Besides the furniture mentioned, there was a stool and a wooden flap hinged to the wall and propped with an iron crutch that served as a table. The hammock was a comfortable thing enough, and there were two sheets and two blankets. By-the-by, I mustn't forget the books— three in number—a Bible, a Prayer-book, and a Hymn-book, ranged in a row with the copper bowl and the other things.

It was half-past two when I was locked in, and at five the warder brought me a pint of gruel and a good slice of bread for my supper. "Make the most of it," said he; "you'll get no more till the morning." But he needn't have troubled on that score. I was too stunned yet awhile, and too heart-sick to think about eating and drinking. I had never made a bed in my life—and how I made that one in that awkward hammock, how I got into it and passed my first night in Newgate, isn't worth while to dwell on when there's so much more to be told.

At half-past six next morning the prison bell rang for getting up, and as soon as I was dressed a warder opened a little trap in the door, and put through into my cell a small brush and a dust-pan, at the same time telling me to make my place tidy, and when I had swept up, and folded away my hammock on the shelf, he brought me a piece of cloth and told me to polish the floor, which, as before mentioned, was of asphalte, and would take a sort of shine if rubbed long enough. When that job was done, my day's work was brought to me, consisting of a pound and a quarter of oakum. Along with the oakum was an iron hook, with a strap to it, and this was to fasten to the knee to help tear the tarred rope, which is as tough almost as

The chairman was not at his post, a circumstance that seemed to puzzle the company generally not a little, as Mr. Lemike was known to be the most punctual of men, and always proud and happy to bring his pets to a show. But, alas for poor Mr. Lemike! his absence was presently accounted for. It was sorrow and deep distress that kept him away from the Ship that night. Himself a publican, the police had most provokingly paid an untimely visit to his house a day or two before, and there discovered *fifty-three* young thieves and their sweethearts engaged in a raffle in Mr. Lemike's tap-room; jQ$ was the penalty in which the unfortunate publican was mulct, with the magisterial intimation that it would be wasting his time to apply next March for a renewal of his licence. No wonder that Mr. Lemike had no heart for dog-shows that Sunday night.

The place was crowded, and there was scarcely standing room, so that, until you took courage from the indifference displayed by the company generally, one could not help feeling slightly nervous at the close proximity of furious bull-dogs, with glaring eyes and lolling tongues, savage at sight of each other, and not improbably hard-pressed by thirst in that hot, close den, and panting for the blood of the first creature they could plant their teeth in. True, their masters, not caring to trust to their leash, held them each by the collar as a policeman holds a thief; but this seemed only to increase their fury, and they strained and strove, as only a bull-dog can, to break away, and then, with one's calf within a foot of the monsters' jaws, and not even the protection of a Wellington boot, came the thrilling reflection, " If it should!"

Different, too, from the bird-show was the present exhibition in the matter of passive enjoyments of the " fancy" involved. Louder even than the barking of the bigger dogs was the uproar of shock-headed, loud-mouthed ruffians extolling the qualities of their canine pets, and staking the security of their eyes and limbs—of their lives even— on the truth of the barefaced lies that came so freely from their blasphemous mouths. Matches for dog to fight dog, for dogs to kill rats against time, and against each other, and for dogs to "show for points," were yelled out with many oaths, and with a horrible din that made one shudder. And in this precious amusement, in this one foul pot-house, were engaged at least sixty men, all on a Sunday evening.

There is always to be met an exception to the prevailing rule, and it was not wanting on the present occasion. This was a man with a bull-dog pup, who sat in a corner nursing his pet, and speaking not until he was spoken to. He was a middleaged man this, with long, well-oiled hair, the ends of which were trained to turn under, and, as was plain to be seen, his hair and his pup were that man's chief treasures on earth. It was almost melancholy to reflect that human hair *will* decay as age creeps on— that puppies will grow and assume the stature of mature dogs. It was a white puppy, and he nursed it like a baby, with its hideous head resting against his greasy bosom. Alternately he sleeked his hair and coaxed it to remain turned under at the ends, and fondled the bull-dog, and tenderly rubbed its gums with his forefinger. "That's a pooty thing," remarked a connoisseur; "what might be the age on it?"—" Seven months and a week," replied the oily man, looking up with almost maternal pride in his eyes; "it's pooty, as you say, now, but what will it be bimeby?" THREE YEARS QF PENAL SER VITUDE. TT is not necessary for me to tell my name, the exact nature of the offence of which I was convicted, or the precise date of the conviction. I may say, however, and the reader may take it as truth—as indeed he may every line that is here printed —that up to the time when I was arrested I never before in my life knew what that sort of trouble was—never was locked up for so long as a single night, or saw the inside of a stationhouse cell.

How my misfortune came about is easy enough to explain. I was a young man, and I lodged away from home; and I liked to do as other young men, go about a bit of evenings to see a play, or hear a song along with two or three mates employed at our firm, and young fellows like myself. That led to my picking up a sweetheart—a thorough good girl—and we kept company. She worked in the day, and had her evenings, and of course I took her out. Then the game that cost me three years' liberty began. My wages were only eighteen shillings a week, and out of that I paid twelve for board and lodging and washing, so that there was only six left for clothes, going out, tobacco, and everything. I won't state the nature of the goods our firm dealt in, but half a crown's worth might easily be stowed in the waistcoat-pocket, and in a manner of speaking you were free to help yourself out of thousands of pounds' worth.

The young woman just mentioned was very respectable, and dressed well; and so was I well-dressed, and, as she thought, respectable too. I went on courting her honourable, and from the first meaning to marry her, but I didn't have the pluck to tell her how small my wages were. If I had it would have opened her eyes at once, so I kept it dark, and by-and-by we got married, and still I didn't tell her how much I got a week. I asked her what she thought she could do comfortably with, and she said she thought she could do with a guinea if I bought my own tobacco and beer. "Very well," I says, "then it shall be a guinea a week, my dear."

That was three shillings more than I was earning, and of course it had to be made up, and I needn't again mention how, and things went on pretty comfortable (barring the thought that would at times come across me of the kick-up there would if I should be found out) for a year. We had two rooms nicely furnished (for Jenny was a beautiful little manager) and come the time a baby was born—a boy it was. That seemed the beginning of the down-hill. Everything was more expensive, she was ill a longish time, and the firm suffered. I was wretched for weeks and weeks before the blow-up came, and in my own mind was not at all surprised when on leaving the warehouse one evening a man whom I knew in an instant, in spite

ble without moving the lips, there were certain muscles in the region of the ear that could not be kept still during the process, and that keeping a sharp lookout for this tell-tale led to his success.

The food at Pentonville is very fair both as to quantity and quality. You get beef and mutton on alternate days, with enough bread and vegetables; and cocoa for breakfast and gruel for supper. The labour is performed in the privacy of your own cell, and if you don't know a trade they teach you one. They taught me shoemaking. I never made much of a fist at it; firstly, I suppose, because it was a trade into which I could never get my heart; and, secondly, because the work I had to practise on was of a particularly plain and unfashionable kind. But, if I may be permitted to express an opinion on the subject, I may say that I consider it a great advantage and privilege to be allowed to work when in prison at some trade *free men* work at. It saves you from sinking as low in your value of yourself as when you are set at spending an entire day at tearing a lot of tarred rope in pieces, all the while knowing that a machine would do the work in five minutes or less. Of course I can't answer for other men, but I can for myself; and although I always detested shoemaking, when I saw my " seat," all ready prepared for me, with a regular set of honest, hardworking tools ready to my hand, I felt more grateful than I could have expressed.

Nor is your work altogether unprofitable to you as regards wages. For the first six months—until, indeed, as I suppose, they think you know your trade—you get no remuneration at all: but after six months you get pay—sixpence a week if you are simply industrious, and eightpence if you are classed with the first grade, and known as very industrious. There is a third grade—the idle grade. Every day a mark is set against the names of the idle ones, and after these have been allowed a certain amount of rope, as the saying is, they are taken before the governor, who on a first charge simply warns them; if they continue idle, the effects of a week of bread and water is tried on them. There is another good thing, besides coming to be a wages man, that happens at the end of six months— for the first time since leaving Millbank he is allowed to see a visitor. I needn't mention the name of the visitor that came to see me.

You get a clean shirt and stockings and neckerchief once a week at Pentonville, and a clean flannel shirt and drawers once a fortnight. A bath once a fortnight. For exercise you are allowed to tramp round a circle made of paving stones in the yard. There are three circles, one within the other, with warders outside and within the circles, and you go round and round for an hour. At one time, in order to be sure that every man kept at a proper distance from his neighbour, there was a rope long enough and with knots in it at equal distance; while he was taking his walk, each convict held one of these knots in his hand, and it was the warder's duty to see that the rope through its whole extent was kept "taut." In wet weather you get no exercise in Pentonville, and sometimes when it sets in for a long spell of rain—the weather being always dull and heavy at such times—you have a rather miserable time of it. However, all get exercise when it is possible—even the refractory ones do who are condemned to the dark cells. There is a sort of round-house, divided into sections, with partitions too high to be overlooked, and up and down this "chicken-walk," as it is called, this class of prisoner tramps his allotted time in company of two warders.

There are certain inducements held out to the well-behaved three years' man, for which a prisoner with a longer sentence is not eligible. On certain mornings a " cleaners party," composed of prisoners, is mustered and taken down to the apartments of the prison officers to scrub, and clean windows, and make matters neat and tidy. I needn't say that every such party is accompanied by a sufficient number of warders. Even when one of a "party," you must not say a single word to any one else, except it is to a warder to ask directions about this or that. But although this of course is regarded as a rare treat, there is another "party" to be preferred to that of the cleaners, and that is the " cookhouse association," or in other words, a number of prisoners told off to assist in the cook-house. Here you may talk without much restraint, and besides come in for odd luxuries in the way of tit-bits and crackling, rarely to be found in your regular meat rations.

I remained at Pentonville through eight months, earning 4s. 6d. during the last nine weeks of that time, which was put down to my account. My schoolbooks were examined on the eve of our removal, and if it had appeared that any of them had been injured beyond fair wear, the damage would have been deducted from my 4s. 6d. My other books—the Bible, Prayer-book, and Hymn-book—I made a parcel of, that they might accompany me to Portland, for that was the next prison to which we were drafted. Once more came the early breakfast that invariably marked a "moving" day. After that we were paraded and examined, and decent garments substituted for those that had grown shabby, in order, I suppose, that we might make a respectable appearance as travellers, and not discredit Pentonville; it could have been nothing else, since the respectable clothes were only for our wear on the journey, and were taken away when we reached Portland.

It was a bitter cold and frosty morning when, chained as we were when going from Millbank to Pentonville, we rode in private omnibuses to the railway station and took train for Weymouth. Every man carried with him a little bag containing some bread and a quarter of a pound of cheese for refreshment on the road, and there went with us as well a biggish can of water, that we might not go thirsty. Once started on our journey, I was aware of the sort of companions I might reckon on when I got to Portland. I had mixed with similar gangs to that which I now made one of, but they were bound to be quiet and well-behaved; now, however, that their tongues were loosened, they seemed determined to make up for lost time. There were armed Warders in charge of us, but they were no check on the laughter and swearing and singing. "Look here, lads," said the warders, "keep it going just as you like, but draw it mild when we come to a station." They promised that they would, but the mildest that they drew it was tremendously strong, and must have considerably astonished respectable passengers who happened to hear it.

We reached Weymouth between two and three o'clock, and, still chained, entered other omnibuses we found in readiness for us, and drove away to Portland. Portland Prison is on top of a hill, and the public works cover the surrounding slopes. It was quite a long drive before we reached the prison gates.

If I disliked the outside of Portland Prison, I found its interior even less inviting. It is a second Millbank, making up in chill and bleakness what it lacks in gloom. Here for the first time I found myself a *branded* convict. We were stripped and bathed, and a Portland suit was laid before each. This was the suit—a pair of moleskin trousers stamped all over with staring red "Ps," a jacket ditto, a blue "slop" striped with red, a black japanned hat adorned in the same manner, a cotton pocket and neckerchief, a flannel shirt and drawers, a pair of thick worsted stockings, a pair of stout hobnailed boots, and a pair of light shoes.

Being winter time, it was growing dusk when I was shown to what was to be my "home " for a year and a half. It was a frightfully dismal-looking little den, and like nothing so much as a dog-kennel on a largish scale. Its dimensions were, as nearly as I can call them to mind, about seven feet high, eight long, and four broad. Its sides and roof were of corrugated iron, and its floor slate. With the frost increasing as night approached it was enough to make one's teeth chatter to look in.

My privilege, however, extended beyond looking in, and when the bolt was shot on me I had opportunity to take inventory of my furniture. Zinc entered into it considerably. There was a zinc washing bowl, a ditto water jug, &c., and a candlestick (there is no gas in the Portland cells). Beside these, there was a tin plate, an iron spoon, a tin pint-pot, a pair of snuffers, a wooden salt-cellar, a little box with brickdust and rubbing rags, and a small hearth-broom. The hammock was the same as elsewhere, with two blankets, two sheets, and a rug. Not a bad allowance of bed-clothing, it may be said; but still, the place was frightfully cold. This I found to be the universal complaint, though I believe nine men out of every ten went to bed in their flannels. It was impossible to get warm. The corrugated iron seemed full of deadly-cold damp, and everything that touched it took the same quality and kept it. Necessity is the mother of invention, and after I had been there a little time, I contrived "a foot-warmer." They are not stingy in the matter of candle at Portland, and, since there is nothing to burn in a man's cell but his bed and himself, not so strict as to lights and fires as at the other prisons. At eight o'clock the bell rings "lights out," and you are supposed at once to extinguish your candle, but it is possible to "dowse" it by placing the zinc washing bowl over it so that the light cannot be seen from the outside. There you have your foot warmer at once. The flame of the candle speedily makes the zinc so hot that you cannot hold your hand against it. Then you place it between the blankets at the foot of your hammock, and you are tolerably sure of warm toes at least till you fall asleep.

"Early to bed and early to rise" is the maxim at Portland, though, by-the-by, and as I discovered on the very first night of my imprisonment there, that early to bed does not of necessity mean early to sleep, for want of companionship. The walls of the cells, though of iron, are not very thick, and scarcely had I laid down in my hammock when a gentle " tap, tap," close to my head gave me notice that a neighbour would like a few words with me. I put my mouth to the wall and whispered, "'What do you want?" on which my neighbour (an old burglar, as I afterwards found, and now undergoing five years for a murderous assault) kindly inquired how I liked myself by this time, and where I came from, and what I was there for. His hope was that I might have come from his neighbourhood (he was a London man), and possibly be able to give him some information concerning his pals; but after a few questions he found that I could tell him nothing that interested him, and so he bade me goodnight. Then my neighbour on the other side gave a tap, and with him my conversation lasted longer. He informed me that he had only five months longer to serve, and comforted me with the assurance that I should find it a little hell at first but would soon grow used to it.

I dare say it was eleven o'clock before I got to sleep, and at five o'clock the bell rang for getting up. It was, of course, quite dark, but as soon as I had turned out there came a knock at my door, and there were two men who carried a tub between them and some candles and a light. The light was to ignite your candle (they give you a fresh one if the last has burnt out), and the tub was for the reception of your slops. I may here mention that out of every convict "party" (distinguished by a number or a letter, and located in a part of the prison known by the same) there are always two who have an especially unpleasant time of it. The office falls on every man in his turn, and lasts for a week. The pair whose turn it is are the servants of the "party." They go round with the slop tub in the morning, they fetch up the great cans for gruel or cocoa, and they carry up the dinners—and all in the time they would otherwise have to themselves. The part of the prison where our gang was, was four long flights of stairs from the basement, and it was no joke to toil up them with a load three or four times in your dinner hour.

When you get your light from the tub men, and the cell door is open, you take the opportunity to hang your tin pot on the outside handle, and stand your tin plate on edge just outside. Then, when you have "tidied up" a bit, your breakfast is brought, and your door being unlocked, you find on the floor a 12 oz. loaf and a pint of cocoa. At half-past six the chapel bell rings. The first morning of my going to chapel it was clear and frosty, with a bright moon, and it was a rather curious sight to see the candle-light within the cheerless place, and the moon without, and the breath coming out of the parson's mouth in a cloud, like tobacco smoke. The service lasted only half an hour, however, and then we were marched back to prepare for work.

And here I may mention a very simple way they have at Portland of telling whether a man is within his cell when he should be, or rather of ascertaining whether the warder has locked you in, as is his duty. I have mentioned that each cell is provided with a small hand-broom; every time a prisoner returns from chapel or what not, as soon as his door is locked,, he is bound to poke the handle of his broom out at the bottom of the door, so that the chief warder, casting his eye along the row of cells, and finding the broom handles at proper range, knows that everybody is "at home." The broom-handle is the only means of communicating with the warders, and it sometimes happens that your signal is held out some considerable time before it is noticed; in the case of a man being taken suddenly ill this is awkward.

Not that there is much real sickness at Portland Prison, though there is a tremendous lot of shamming. I have known men who by a process too disgusting to describe have manufactured such evidence of blood-spitting that the doctor has been deceived, and the cheat allowed a spell of rest and superior food in the infirmary. I have likewise known men to make themselves a genuine bad leg, in hopes of the same reward. The process is simple, and consists in threading a needle with thread well rubbed with copperas, making a large stitch in the fleshy part of the calf, and allowing the thread to remain in the flesh an hour or so. I have known a man play this trick to such perfection that it was the mere turn of a straw, as the saying is, that saved his leg from being sawn off at the knee. It must be the warm clothing and regular diet that keeps the Portland convicts in health. It certainly is not the medicine they have given to them. All that the majority ever see in the shape of physic is a tablespoonful of treacle twice a week. You can, however, see the doctor whenever you feel poorly. A warder takes you to him, and you find him in a sort of cage with wooden bars in front, with enough room between the bars to admit a man's hand. It is rather an odd sort of consulting-room; but the more open one that used to be was found not without objections. Of course, the doctor is the mortal enemy of the prisoner who wants a skulk in the infirmary and enjoys such confoundedly good health that do his best he can't get himself up as a fit subject. Such men have been known to conceal stones about them, and to fling them at the doctor's head as soon as he began to "pooh-pooh" their ailments. So, now they put the doctor in a cage; and, if it is necessary for him to feel your pulse, you have to put your hand between the bars. Looking at your tongue, however, seems to be the great health test at Portland. I remember after I had worked a fortnight at barrow wheeling, I felt such terrible pains in my shoulders and loins that I thought I had somehow hurt myself seriously, and I asked to be taken to the doctor. Before I had told him half my symptoms, "Put out your tongue," said he, and I did. "Be off, be off!" said the doctor, "there's nothing the matter with you;" and he was right, as it turned out, though at the time I thought it monstrously cruel to be made sport of, for I could make nothing else of the notion of looking at a man's tongue to find whereabouts his back was sprained.

There is no mistake about it, the work at Portland is terribly hard to a man whose hardest day's work, before misfortune overtook him, was performed in a drapery warehouse or behind a clerk's desk. It is simply " navvy" work, and that of a by no means easy kind. The labour consists in drilling the rocks for blasting, shifting the great lumps of stone blasted, digging trenches, and wheeling big barrow-loads of earth up a 9 in. plank; and there is no fear but the old hands will take care that you do your share of labour, even if the overseers don't. If it rains you knock off. There are sheds at all parts of the works, and if the rain comes down as though it meant lasting some time you are ordered to shelter. The longer the rain lasted the better we liked it; not only did it give us a chance of a gossip, but also of playing the only game we could ever indulge in, which was that called "coddam." Of course we had to play very quietly, and the game itself—simply guessing which out of a group of fists holds the "piece," which is a button or a bit of stone—is not a particularly lively one under ordinary circumstances, but we got a tremendous lot of fun out of it. When it set in for a wet day we stayed at home idle, but I would a precious sight rather be at quarry work than moping in a half-dark cell.

When we were out working, at twelve o'clock we knocked off and went back to the prison to dinner. We got a pint of soup, a pound of potatoes, 6 oz. of bread, and 5 oz. of meat. Not a bad dinner if it was all as it should be, which it is not. I can conscientiously declare that I have stuck to the truth in the strictest manner in all I have related, and I do so now when I say that the meat at Portland is very bad indeed. Not as to freshness, but quality. It is coarse, insipid, and so tough that nothing is commoner than for the prisoners to chew it for the little good there is in it, and spit it into their slops. It is almost a waste of time to cook such stuff, and, I shouldn't wonder, a waste of Government money as well. I don't speak from my own single experience; it was the universal complaint, and that amongst men of such tremendous appetite that they would beg; the food out of your mouth. There was one convict there—ai Lancashire man, an awful glutton. He was a great ruffian, and selected his companions, to whom he sometimes afforded a little amusement according as they contributed a trifle towards satisfying his everlasting hunger. They would smuggle him out a bit of pudding or a potato, and in return for the present each one was permitted to give him as hard a punch on the body as he pleased. These sort of larks, however, could only take place when the fellows were working in trenches and not in sight of the officers.

You are allowed an hour to your dinner, which gives you time for a read or a doze, and then back to work until four o'clock in winter time, and about six in summer. Soon as you return you wash and " dress," taking off your heavy hob-nailed boots and putting on the light shoes before mentioned, and then you go to chapel again, and spend twenty minutes there and return to supper, which consists of 9 oz. of bread and a pint of gruel. I may state here, as regards victuals, that the individual who is known as a "second-stage man "—that is, one who has served half of his whole term—has, provided he is well behaved, considerable advantage over the others. He gets 2 oz. of cheese on Sundays in addition to his dinner; and, what is of more consequence to him if his tastes are anything like mine, he gets a pint of tea, with milk and sugar, every evening instead of gruel. In summer time this is indeed a luxury; for, as may easily be imagined, to come sweating in your flannels from the quarries to your iron cell (which is just as hot and oven-like in summer as it is cold in winter) and find nothing more refreshing to drink than a measure of warm thick gruel, is not all that could be desired. When a prisoner has served another length of time he becomes a "third-stage man," and is entitled to further privileges. He is allowed, in addition to the tea and the cheese, to sit up an hour after the ordinary bedtime, and three times a week he has baked meat for dinner; whereas, as I should before have mentioned, the ordinary convicts never get anything but boiled meat—and always beef. If it was salted it would be less insipid, but it is fresh beef.

It will hardly be believed that there are "swells" and dandies amongst the Portland convicts; but such is the fact. I have known men obtain a needle and thread on the sly and alter the set of their trousers—the trousers stamped with the red Ps—to what was the prevailing fashion when they were last in the world. I have likewise seen as much as a precious "quarter" (a quarter of an inch) of tobacco paid by a swell for the privilege of exchanging his trousers for another convict's, because the swell "liked the cut of 'em." The swell convict greases his hair by means of a bit of fat saved from his dinner, and curls it if it is long enough. Saturday night is the convict swell's greatest time. Once a fortnight on a Saturday every man gets his clean flannels, in addition to socks, shirts, and neckerchief, and these he finds in his cell when he returns in the afternoon from work. On a Saturday the blacking and brushes go round, so that the men may polish their light shoes: then, what with his shiny hair and his shiny shoes, and his nattily tied neckerchief, and his fashionable fitting trousers, the convict swell looks quite grand marching to chapel on a Saturday evening.

I have spoken above about a precious bit of tobacco. I need not say that tobacco is not allowed by the authorities—it is smuggled in. Working in the quarries are free men as well as convicts, and it is through these free men that the tobacco is procured. It is managed in this way. Supposing a man has friends able to send him half-a-sovereign, he scrawls on a bit of paper, "Write to So-and-so for so much, and have it directed to you;" and then, catching the eye of one of the free workmen, the convict tips him a wink, and dropping the morsel of paper to the ground, kicks a stone over it, and goes about his work. The free workmen knows what is meant. In the course of the morning he picks up the paper, and speculates a penny in writing as the convict desires. If the money comes the free man keeps half for his trouble, and takes on himself the laying out the remainder for the convict in tobacco. It is leaf tobacco, and is conveyed to the convict by his agent just as the "order" was conveyed in the first instance—the free man slips it under a stone, and the convict picks his time for securing it. It is wonderful how it is prized. There is a regular scale of value for it. "One wing" (just a skiver of a single leaf) is worth a "sixer" (a 6 oz. loaf); "one chow" (or chaw), "a twelve and a bull" (a 12 oz. loaf and a 5 oz. ration of meat); a " quarter" (inch), "two bulls and a pudding" (two meat rations and the 6 oz. of suet pudding allowed on certain days). Of course, there is no chance of smoking a pipe at Portland; the tobacco can only be chewed, or I dare say it would fetch still higher prices.

The clothes worn by the convicts are all alike, whatever their term or their crime, except in special cases. Amongst the gangs in the quarries may be seen here and there a convict with one leg yellow and the other of a cinnamon colour, and the same as to his arms and each half of his body. These men work in irons, having "anklets" and a chain long enough to hitch up to their waist strap, and which for further convenience is likewise gartered to each leg below the knee. These are known as "canaries," and are convicts who have attempted to escape. There is another class of chained workers called "magpies," whose dress is black and cinnamon, and these are so punished for assaults on warders and other crimes that may not here be mentioned. Every Portland convict wears on his arm a leather shield-shaped badge backed with white drill, and with his length of service cut out in the leather, and showing white. Besides the numbers "3," "5," or "7," as the case may be, a convict's badge likewise shows what his behaviour is; thus, "V.G." is "very good," "G." "good," and "O." nought, or good for nothing, I suppose. "L." signifies that the wearer's sentence is to last during his life. This letter of the law, however, is not invariably adhered to. I was on intimate terms with a gentleman there who had already served "a life," and who was then undergoing ten years for a crime committed since he got his pardon.

Having the good luck to be considered a "V.G," after eighteen months at Portland, I one evening had the great gratification to find myself ordered before the governor, who told me that in consequence of my good behaviour I was to be sent with a batch next day to Broadmore, and as I heard Broadmore spoken of as something like Paradise as compared with Portland, I thanked the governor very heartily for the information. Broadmore is in Berkshire; and ironed, as on all the previous journeys, next day we were packed there by rail. I had not been misinformed as to the sort of a place it was. At Portland no two men were ever trusted together out of sight of a warder—three men on rare occasions might be, but two never; whereas at Broadmore there was a great barrack room, and with beds ranged round, and there we slept and messed, free to talk and amuse ourselves in a quiet way as though we were lodgers at a lodging-house. The food was plentiful and excellent, contrasting strangely with that allowed the poor folks at the workhouses sometimes exposed in the newspapers.

At breakfast time we got a pound of bread, a pint of cocoa, and 2 oz. of cheese. The hungry ones ate the lot up at once, but the prudent ones reserved the cheese and a piece of the bread, for at eleven o'clock there was half a pint of beer for lunch, and that with a mouthful of bread and cheese, made quite a comfortable snack. At dinner we got a pint of soup, a pound of potatoes, and 5 oz. of boiled meat for three days, and the other four days 5 oz. of roast meat, a pound of potatoes, and 6 oz. of suet pudding. In the evening a pint of tea, and 8 oz. of bread. They allow your hair and whiskers to grow at Broadmore.

The work there is field and garden work, and they keep you to it stiffly. You get half a day's schooling a week, chapel twice a day (the service is held in the schoolroom), and two hours' exercise on Sunday. I was at Broadmore three months, and, speaking as a prisoner, I liked it very much indeed.

Altogether I had now served two years and seven months of my sentence, and as a well-behaved man was entitled to my "ticket." To get it I had to be taken with the rest (no chains this time!) back to Millbank, where I remained nearly a fortnight, and one never-to-be-forgotten morning, after having my photograph taken, I was discharged, and let out at the gate a free man to go wherever I pleased. I did not get my own clothes back, but corduroy trousers and waistcoat, and a tweed coat, and a black billycock cap. My earnings in prison had amounted to £j 10s., which, however, is not come-at-able all at once; it is doled out to you a pound or so at a time, which, I think, is not a good arrangement. If a man means to be honest he wants all he can get to set his home to rights again, and buy a few tools to follow the trade the authorities have taught him; if he doesn't mean to be honest, you may as well give him his money first as last for all the difference it is likely to make.

After all, however, I did not wait for my bit of money. I found out the Prisoners' Aid Society, and they advanced me the £1 1 os., and I did the best I could with it. The best was not much, I am sorry to say; however, I live in hopes of matters coming all right again by-and-by. It shall be no fault Of mine if they do not, I will venture to say.

AN EXPLORATION INTO "JACK KETCH'S WARREN" FEW days since it was my good fortune to receive a rather curious and interesting letter. The writer was a City missionary, and the communication was dated from the "Mission House, Turnmill Street, Clerkenwell." It was a remarkably blunt and plain-spoken communication. It set forth that in a story of mine recently written and published mention was made of Frying-pan Alley, and an attempt made to describe that place and its inhabitants, whereas nothing could be plainer to any one well acquainted with the locality than that I in reality knew next to nothing about it. "Not that it is in any degree wonderful or surprising that it should be so," was the text of my friend's epistle, "since it is almost impossible, except from one or two sources, to obtain anything like reliable information as to Frying-pan Alley, or the other disgraceful and disgusting alleys and courts adjacent. It is a waste of time to make inquiries of the police. A single policeman is rarely, if ever, seen in Frying-pan Alley, Bit Alley, Rose Alley, or the Broad Yard, in the course of his perambulations 'on beat:' it would be scarcely safe in riotous seasons for him to show a face there, and secure harbour is thus afforded to thieves. The sanitary officers of the parish are even more timid than the police, so that year in and year out the alleys mentioned are the undisturbed breeding-places for fever and pestilence, and though sickness and disease in one form or another is never absent, a Scripture reader is almost as unknown to the wretched creatures who herd there as a breath of pure fresh air. There are but two persons—the parish doctor and myself—who have a perfect knowledge of the extent of vice and misery constantly to be met with in these alleys." Further, the writer intimated that if I could only find courage to enter into an investigation of these Turnmill Street horrors, it might be the means of working a good he had been, single-handed, long endeavouring to accomplish; and further still, and better than all, he generously announced his willingness to become my conductor and guide if I decided to entertain his proposal. So tempting an offer was not to be neglected, so I wrote back and fixed a day.

I found the mission house in Turnmill Street a very modest and unpretending place. It had evidently at one time been a shop of a small sort, and its windows were now closely placarded with Scriptural notices and temperance lyrics, and announcements of missionary lectures and "mothers'meetings." I knocked at the door and inquired for Mr. Catlin, and that gentleman promptly made his appearance.

I trust when he reads this that he won't be offended at my remarking that he was not at all the sort of man, as far as personal appearance goes, I had reckoned on making the acquaintance of. I had got it into my head (chiefly, as I believe, from the nature of a tract and a little poem composed by that celebrated philanthropist and lenient judge, Mr. Payne, that accompanied the missionary's letter to me) that I should find him a prim and precise person in glossy broadcloth of raven black, and the stiffest and most spotless of neckcloths. But he did not in the least resemble this picture. He was a shortish, thick-set, and muscular man, with a brown and weatherbeaten face, short crisp hair, like that of a blacksmith, and a pair of bright restless eyes, and a hairy, knuckly fist that could have come of nothing but hard labour. He came downstairs, ready attired for walking, in a shaggy brown overcoat and a black billycock hat.

We went into the shop, and after ten minutes' chat were on the easiest terms imaginable. It was a largish shop, as though the parlour behind had been added to it, and in the rear of this again was a tolerably commodious schoolroom, capable of accommodating a hundred and fifty persons, I should say—the rent of which, together with the whole of the premises, had been guaranteed to the owner for the space of three years by a kind-hearted stationer in the City. Very much more he told me concerning his labour and its field, with which I will not trouble the reader. I may mention, however, that he was not always a missionary, as he gave me to understand, having in his young manhood engaged in the prize-fighting profession, lodging in Seven Dials along with a now celebrated "pug," who, so far from despising his old friend, on high days and holidays dropped in and took a cup of tea with him and his wife. Putting a packet of tracts in one pocket and a small Bible in the other, and humming a lively tune with the air of a contented carpenter or any other sort of handicraftsman setting out to an easy job, he came out of his house and led the way.

"There are two places I should like you to see before we begin the alleys," remarked my guide, "not so much that they are worse than we shall find elsewhere, as that they form part of the house property of one of the most advanced ' reformers' in our parish."

With that he pushed open a door opening sheer on to the highway, and when we had entered in at it and traversed a long and narrow passage, we came upon this spectacle—a building that at one time of day might have been a washhouse, about twelve feet in length, eight in width, and of the height of a tall man. The walls were of bare brick, and stained in great black patches where the rain had trickled through the shattered roof, and the floor was broken and of a dark slate colour. In the corner to the right, and in a line with the door, a rickety bedstead, with its posts aslant and thickly barked with dirt and grease, bearing a spread of foul rags and tatters that served as a bed; a something that served as a table, a broken-backed chair, a couple of stools, and several publichouse cans (borrowed, as I suppose, from taverns in the neighbourhood and not at present returned) as water vessels and cooking utensils. In a sort of hole hacked in the grimy wall a skillet with a fire in it, and huddling over the fire a gray-haired, hungry-faced old man in his shirt-sleeves, and wretchedly old waistcoat and trousers; and an old woman with her skin of a colour with the floor-boards, and, as well as might be guessed from appearance, with no other covering than a shockingly old and dirty cotton gown, with hands like the claws of some huge and unclean bird, and a frowsy nightcap, but ill concealing a head of hair raggeder than any crow's nest; and a young woman tidier and cleaner than either, but still a sight to see; and a little child of two years or thereabouts, amusing itself with one of the public-house cans before mentioned. But stranger than all was the odd kind of litter that strewed the hovel—a litter of paper—scraps of every sort and condition. Brown paper, white paper, printed paper; paper that had served as parcel wrapping, and paper torn off the wall to which it had been originally stuck by the bill-sticker in lively strips and pennons, and showing brilliantly in red and blue and yellow amongst the humbler *d'ebris;* post-office envelopes, handbills crumpled up, and showing traces of the kennel, into which they had been cast; all in pell-mell confusion, on the bed, under the bed, strewing the floor, and in dangerous proximity with the unguarded fire skillet, and filling a great sack lying along on the floor.

"It is my trade, sir; how I gets my living," explained the hungry-looking old man—John Smith by name, and aged eighty seven. "It's a hard way of getting a crust, but it's better than the work'us. I'm up and out every morning by three o'clock. I was up and out at that time this morning. It's no use going out in the daytime; you gets interfered with so. It ain't the streets I look to so much as the dust-holes down mewses, and them kind of places, though, of course, I don't overlook what I see laying about in the gutters. I tears the bills off the walls when I gets a chance—not at the advertising stations, sir; oh, dear no, though I dare say they thinks that I do. That 'ud be a month if they caught you at it, and it ain't worth the risk. Besides, it's the poorest sort of scrap papers that you get off walls; it only fetches a shilling a hundredweight, and they don't care about taking it at that. Eighteen pence a hundredweight is what I get for the other when it is pretty clean; but it takes a long time to pull together a hundredweight out of little bits. Well, sir, as you say, it isn't much of a dependence; but you see it *is* a dependence as far as it goes, and gets us a bit of bread and keeps a roof over our heads."

"Very little more than a bit of bread falls to their lot, poor old creatures, I imagine," I remarked to Mr. Missionary, as we made our way out of the passage into Tummill Street again.

"Yes, it is sometimes a flavour of meat as well, I am almost sorry to tell," replies Mr. Missionary; "he didn't tell you of something else he looks for in the dustholes! He hunts for bones that have been thrown there since the day before. The worst of them he sells, but such as have a bit of meat left on them are put by and *was/ted* and made into a stew."

From Turnmill Street we made our way to Aylesbury Street, as far up as a house just opposite the churchyard, and again my guide pushed open a door, which opened, like that we had just left, into a dark passage, and presently we came on a staircase, so dark that it was necessary to feel the way up; necessary for me, that is. Mr. Missionary evidently knew the way as well as if he lived there, and skipped up with an agility which often left me blundering behind. Up and up, till four long flights were accomplished, and the garret story reached, and at the back garret door Mr. Missionary knocked.

"Come in!" somebody called, and my friend opened the door. That I could tell by the sound caused by turning the door handle, but for all the interior of the room that was rendered visible the door might have been shut as before, with this advantage, that we should not have been choked and blinded by a great cloud of foul chimney smoke that came belching out upon us.

"Oh! it's only you, sir; come along in, sir; we're a little thick up here, you see, sir."

"So you are, and that's a fact," replies Mr. Missionary cheerily, and marching bravely into the smoke. "Couldn't we have the window open a bit, and let a little of it out? Ay, I thought we could; it won't give you cold, Mrs. Grinder, if you put your shawl over your head. And how are we to-day, Mrs. Grinder?"

Now that the smoke had partly escaped out at the diminutive and paper-patched casement, I could see about me. The chamber, like all back attics, was neither convenient nor capacious. At its highest the flat of the hand might be laid on the ceiling, and at parts it slanted down so abruptly that there was barely room for creeping under it. One time of day ceiling and walls had been yellow-washed, now they were sootcovered. I don't mean to say—as regards the ceiling, at least —that it was merely blackened with smoke; it was literally coated with a thick fur of soot, such as is seen in the interior of a chimney-pot.

There were two old women occupying the garret—Mrs. Grinder and her servant. Mrs. Grinder was aged eighty years, and presented as ghastly a picture of humanity as can be imagined. There was a fire-place, with a handful of fire in it, with a breadth of old carpet nailed across the aperture as low as the top bar almost, by way of inducing a little of the smoke to find its way up the chimney; and crooning nose and knees over it sat Mrs. Grinder, her puckered old face deathly white in such places as had come in contact with her hand, but otherwise smoke-dried to the brownish sallow of a Chinese. One of her eyes had faded right away, and the other was following rapidly, and on her head she wore a plain skull-cap, secured under her chin, grimy and festooned with sooty cobwebs, as was everything else in the pestilent den. She had a drop of weak slop of tea without milk before her, and she was mumbling a slice of dry toast.

Mrs. Grinder's servant was not in such bad condition; indeed, although, according to her own statement, she was sixtyseven, she was by no means past worldliness or looking after the main chance. I call her Mrs. Grinder's servant, though, perhaps, it would be more correct to style her that poor old woman's partner. She was used to Mr. Missionary, but seeing a stranger with him she instantly busied herself in improving her personal appearance by dipping a dishclout in some strange liquid that stood by in a broken basin and nibbing her face and hands with it, and I suppose by wayof impressing me with what a particularly cleanly old person she was, she never ceased to chafe either her face or her hands with the rag the whole time I was there.

Mr. Missionary being engaged in reading a chapter out of the Bible to Mrs. Grinder, I had some whispered conversation with the other old woman. "She's a-goin' fast, that's my belief"— (this with a jerk of the thumb towards poor Mrs. Grinder). "I thought she was off last night, but lor! I wasn't a bit frightened; a Christian woman ain't got no call to be frightened, has she, sir? That's where I sleeps, on that box. She sleeps on the ground, on that there nice new bed, what Mr. Catlin bought for her, but she used to sleep *ralcy* on the ground —on the bare boards—afore that time. I does for her, don't you see, sir. I has eighteen pence a week from the house, and I gives her ninepence out of it for my lodging, and I waits on her, and has my bit of wittles for it. She has a shilling a week from the house and a quartern loaf, and I goes to church o' Sundays to get the bread. She don't get the bread from the house, don't you know, sir, but from the church. When the service is over, we goes into the vestry, and there's the bread. Meat we never gets, nor yet beer, 'cept when all unexpected somebody pops in and gives the old woman a trifle, and sez, 'Get a bit of meat with it,' and then I gets a mouthful."

"But surely you don't both live through the week on half-acrown and a quartern loaf!"

"Oh no, sir. The old woman gets a shilling a week from Mr. Catlin; but arter all, it's less than half-a-crown, because there's eighteen pence a week to pay for rent. Werry hard pinchin' for two poor old women, ain't it, sir?"

"But do you really get nothing else?"

"Notting else—'cept the rice flour from Mr. Catlin. He's got a sackful on it; leastways, there was a sackful on it at first, and there it is for the askin' to them as he knows stands in want of it. Many a basinful of it for supper has the old woman and me had."

"But why don't she go into the workhouse?"

"Hu-ssh!"

But it was too late. The poor old half-dead woman, who had sat moaning and groaning with her cheek against the sooty carpet that hung before the chimney as though she had no atom of strength to do anything else, instantly fired up as though she had been galvanized, life flashing in her weak remnant of an eye.

"Go to the house yourself! I shan't go to the house. I won't go. What do you mean by it?" It was shocking to witness the poor old creature's fierce energy, and to hear the high-pitched passionate tones in which she spoke.

"Lor a mussy, who said you was a-goin'?" remonstrated her partner.

"I won't go. I'll never go. I'd sooner die."

"No, no, you shan't go to the house, I'll see to that," remarked Mr. Missionary soothingly, whereon the old woman, comforted, leans her cheek against the sooty carpet again, mumbling her thanks, and begging her comforter to come again soon and read some more of the "blessed words" o' promise to her. And then, after gladdening the heart of the poor old things with a prospect of meat for dinner, we bade them goodday, and found our way downstairs again.

"Now we'll pay a visit to Jack Ketch's Warren," remarked Mr. Missionary; "don't imagine that I gave it that name, it's been known as such these fifty years. We'll go through the three alleys, and then we'll look in at Little Hell."

On our way from the house where poor old Mrs. Grinder resided to the first alley on our list, my guide discoursed of the petty thieves of his neighbourhood, and what a cunning and desperate set they were. "Snatching" from passing vehicles appears to be their staple of business, and a very safe and simple staple it is. The "Warren" has many mouths, and a single jump from the highway will reach any one of them, and follow who dare! Even should a sufferer find the hardihood to pursue a delinquent he can by no possibility be successful, and this not so much that a thief will be screened by the general populace (indeed, as will presently appear, the whole locality would be better named "Squalor's Warren" than Ketch's), as on account of the endless facilities that favour the thief's escape. Such a thing as a closed street door is scarcely to be met with in any of the alleys, and every house has cellars below, and a trap in its roof, and low walls in its rear, a scramble over which will take the pursued into the back premises of a house in another alley. The best plan is to bear with your loss with all the patience at your disposal, and go your ways quickly as possible out of such a desperate place, as you always may unless your case should be as peculiar as that of one unfortunate Mr. Missionary told me of. There was a waggoner and an empty waggon coming up Turnmill Street, and the waggoner, who was a cripple, had a call to make at a shop there. He was unable to walk any distance without crutches, but as it was only a couple of steps or so from his waggon to the shop-door, he left his crutches in the waggon, and hobbled in without them. In a minute or so he hobbled out again, and lo! his crutches had vanished. Mr. Missionary told me of another case in which a chandler's shop in the main street had been entered in broad daylight, and while the proprietor sat in the shop parlour with the door open half a tub of butter by some means was spirited away.

Shortly after hearing this last little story, it was my good fortune to find myself in the midst of a gang of this lightfingered gentry. We went into a certain house, and the young gentlemen, having no serious business on hand at the moment, were larking in the passage. My friend knew them every one by name, and they knew him, and I must do them the justice to say that their treatment of him was highly creditable to them. "Ah! Mr. Catlin, how do you do, sir?" "Mornin', Mr. Catlin, hope you're well, sir!" "I wish you were all as well, my lads," replies my friend, turning his bold, blunt, honest face to them. "Why, now, why don't you great strapping chaps turn out and look for a job?" "Can't get nothink, Mr. Catlin; there's lots of coves out of work jes now, sir. " "There always are, Joey, of one sort and another. If you want work you can have it. I'll tell you what I've done. I wrote to that brickmaker I was speaking about the other day, and I'll answer for it you can get on if you'll go and see. Why don't all of you go, now? It would be company to work all together, and you'll earn eight or ten bob a week!" The proposition, however, though civilly received, was not palatable. "I'd have a turn jolly sharp," at last remarked a stag-eyed, bullet-headed youth of about sixteen, "on'y I'm afeard of spiling my hands for gold chain makin', which is my trade." And the rest very gladly took refuge in the little joke to laugh uproariously, and bustle out of the embarrassing presence of the good man.

"Did you ever hear of a poor creature whom the police call the countess?" inquired Mr. Missionary.

I had heard of her very frequently. I distinctly recollected that the last time the titled lady appeared in a police-court the case was headed "The Notorious Countess Again—*her Hundred and Seventy-eighth* Conviction." I have since mentioned the countess's case to an elderly friend of mine, and he informs me that more than a quarter of a century ago she was about as handsome a wicked woman as might be met between Pall Mall and Piccadilly. At that time she was receiving an annuity from the nobleman whose name she borrowed, and was the gayest of the gay—splendidly dressed, sparkling with gold and jewels, riding in a carriage, eating of the daintiest, and drinking wine at a guinea a bottle. Even at that time she was a violent-tempered woman; and, being gifted with enormous muscular development, was not the pleasantest of companions; but it was not until fortune took fright at her fading beauty that she gave way to her pugilistic tendencies. She is an old woman now, but for many years a single policeman would almost as soon think of tackling an escaped tigress as the countess, and out of her one hundred and seventy-eight commitments it may be safely said that at least a hundred out of the number were for assault as well as drunkenness. It is a wonder that the countess is not dead years and years ago. But she is not. A gaunt, grey old woman, she lives in a Turnmill Street alley, under the protection of a gentleman in the bullock-driving interest. The pet of the saloon, the belle of the dance, the dashing beauty is at present domiciled in a Wretched little den, to reach which it was difficult work, groping a way up the dark rickety stairs. In reply to a tap at the door, a gruff, muffled voice growled "Come in," and we went in. No fire, little or no furniture, and a few blackened potatoes left cold from yesterday on a plate on a shelf. To the countess's praise be it spoken, however, the place was clean.

The countess was not at home, but the count was. Behind the door there was an erection in bedstead shape and a great heap of rags and tatters piled in the middle of it. Under this heap lay the count. It was nearly noon, but his lordship was not disposed at present to quit his couch, and hearing the missionary's cheery voice at once ducked his head beneath the rags, rendering himself quite invisible. He remained invisible, his bulky shape curled up dog-wise under the bed clothing. My friend imagining that he must be ill advanced to the bed-side and inquired solicitously as to his health.

"Well! course I'm well," growled the count.

"Missus out?"

"Dun no and don't keer?"

"She isn't drinking, is she?"

"Dun no and don't keer?"

"It's such a lovely morning; quite hot in the sun." "Humph!"

"Ah! you won't own to being queer, that's where it is, You wouldn't lay here when you might be up and looking for a job if you felt all right. It's that rheumatism hanging about you. Ah! it will be all right by-and-by, my friend, if we only mind ourselves and look up. There's no pain or poverty in heaven, hey?"

"Werry likely."

"Don't you think it would do you good to get up and have a walk?"

"Good-mornin'."

"This bright weather will make the work stir, don't you think?"

"Good-mornin'!"

S—2

Not a bit more uncivil than this was the count towards my friend, although, as I was informed, he was amongst the least amiable of the alley dwellers. But for that matter, and as I have before remarked, everybody was civil to Mr. Missionary, from the blear-eyed old sinner of eighty to the hideously dirty small creatures of tenderest age, who left dabbling in the gutter or delving in the reeking mounds of vegetable offal to pluck him by the coat-tail and say, "Hallo, Mr. Tatlin I" That any man single-handed should be able to conquer the deepest of all prejudices in the minds of a people of the stamp such as his daily dealings lie amongst, and bring them to regard him as their disinterested friend and counsellor, the arbitrator in their fierce disputes, and the peace-maker in their quarrels, is simply marvellous, and shows what indomitable energy and singleness of purpose may accomplish. Without the happy gift of tact, however, even under the favourable conditions mentioned, a missionary might easily fail. Mr. Catlin has this happy gift. With all possible respect and admiration for him, I should say that he is the jolliest missionary in the service. He doesn't go about sad, solemn, and with his dismal opinion of the miserable world he is for a term compelled to sojourn in imprinted on his countenance. He knows—and it is a thousand pities that all pastors and teachers similarly engaged do not know it also—that these alley dwellers are not far-seeing—their existence is essentially what is known as a "hand-to-mouth" existence, and that principle is sure to contaminate any higher views they may be brought by easy gradations to arrive at. They expect immediate results to appear after any undertaking they may embark in. I heard a story the other day of a man of this class which fully illustrates what I mean. He was a painter by trade, and so ungodly that never since the time of his marriage had he once entered a church. One day his wife fell ill and a Scripture reader came to her, and at the same time took opportunity to address a few words of advice to her husband. "How can you expect the Lord to look after you when you so completely neglect Him?' remarked the Scripture reader in reply to an observation of Mr. Painter that "he hadn't flicked a brush this eleven weeks." "If you were to attend church regularly all that would soon be altered." "Do you really think it would, now?" "It is certain." "Then I'll give it a trial." So he did. He went to church three times on the following Sunday, and because he didn't immediately fall on a comfortable job at good wages, when the Scripture reader came the following Wednesday he flatly declined to let him into the house, alleging as a reason that he always suspected that preaching and praying was just a parcel of cant, and now he had tried it and proved that it was.

The alley dweller believes in what he sees, and if you show him a good man and tell him that because of his sinless life he is without a single care or sorrow, the alley dweller won't believe you unless the man in question is rosy and smiling and comfortable-looking. Such a man he finds in the missionary of Turnmill Street. He carries a smile and a cheery and encouraging voice wherever he goes, and he claps shoulders or shakes hands with any thief or ruffian that crosses his path with an air of brotherly kindness that carries weight with it. Not the crushing weight of conscious superiority brought to bear against branded depravity and vice, but a lever weight, that for the time at least raises what is left of the man out of the slough in which he is wasting and brings him face to face with a friend. Always bright, always ready with a little joke, always in cue for a snatch and a tune (sacred of course), such another man is never seen in the alley except on very festive occasions indeed—at a wedding for instance, or a christening. And when the alley dweller marks this he finds something very potent indeed in Christianity.

We went up an alley and into a house where lived a man whose wife had been ill during six years. She was abed, with her head bound up, poor thing, and looking pitiable enough with her white face and her great despairing eyes looking out from the gloomy corner where she was lying. Her husband had at one time been a master sweep at the west end of the town, but now followed the trade of a chair-caner. Their room, although scantily furnished, was more decent than any we had as yet been into, and the man was at work shaving cane as he sat on a stool by the fire. As became him, my missionary friend at once gave his attention to the sick woman, and in an undertone I chatted with the cane-shaver. Things were very bad with him, he informed me. If he earned eighteen pence a day he was lucky—a sum, as he truthfully observed, the inside of enough to pay rent and buy bread, to say nothing of the bit of nourishment the missus ought to have. "She ain't so well to-day," explained the cane-shaver, sinking his voice, "and I'll tell you how I thinks that happens. You must know that she fancies a bit of buttered toast at breakfast —she'll eat that when she can't eat anything else—and we generally manages to get it for her. Well, somehow, the ha'pence wouldn't run to butter this morning, and I was 'bliged to send for a bit of drippin' instead. That did it. Her poor stomach, don't you see, sir, won't bear trifling with, and the drippin' toast turned her off sick as a horse. Things ain't as they used to be, sir, or else I'll wager she shouldn't want for nourishers. Why, one time o' day I was doing as good a bizniss as any one in the trade. It was me, with eleven other master sweeps, as gave evidence before Parliament about the climbing system." And with that with an air of pride he strode across the room and fetched an old bag made of bed-ticking and carefully secured at the mouth by many wraps of twine. It was quite a sight to see the changed expression of his face as he dived his hand into the bag tenderly, as though its contents were live birds, and one at a time brought out for my inspection the credentials of his old respectability. There were letters from Somerset House—letters gloriously branded, "On her Majesty's Service," and with the Royal Arms at the back, and Acts of Parliament, and other deeds and documents, the nature of which he would cheerfully have explained had not my friend, who by this time had ministered to his patient, hinted to me that we had farther to go.

And here I may relate a rather singular fact that the mention of documents has put into my head. The institution of matrimony is one that is much neglected in the Turnmill Street alleys, and this, despite the efforts of their best friend, who is generally understood to be at any time willing to give a bride away and pay the fee for putting up the banns, and of the generosity of the minister of St. James's, Clerkenwell, who charge's nothing in such cases for his clerical services. Difficult, however, as it is to induce them to undergo the ordeal, they by no means hold the marriage state in contempt, as is evinced by the fact that in almost every case where it has been performed between the couple residing together you will find the certificate, either framed or plain, hanging against the wall; though why the spot selected for it should so invariably be *beneath the clock,* should that useful article of furniture be present, is more than I can guess.

The sanitary condition of the Turnmill Street alleys is a disgrace to the parish in which they are situated, and shows something monstrously defective in the working of all the various Acts of Parliaments passed for the wholesome housing and cleansing of the very poor. The houses in the alleys are lofty, each containing ten rooms, and in the majority of cases every room harbours a family. In one of the houses (only for Mr. Missionary's sake I would most gladly give its number and the name of the landlord) *fifty-six* individuals find shelter, and the rent of the dilapidated, dark, and miserable structure amounts to *2 &s.* a week. "Rents are going up too," a lodger who paid *is. yd.* fqr a mite of a room, which whitewashed and otherwise rendered decent, might serve as a kennel for a mastiff, ruefully informed me. "There have been a thousand houses pulled down for the railway within half a mile of this, and they come swarming down here after lodgings because there's nowhere else to look for 'em. I was threatened to have another threepence put on me last week." "Where's the use of making a fuss about it?" said another. "There was a fuss made about two years ago when we was a-dyin' up of fever here like rotten sheep, and the police came with their chloride of lime and their brushes, and their whitewash pails, and it was 'Move on there,' and turn out here, and there wasn't to be no living of two families in a room, nor no chuckin' your waste of vegetables and that into the cellar, when the dust heap was a-runnin' over, and we was all to be made that respectable that we wasn't to be allowed to go out without scented ile on our hairs, as a feller may say. Well what come of it? They whitewashed every mortal *outside* thing they could dab a brush on, and they turned the donkeys out of the parlours, and then they walked off, and we have seen nothing of 'em since, and we don't want to for all the good they are. What happened arter they was gone? Why, the donkeys had to be stowed somewhere on the' premises, that you may be sure, and the parlours, what warn't thought good stablin' enough for a moke, was werry soon let for a couple of families to live in."

One of the greatest evils to be met in the "warren" is the scarcity of water. There is a cistern attached to each alley, and once every week-day the water company allows a limited supply of the precious fluid to run into it. The said supply, to judge from the size of the vessel that holds it, would be unequal to the wants of the inhabitants even supposing that the water was required only for the ordinary purposes of personal ablution and cooking and house scrubbing, but apart from these legitimate-uses the inhabitants, or half their number at least, require water for trade purposes. They are costermongers (as we style them, but "general dealers" as they invariably style themselves), and the commodity in which they mainly deal is green stuff—such as cabbages, savoys, and turnip tops. They buy at a cheap rate such stock as is left over from the day's market and will not keep till the next market day. They carry it home—overnight, perhaps—and stow it somewhere *(where,* one is afraid to hint at almost as regards houses where space is so precious) till the morning. The appearance a bunch of greens would then present may be easily imagined; no one would give a single halfpenny for the flabby yellow things and they must be revived. Every general dealer has a tub that is used for this purpose amongst others, and any one bold enough to look into either of the alleys on a Saturday morning may witness at full blast this process of cabbage dressing. Every coster man or woman is busy over a tub, soaking, trimming, and selecting, batch after batch, until the stuff in the vessel becomes too thick and nauseous to be of further service—a fact lothfully recognized by the green-washers, since no more than that one tubful of water may be obtained. In the evening this precious "green-stuff" is carried on the barrows to the Aylesbury Street or Leather Lane markets, and there disposed of in "lumpin' penn'orths" to economical mothers, who take home the vegetable and boil it for their husband and children. It might be worth inquiry how much disease and death may be traced to this source. "I have known the neighbourhood through several years," said an individual with whom I had some talk on the subject, "and I never yet knew a time when sickness in some shape or another did not exist amongst us. In summer time it is frightful. I have seen as many as *thirteen* children buried out of the alleys in the course of a single Sunday afternoon."

Very shocking—incredible almost coming from the mouth of any one except that of a credible eye-witness. Incredible that is to the thousands and tens of thousands whose knowledge of the poorest of the poor is confined to what they may happen to read in the newspapers concerning them. If they could for once in their lives and for humanity's sake screw their courage to a pitch that would enable them to become spectators of what is to be daily and hourly seen in these alleys their wonder would be rather how that death laid his hand on the inhabitants with such lightness. Soon as one unused to so pestilential an atmosphere puts his head in at the dark, ugly mouth of one of these alleys—not so wide in one case as an ordinary wash-house door—the odour that assails his nostrils is of so sickening and deadly a nature that to proceed seems sheer foolhardiness. The walls on either side are black and damp, as is the vaulted roof overhead, and the broken paved way under foot squelches up foul mire as the foot presses it. A little way between the walls and you come on the houses, black as the entry and as unwholesome-looking, and so close on either side that without exaggeration it would not be at all difficult for opposite neighbours to shake hands out of their respective windows. The door sills of the houses are broken and worn down to the gangway, and the thresholds are mere traps for unguarded feet to stumble over, and over head, increasing the wretchedness and gloom of the place, hang suspended from props and brooms thrust out at the upper windows,

the rags that have undergone the mockery of washing, and now trickle down melancholy splashings, augmenting the filthy gutter that rolls sluggishly down the middle of the alley. Everywhere is stench, everywhere uncleanness and squalid misery.

Nor must one other feature standing out with terrible prominence in these foul dens be overlooked—sufficient of itself to account for all the sickness and death that there take place, ay, and far ten times more even though the cold of Siberia reigned there constantly. I should always desire tQ be well within the mark in making statements of this nature; and when I say that the average number of houses in each alley may be taken at twenty, I believe I allow a margin. I think I may also state, with as little fear of contradiction, that in each of the houses four families reside, consisting each of five individuals, giving a total for each alley of *four hundred* human beings, men, women, and children. For the accommodation of all these there is but *one water-closet*. "It is impossible to keep them clean," I was informed (not by Mr. Missionary, but by a person whose knowledge of the subject was beyond dispute). "There are a goodish many people living up here of a reg'lar clean and decent sort, and a goodish many who are as bad as the beasts of the field. Up this alley it is one man's job to give the 'place' a wash down every morning, and he gets the rent of his room forgive him for his trouble, but it's never fit for a decent person to pass, let alone go into; and how can it be wondered at? They can't get a man to do the job down the next alley because the landlord won't pay for having it done; so an old woman living up there does it, and the people what lives there *give her their cinders* for her trouble. You see what it is now, sir, and this is March and not a particularly warm day either. You should pay a visit to this quarter some hot afternoon in August. Why, even the reg'lar lodgers can't stand the awful smells there are here on summer nights, and you may see 'em squatting out on the kerb and laying on their barrows in Turnmill Street till the

air has got a bit cool." I cast an eye into one of the "places" as I passed it hastily, and all I can say is that if every cinder that old woman had given to her was converted into a golden nugget, the value realized would still fall very short of the service expected of her.

Scavengering in the alleys, as I was given to understand, is but a shade better cared for than the sewer business. I went into a hovel in a corner where lived an unlucky little man whose sole subsistence was the manufacture of such skewers as are in requisition at cat's-meat shops. There was a bed in the room, as, indeed, was without exception the case as regards every room I entered that morning; but in this case there was a young boy lying desperately ill on it, and the father sat by the fire ragged and unshaven, and with a leathern apron on, cutting up the billets with a sharp knife, while mother sat at the other side sharpening the blunt sticks as father cut them. The price obtained for the skewers was sixpence a thousand, and out of that they had to buy material—wood-billets and string. The wood per thousand cost them twopence, and if they both sat at work and stuck to it from morning till night, they could cut and point three thousand skewers, and so earn a shilling short of a halfpenny that went for twine to tie the three thousand skewers into thirty bundles. "We're obliged to tie 'em in bundles, because it's only the respectable shops that we serve," explained the skewer cutter.

"Your little boy appears very ill," I remarked.

"Ah, but he's better since they've moved the heap," replied the child's mother, "the dust heap, I mean, you know, as you might have noticed just at our door as you came in."

"It won't be long before it requires to be moved again, I should imagine, judging from its growth towards your doorstep."

"Lord bless you, sir, that's nothing. The scavengers come once a week or so in the winter, and are able to keep it under a bit; but whether it is because they are extra busy, I don't know; but the way they let that heap grow there in summer weather is astonishing. It tells up, you see, sir, when the fruit glut sets in; and there is a deal of waste in plums, and such like, to be chucked away, and there is nowhere else to chuck it but just here. Why, many a time I've seen the heap so big that it run over and fell all into our passage, and when they found that they've gone on chucking it into our passage as they brought it, and we had to make our way through it passing in and out. It ain't so much the inconvenience, but the smell, sir, is something awful."

"In the walnut season when they bring their wet muckyshells here, and chuck 'em out by the bushel! phew! it's grand then, I can tell you," put in Father Skewer-cutter, looking up for an instant with a wry face.

"But why do you stay here?" I asked.

"Why? we must, because we can't get a place at the rent we can afford to pay anywhere else. That question's very soon answered."

"What rent do you pay?"

"Two shillings a week."

"Why they tell me that for that sum you may get a threeroomed cottage and a good bit of land to grow your own vegetables in the country."

"Ah, but they don't use many skewers in them parts," answered the old man, with a knowing shake of his head, as he bent with a will over his work again.

"It is very little the poor fellows in this quarter see of the country, I presume," I remarked to my informant, as we made our way round to Broad Yard.

"Well, sir, we try to do a little good in all directions, and the one you mentioned has not been forgotten. Last year I beat up amongst afewfriends, andgot enough money to take a hundred and fifty of them down to the sea-side. We went to Brighton, and a very pleasant day we made of it. I think not one in twenty had ever seen the sea before. In the carriage where I was one man said to another, just as we came in sight of the sea, ' See them there fields, Joey? I'm for a quiet stroll and a pipe over them as soon as we get out,' nor could he be persuaded that what he saw was the water till we got near enough to see the waves rising and falling."

"That," continued my friend, as we passed a cellar door, "is where I once had an interesting interview with a sweep, and nearly lost my life. He was a very hard character to deal with, and the worst of it was that you could scarcely ever catch him to have a few words with him. When he wasn't out, and in an unfit state to talk with, he was down in his cellar here amongst his soot. 'But one day I was coming past, and I heard him at work, and as I thought in a good humour. I couldn't see him, because the cellar runs a good way under, and is as dark as night, and there wasn't any ladder. 'Never mind,' thought I, 'I'll have a jump for it,' and so I did, and alighted fairly in the middle of a heap of soot as high as my waist. I thought I should have been smothered. In an instant the soot flew up and filled my eyes and nostrils, and there I was floundering until he came to help me. I shouldn't have been surprised if he had grumbled a bit, but as soon as I was able to speak and make some sort of explanation, 'And d'ye mean to say that you've took all this trouble over me?' said he, and from that time we have been the best of friends."

In the alley adjoining we found the house where lived the man and his family last on our visiting list.

"I think you will admit after you have witnessed it that a more distressful sight you never saw," remarked my guide.

And without doubt he was right. The house was the dirtiest of all the dirty ones I had entered. There was a strong stable flavour in the air that pervaded the basement, and a sound of snorting and stamping of hoofs that declared the proximity of donkeys. But the smell was very much to be preferred to that which grew on you as you ascended the tumbledown staircase. Dirty suds seemed to be the chief ingredient of the sickening stench proceeding from the open door of the first floor, which betrayed its whereabouts. This was the room where Mr. Burke lived. Mrs. Burke was washing—that, at least, was how she described her occupation, though from the colour of the rags she was dabbling and sluicing about she might have been dyeing. Mr. Burke had just risen from his bed and was in the act of pinning and tying on a few rags to fit him for hobbling to the hospital on account of some complaint that afflicted him. In the corner there was a bedstead, a bed dirty as dunghill rags (I trust that the reader will regard this as plain, simple truth, and acquit me of any attempt at word-painting), and three or four sacks, such as potatoes are brought to market in, only fifty times dirtier—being nearly black, in fact; and on the sacks, naked as they were born, except for their tremendous shocks of dirty, tangled hair, squatted three children, varying in years from, say, four to ten. Not only were the poor little creatures shockingly unclean, but the dirt on them—all over them, on their legs, on their chests, on their prominent ribs—was of that dry and polished sort, such as may be seen on the hands of a workman at a dirty trade. "Why don't they get up?" I asked.

"Cos they ain't got no clothes," replied Mr. Burke; "they ain't had no clothes for ever such a while."

"But what do they do all day?" I asked.

"Oh, I don't know; they 'mooses themselves somehow. I can't help it. I'm so crippled, don't you see, and can't do no work, and the work'us won't help us to no more'n a loaf. They thinks themselves lucky if they gets wittles, let alone clothes, poor kids."

"Hallo! why, where's the baby *f* inquired my friend, as a shrill, though muffled piping made itself heard; "why, I declare it's right down Under the sacks *f* and heroically approaching the heap of foul rags, he made a dive and fished up Mrs. Burke's last suckling, kicking and squalling, and not a bit more like a baby than a skinned rabbit, and with an apology for a flannel petticoat slouched about its poor little body.

"Give her to mS, please, sir, and I'll give her a drop; arid then baby must be good while mother rences out her clothes and gets them out o' winder."

That baby, and poor Mrs. Burke "giving it a drop," and the terrible smell the suds emitted, and Mr. Burke's rheumatic groans as he tortured his arms into his tattered jacket, and the gambols of the naked children on the sacks, brimmed the cup that had been filling since I began my explorations, and taking leave of the Burke family, and shortly after of the gentleman who had been so kindly instrumental in letting me into these little secrets, I gladly hurried away to where the air was fit to breathe.

AT THE EARTHING OF A FELO-DE-SE.

'OR a period of three years or nearly, a harmless and quiet -fellow—an odd jobber at carpentry—lodged at a common lodging-house in the neighbourhood of Whitefriars. Like all odd jobbers at a trade, his means of existence were by no means certain; but he was not a communicative man, and whatever were his privations he kept them to himself, paying for his bed in the kitchen with a punctuality that won him the esteem of his landlord. He was an eccentric kind of man, and had a great fancy for experimenting with firearms. It was not uncommon to hear him banging away of a night in his bedroom down below, but as there was nobody down there that he could shoot but himself, this, amongst several other whimsies of his, was winked at by the people of the house on account of his general good conduct.

One morning he was discovered horribly maimed and dead.

That his death was the work of his own hands was beyond a doubt. It appeared that his curiosity concerning engines for the destruction of human life was not confined to guns and pistols. It entered his fantastic brain that the guillotine was a machine worthy of his study, and he at once set about constructing one which should be an improvement on the upright posts and grooved-knife contrivance as used in France. The cunning and ingenuity exercised by this poor fellow in bringing his new and improved guillotine to perfection is without parallel in civilized countries, the nearest approach to it being the skill displayed by certain African savages in trapping and slaying the hippopotamus. The engine of destruction the Bayeye brings against behemoth is called a "downfall," and is conrived in this manner:—An iron blade is fixed in a beam and the beam is hauled up by a bark rope over a limb of a tree that projects across a path the hippopotamus is known to perambulate on his way to the river; the bark rope is brought down and secured across the path under the grass, so that when hippo comes shuffling along he kicks the string, and the bladed beam is released, and comes plump down atop of the amazed brute's back.

Success is not invariable. Sometimes the beam turns a sommersault in its descent, and does no more than expedite hippo's movements by catching him an ugly knock, and sometimes hippo will give a lurch to the left or right just at the wrong moment, and the blade will inflict but the merest scratch on his ribs.

The device of the poor crack-brained jobbing carpenter was wonderfully like the Bayeye's " downfall." He procured a stone weighing thirty pounds or thereabouts, and he chipped it into shape so that it might "fall true." He suspended this stone by a string over a bar driven into the wall above the cupboard, against which his bedstead came. He sharpened a chopper; he bored a hole in its handle, and hinged it on to a screw taken out of his bedstead, securing it with a nut, so that the weapon might stand steady on the edge of its blade. He procured a form and placed a pillow on it, and taking a razor-blade in his grasp, laid his head down on the pillow, and immediately under the hanging stone. He brought over the chopper (the handle of which was secured to the jambs of the open cupboard door) and rested its sharp edge on his wind-pipe. He raised his hand with the razor-blade in it and cut the cord that held the stone, and down it came—not decapitating the madman, as he no doubt expected that it would, but merely indenting his throat to the depth of about an inch.

Enough, however, to cause his death, and to occasion the summoning of a coroner's jury to investigate the matter and settle the manner of death the unlucky wretch had died.

There were sixteen jurymen and the coroner, and the evidence laid before them was of the simplest sort. Nobody even suspected that he was "wrong in his head." The last person who conversed with him found him rational and in no way excited. So far from showing symptoms of insanity, he had always appeared a very sensible man indeed. As to the firing of pistols in his bedroom and that sort of thing, if every man given to such pranks were pronounced mad, pray how many sane men would be left in the world? Besides, look at the deliberation—the cool calculation' and sound judgment that marked the. performance? Could any madman construct a machine like it? Could any man, except in his sound and sober senses, have so nicely adjusted the hatchet and hung the stone that it should descend as true as a plummet? If you wanted motive, there was motive enough surely. In the self-murderer's pockets were discovered fifteen pawnbrokers' tickets for tools —indeed, it seemed that, hard pushed by poverty, he had parted with all his.tools except the one he reserved for such fatal use.. He owed some rent. lie was steeped *to.* the eyes in poverty; he had no friends; it was nQ use his looking for a job, since if he found one he had no tools to do it with. A1J these matters pressed on his mind, and he.resolved to make an end of it.-.: ,. Just as plain as here set down did the.whole affair appear to the minds of twelve of the jurymen out of.sixteen. The minority were of a different way of thinking. Possibly it occurred to them that nobody but a man bereft of reason would dare dally with death as this man had. There is no greater coward than the sane man who slinks out of the world. He invariably seeks sudden death—dodges over the threshold of existence in as little time as it takes to make a sweeping cut with a keen razor, or to pull a pistol trigger. He does not loiter at the gate of the grim toll-taker, as did the unlucky jobbing carpenter, pulling bobbins and arranging pretty contrivances, as though preparing for the opening scene of a peep-show. He —the sane man urged by desperation to bring his miserable existence to a sudden end—might, at half-glance, as it were, take kindly to a scheme of the guillotine order, but by the time he had brought it to face him fully, he would of a surety take fright and run for his life; whereas, the madman, delighted with the progress made in carrying out the conceptions of his disordered brain, would grow madder and madder each moment, till, when the time came for his laying his head on the pillow and severing the string that held the heavy stone, he, in all probability, was as delighted as a boy for the first time in his life about to fly a kite or despatch a fire-balloon. Cool and deliberate! No doubt of it. Had any one been nigh enough to listen, it is not unlikely that they would have heard the poor maniac laughing pleasantly to himself, or humming the burthen of a funny song, the minute before his life slipped from him. However, the majority of the jurymen were of opinion that the suicide was in perfect possession of his senses to the very last, and there was no more to be said about it, except that as he had shown himself to be a felon of the very worst degree—a guilty wretch who by his own act had so offended Heaven that nothing but the prayers and intercession of all good men could save him from everlasting torment—such prayer and intercession should be denied him, and he should be flung into a hole at night-time, with no more ceremony than attends the throwing a dead dog into a ditch. Law is law, there is no denying, and 4th Geo. IV., c. 52, and not twelve intelligent men of the present enlightened times, is responsible for the wrong if any exist; but one cannot help thinking that a law permitting a dozen cheesemongers and tailors and butchers to ape the functions of the Last Awful Tribunal, and sentence a fellow-creature to everenduring punishment, cannot be too soon repealed.

On this occasion, the law, as represented by its coroner, thought the verdict a very proper one, and, calling in its beadle, confided to him the responsibility of seeing that its dignity and majesty was maintained. It happened to be the first time that the beadle, who is a modest little man, and keeps a walking-stick shop, had ever been entrusted with a business so tremendous, and he was, not unnaturally, somewhat nervous over it. However, when it was explained to him that if he didn't take the matter in hand his churchwarden must, his fidelity overcame his qualms, and he undertook the commission, and at once put himself in communication with the undertaker, as the suicide had to be put in the ground that same night.

"We shall call for it and take it up at half-past seven," I was informed, and was honoured with an invitation to "ride down with us." This however, I declined. It is unpleasant enough in all conscience to make a business jaunt to a graveyard, but to ride thither on a hearse at night—seated on the black, shiny roof, and holding on by the stumps that on ordinary occasions support the funereal plumes, was not to be thought of; especially as the journey was to Ilford, a dismal country road in part and ten miles from London. So I elected to go in a vehicle of my own choosing.

They took "it" up punctually at the time appointed—Mr. Beadle and two men of the staff of the contracting undertaker who undertook the job. The box they put " it" in was composed of half a dozen unplaned boards scantily smeared with a blackish pigment and roughly nailed together. It was scarcely of the ordinary coffin shape even, and being without plate or inscription might have been carted to a railway with other luggage without exciting particular attention. When " it" severed the string, it still retained in its grasp the handleless razor, and it would have been bundled into its hole still grasping it had it not let it fall while being hoisted into its box. The villanous and felonious article had no friends, not a single one. So, stowed in the hearse, and with the beadle, and the driver, and his friend perched on the box, the funeral party was complete.

A pair of stout horses were attached to the hearse, and whirled it over the stones at a spanking rate, so that my coachman had some trouble at times in keeping it in sight—especially as it was so very black—horses, carriage, and men—and the moonlight but fitful, skulking behind cloud-banks sometimes for as long as two minutes together. I don't know how Mr. Beadle (being, as before hinted, a somewhat nervous man) found it on the hearse roof, with the felon's body within two planks' breadth of him, hurrying along the dark road, with the wind whistling across the bleak flat country. I know that I found it anything but satisfactory, and was not at all sorry to hear my man say, "I can see the Rabbits, sir; the Rabbits is the house where all these black jobs puts up for a freshener, sir."

The Rabbits, a white and ghostly house, crouching back from the highway, is within a stone's-cast of the cemetery gate, and being the only "public " for a considerable distance, is much patronized by travellers returning from the melancholy duty of interring their friends. Likewise it is the resort of the servants of the Cemetery Company—the grave-diggers, &c., of whom there is necessarily a very considerable staff. It was about half-past nine when the hearse drew up at the Rabbits, it being thought in no way indecent, since the poor corpse in their charge was merely a *felo-de-se,* to leave it outside the gin-shop a little whilst its custodians took a drain at the bar.

This, after all, was fortunate. At the bar, imbibing rum, was a tall man, with a check shirt and clay-stained corduroys, whom one of the hearse party at once recognized as a gravedigger.

"Here you are, then!" exclaimed the hearse driver. "Yes, here I am; what o' that?" returned the grave-digger. "Well, you're all ready for us, I suppose?" said Mr. Beadle.

"Me ready? Ready for what? I've just come in for twopen'orth of rum after my supper, and now I mean to toddle home to bed."

"What! d'ye mean to say that they didn't send you word down that we should bring you a job here to-night?" demanded Mr. Beadle, in alarm.

"I mean to say we haven't heard a word about it," returned the grave-digger, decidedly. "There'll be no burying here to-night. There can't be: everybody has gone home long ago."

The poor little man with the majesty of the law to uphold, though fully armed with the awful authority of 4th Geo. IV., c. 52, was in a predicament. The gravedigger, having drunk up his rum, was buttoning his jacket, and would be off and abed before a policeman could be found to enforce the Act of Parliament for such cases provided; to drive the *felo-de-se* back to Whitefriars, or to take out the horses and stable the body for the night at the Rabbits, were courses equally objectionable. Mr. Beadle thought he would try severity.

"Very good; then I shall lay it at the gate and leave you to answer for it."

"You'll please yourself, I suppose," replied the cool gravedigger, lighting his pipe; "it's no business o' mine what you do with it."

The case was growing desperate,— 4th Geo. IV., c. 52, was in jeopardy, and the law's majesty in danger of being outraged. As a private individual he never would have done it; but for the sake of his country's rulers, for the sake of the dignity of the Houses of Lords and Commons, and the safety of the lion and the unicorn, Mr. Beadle relented, and resorted to persuasion and entreaty, and finally the grave-digger yielded so far as to consent to ask permission of the lodge-keeper to pass "it" through. "It" was passed through without difficulty, and at a distance of more than a half mile from the entry, in the unconsecrated part, a hole was found. It was fortunate that at this time the moon struggled out of the clouds, otherwise there might have been some bungling, for, being but an amateur at *felo-de-se* burying, Mr. Beadle had forgotten all about the torches. Had it been pitch dark, with torrents of rain falling, the job would have to have been got through somehow.

As it was, it was got through with neatness and despatch. The grave-digger was an old hand, and had his ropes about the box in a twinkling, and held one while the undertaker's men held the other. "Lower," said the grave-digger, and they lowered, and the box rested on the clay. Then the gravedigger threw a few shovelsful of earth on the box— enough to cover it—and replaced the planks over the hole, and we went away.

"Why didn't they cover him in entirely?" I asked.

"What for? We couldn't spare a regular interment a grave all to himself, let alone one such as him," replied the gravedigger.

"But surely you won't put another body over his?"

"Surely we shall," answered the grave-digger. "Not a Christian, you know," he hastened to explain—" one of them sects what don't care about being buried in consecrated ground. Why, what's the odds? He's as good as they are now anyhow, if he wasn't before."

And discussing kindred matters, the hearse bowled out of the cemetery, and once more we put up at the Rabbits, where the party invited the grave-digger to the social glass and the friendly pipe, and, the undertaker's men as well as the grave-digger being well versed in sepulchral lore, quite a jolly hour ensued, when, hey for London! with our noble work accomplished, and the law's majesty and dignity vindicated.

AMONGST THE MUSIC-HALL LUMINARIES.

TV/1 USIC-HALLS so called, as places for the amusement of the working classes of London and its suburbs, have of late advanced rapidly into public favour. Twenty years ago the number of "singing and dancing" licences issued by the magistrates numbered scarcely fifty, and now they amount together to upwards of three hundred and fifty. The managers of these "halls" conduct their business with much spirit, and it may be assumed considerable financial success. Their placards are prominent at every bill-sticking " station," and on every wall and hoarding sufficiently capacious to contain their gigantic dimensions. In six-feet letters of green, on a yellow ground, the public is informed that Peter (the Great) Wilkins will, all next week, and till further notice, continue to enchant crowded audiences with his eminently successful song of "All round my hat; or, Who stole the donkey?" Likewise that the Inimitable Brown, the Irresistible Smith, and the Delightful Robinson will variously "electrify," and "convulse," and "occasion shrieks of mirth," amongst their kind patrons. Portraits of these celebrities appear, highly coloured, in the music-shop windows. There is the Delightful Robinson in his last hit of "The Perambulator; or, Jemima's Young Guard," and of the Irresistible Smith in the act of delivering himself of that famous and soul-stirring melody " Matilda Toots; or, You should see her Boots. " So enormous has been the success of the music-halls that theatrical managers have grown alarmed, and sued the law for protection from their formidable rivals, and grave magistrates, by way of settling the matter in the fairest possible manner, have for a while sunk their dignity, and, all unknown to their friends and relatives, stolen off to the Cambrian or the Isis to see the fun and judge for themselves; and when next the case came before them, as they sat on their judgment seats, they have not hesitated to declare their approval of the entire entertainment. Where a magistrate ventures any man may follow; so the other evening being in that quarter of the town where is situate that celebrated place of entertainment, the Grampian, I thought I might do worse than invest sixpence there.

I might have got in for threepence, that being the sum charged for admission to the body of the hall, but observing stuck about the walls in the neighbourhood that Ezekiah Podgers was to appear for the first time that evening, in addition to the powerful and talented company always to be found at the Grampian, I thought it possible that there might be some little crowding. Sixpence admitted me to the gallery, and if I had gone as high as a shilling I might have taken a seat in the stalls on a form covered with red baize, and smoked a cigar in the distinguished company of Paddy Finnigan, the chairman. In addition to these advantages, I might have secured a spitoon all to myself, as well as a glass bottom to the pewter out of which I drank my beer—paying no more than an extra twopence per pint on account of the indulgence. However, it is not every man that can afford luxuries in this hard driving world.

I was half sorry, indeed, that I was tempted to invest that extra threepence, since within ten minutes of taking my seat and some time before the performance began, the gallery was packed and crammed as full as the cheaper space below. However, this only confirmed my expectations of the rare treat in store, and I allowed the heavy young man immediately behind me, with his arms comfortably folded and resting on my shoulders, to remain undisturbed, and banished regret for my unfortunate hat that was rapidly yielding to the enormous pressure brought against my knees.

The orchestral arrangements at the Grampian, though modest, are creditable, and, as a prelude to the more important performance, executed some popular airs in a neat and dexterous manner. After that a young lady, who on the bills was vaguely described as "serio-comic," favoured the audience with a funny song descriptive of the miseries of ancient maidenhood, which was highly relished, judging from the applause that followed. The singer was recalled, and as a set-off to her former song sang a ditty concerning roguish married men and the barefaced swindles practised on muchenduring wives. It might have been that the laugh would have been against the men this time, but there was no room for the change; in the former song the female portion of the auditory had laughed the loudest and longest, and now there was nothing left but for everybody to clap their hands and jingle their glasses unanimously. It was curious as the song progressed to note the gentle elbowing administered to the husbands by the wives in all parts of the hall by way of reminder of some bygone delinquency suggested by the singer, as well as the good-humoured winkings with which the nudgings were received. This must-have been instructing as well as amusing to the sweet-hearting portion of the audience.

After Miss Maclachlan had sung for the third time, three "niggers" bounded in, and it augured well for the sympathy of the working men of England with the genuine down-trodden slave that they so kindly tolerated the wretchedly threadbare quips and cranks of these worn-out make-believes. They were funny "niggers "—jolly, well-fed; all play and no-work darkies, whose sole business in life appeared to be to sleep away the morning, and throughout the afternoon play upon the banjo, and sing of what they had for dinner and what they expected to get for supper, varying the amusements by inventing conundrums. Their jokes as a rule were not original. The majority, as they rolled out of their capacious mouths, were as familiar to the audience as the story of Jack-the-Giant Killer, and when they essayed something new, it were preferable that they once more slew Blunderbore, though for the thousandth time. Nor were their doings a bit newer than their sayings. Jumbo artfully withdrew Mumbo's chair, as of old, bringing Mumbo with a crash to the ground, and whereon Jumbo, as of old, promptly delivered himself of an *apropos,* though not over delicate riddle, concerning the railway engine and the tender behind. Gumbo played the bones over his head, and under his legs, and behind his back; and Jumbo played the banjo over his head, and under his legs, and behind his back; and Mumbo cried, "Gor 'long, nigger!" several times, and in very effective style; and at the termination of the performance there was a burst of applause provocative of the suspicion that, although by no possibility could Britons voluntarily become slaves, still, if the dire day ever did fall, and a choice were allowed the conquered, they would to a man elect to be slaves on a sugar plantation "down Souf."

The entertainment as far as it went was, as has been shown, quite equal to the expectations of those who had paid to come to witness it, but the cream of it had yet to be served up, and here it comes in shape of funny Ezekiah Podgers, who has just arrived in a state of perspiration from the Waterloo Music Hall, and his brougham may be seen waiting at the door of the Grampian to take him on to the Balaklava the moment the Grampian can spare him. The demand for Podgers is enormous. His earnings must exceed fifty guineas a week. It is rumoured that his brougham, with the magnificent lamps and his pair of horses, cost him four hundred guineas.

Podgers' appearance is the signal for a perfect hurricane of welcome. A hundred sturdy voices shout out his name and cry "Bravo, Podgers I" and the shrill tones of women swell the flattering chorus. Podgers is used to this sort of thing, however, and briefly bowing his acknowledgments fires away, and instantly the hall is hushed. He was supposed to be dressed to the "character" he was personating, but what character is manifested by a costume consisting in a threeinch-square check suit buttoned up to the chin, with trousers six inches too short, and a hat about four sizes too large, is not plain. His first song was called "The Ugly Donkey Cart." Every eye brightened as soon as it was made known that this song of songs was the one forthcoming. Simple as the ballads of old, but far surpassing them in point and subtlety of wit, it is descriptive of the infatuation of a young man for a damsel in the fried fish trade, and resident on Saffron Hill. How this young man loved and pined in secret, and how he finally went "4»r0&" 'his'"'? irwrer bones,".-peed, not here be. minutely, described. It came to this, as the fifth verse declared *irr I .-. ... m k '.* -is "She shoved me right bang into a dish of fried Dutch plaice,,

Took hold of a bowl of butter, and threw it in my face;

The driver came in at the time, to make my troubles complete,

, He got all the boys to pelt me as I ran away clown the street.

Doodle de dum, doodle de doodle lum, de doodle lum, de doodle lay." «.,. . ... J-.-

'The last line is the refrain of this exquisitely humorous ditty,, but the people couldn't sing it for laughing..They tried, but the recollection of the catastrophe just related was too much for them, and they broke down to combine in a roar of mirth. They tried again, and broke down to roar and bang the table and ring the glasses with the liquor stirrers, and cry " Encore!" as though but a little more of Ezekiah Podgers were required to fill their chalice of earthly bliss and restore them to old Eden.

Mr. Podgers knew how it would be evidently, since he must have commenced to change his clothes the moment he was roared off the stage. Responsive to the clamour for his reappearance, he came on again in a long coat with a tightfitting dressing-gown made out of cotton chintz of a staring colour, and wearing on his head a tall conical cap with a tassel. He was received as enthusiastically as at first. "He's first-rate in this," a neighbour observed to me, "I've seen the inventor of it do it, but Podgers beats him in my opinion— jumps a good two inches higher."

The song was the celebrated one of the "Cure," which, as the public is probably already aware, is a "dance song," the "cure" thrusting his hands into his trousers pockets *a la* Mr. Clown, and jumping up incessantly, at the same time keeping his limbs as rigid as possible, while he sings. The words of the song are worthy of the action that accompanied it, and subjoined is a sample of the former:— I) ' *r* ' 'r -"'"""

'' Young Love he plays some funny tricks-

With us unlucky elves;, --..
So, gentlemen, I pray, look out,
And take care of yourselves;
-. .For once I met a nice young maid,
, Looking so demure,
And all'at once to me she cried, ---
..'. You are a perfect cure!'".. »

There were ten of these verses— some even more spirited and mirth-inspiring than the one quoted, and during the whole time occupied in singing the song Mr. Podgers never once halted or paused for breath, but continued to bob up and down with the regularity of a steam-engine piston. No wonder that the audience clapped and demanded a repetition. "Just you fancy the presper-ation he must be in!" remarked my neighbour, and clapped his hands more vehemently than before for Mr. Podgers to come on again;

After a lapse of about five minutes the indefatigable Ezekiah once more made his appearance, this time in evening costume and with nothing except three blazing diamond rings on his fingers, a gold watch-chain of "cable" pattern, and a hat with a curly rim, to distinguish him from a private gentleman. He,was sure, he said, that his patrons would excuse him from another song requiring so much exertion as that he had already sung —especially when he informed them that he had already sung it once at the Waterloo, and was bound to sing it yet once more at the Balaklava, "to which hall my donkey cart is at this moment waiting outside to convey me," funnily remarked Mr. Podgers, fingering the cable chain so as to bring two of the diamond rings in a position to twinkle to advantage in the gas-light. "However, I will sing you another song, and that must be the last to-night—it must indeed. Any other night I shall be," &c., &c.

Podgers was the people's pet, and they delighted to indulge him. It was something to confer a favour on a man with three diamond rings and a brougham and pair!" Go on Podgers! Bravo, Podgers! Just one more!" Podgers winked affably, aad advancing to the footlights with an affectation of timidity, requested the married men of the company to protect him from the violence of their wives, and the bachelors present to keep tight hold of their sweethearts, for he was about to sing a song calculated to rouse even that very tiny bit of anger to be found in every fair breast. "Poor Married Man!" cried a hundred voices, at once made aware of the song Mr. Podgers was about to sing, nor was it observable that the owners of the fair breasts greeted the intimation with less enthusiasm than the sterner sex.

The song was an intensely comic one, being descriptive of the shifts and privations to which a poor wretch is reduced with many little mouths to fill and small means to meet the responsibility. It made fun of his rags, of his wife's rags, of complaints of his children, the scanty size of the family loaf. It was fruitful in facetious allusions to his darned stockings and his only shirt. It went on to tell how that—

"No one knows'what he suffers, Poor married man!
He wears *top* boots, for they're all uppers,
Poor married man!
And in that state, oh! what a treat,
Bare footed now he walks the street,
And urchins cry, 'How's your poor feet?'
Poor married man!" and so triumphantly worked up to the inexpressibly humorous climax when

"Grim death comes kindly to relieve him,
And a parish egg-chest at last receives him;
Poor married man!"

"Ha! ha! ha! Ho! ho! ho! Bravo, Podgers! Oh Lor', oh dear, oh dear! What a funny song, to be sure."

I had noted down several other examples of the "comic" songs of the music-hall, but when this last one is recalled to my memory, I feel unequal to the task. I trust, however, that I have fulfilled my purpose, which is to draw attention to the sorry rubbish in the way of comic singing that is put off on the frequenters of places of amusement of which the Grampian is taken as a type. It is an insult to every sane man and woman to set such rubbish as that contained in the " Cure" before them, and a wonder of wonders that the man who first attempted to sing "Poor Married Man!" was not pelted off the stage. How does it happen that such trash is tolerated by the pleasure-seeking Englishman? How is it he is so clever at work and so foolish at play? Is it because his serious energy is so tightly strung all day that he requires so violent an alterative before he can feel comfortable, and able to smoke his pipe serenely and enjoy his beer? Is his appreciation of fun so dull that his risible faculties will not consent to be moved unless they be tickled by some such gentle stimulant as,

"The shrimps you pull in half by the tails,
And eat bread and butter and things like snails,
On the Sanas, on the Sands, on the Sands, on the Sands,"
which was part of a song called "Margate Sands," sung by another funny gentleman in the course of the evening? Either this is so, or, as is more likely, the English workman is just a jolly, good-tempered fellow, who sets out for the Grampian with his "missus " on his arm, determined to "enjoy himself," and is grateful to anybody who will assist him to that laudable end.

TT is my proud and happy privilege to announce to the anxious mothers of England that one of the most celebrated and voracious dragons haunting wicked London is at its last gasp, and cannot, unless by a miracle, recover. Were it anything else than a dragon it must be pitied; its case is so deplorable. Its fangs are worn down to the bluntness of a broomstick; its sting has lost its sheath, and there appears plain to be seen and avoided; the fire has expired in its nostrils, or at least is reduced to the merest smoulder, accompanied by a fume sufficiently disgusting to warn off all who would approach; there is no more fascination remaining in its eyes than in the eyes of a dead flounder, and, more significant than all, its wonderful powers of wheedling and deluding have forsaken it, and it is reduced to idiotic chatter and drivel that can fill its hearers only with disgust and contempt.

Coal Hole is the monster's name. It is one of the most venerable of metropolitan dragons, and may truthfully boast of having devoured a larger number of green young men than any beast of its tribe. For very many years its den was situate in the heart of London, and it had as its chief priest a huge, fat creature of our own species called Baron. These were the dragon's palmiest days, and its renown spread through 7—2 the land. Daring young farmers and graziers venturing up to "Lunnon" in the Cattle Show season were treated to a glimpse of real outand-out "life" by their Cockney cousins, and, after paying a visit to all the minor dragons, "wound up " by diving into Maiden Lane, and obtaining an introduction to Old Dragon Coal Hole. Hailing from regions where gas is unknown, and where the "mop" fair at Michaelmas and the "mummers" at Christmas-time are the only amusements vouchsafed the inhabitants, it were no wonder if the young farmers and graziers were enchanted by the intoxicating splendour of the dragon and. its surroundings. Lights sparkling amid a glory of twinkling glass, velvet-covered seats, waiters more respectable-looking as regards dress than the country parson at home, brilliant champagne, choice cigars, ladies more splendid than Queens of Sheba, spicy meats, spicy songs, and music compared with which the Muggleton brass band was as the braying of donkeys in a pound! No wonder, when young Dawkings heard and saw all these things that he felt slightly delirious, and that on returning home he confided to his most intimate male friends the matchless marvels he had been eye-witness to, and the "pretty penny " which first and last the privilege had cost him. Dawkings's most intimate friends whom he could trust with a secret he would not have come to his mother's or sister's ears for worlds, had *their* most intimate friends who were equally trustworthy, and so the secret spread, and the dragon of Maiden Lane became more terribly famous than ever. Visions of the monster nightly haunted the pillows of parents whose sons were in London, and when kind-hearted Aunt Deborah forwarded to Mr. Charley Wiggles, of King's College, that fifteen pounds he so disinterestedly solicited from her on behalf of his widowed laundress, whose husband had been killed by a fall from a ladder, leaving her with thirteen young children to support, the letter that accompanied the donation, and which contained good counsel against the wiles of dragons generally, hinted broadly at Dragon Coal Hole (" night-house" Aunt Deborah called it) in particular.

But sleep in peace, good country mothers and fathers; abate your alarms, Aunt Deborah; for the ravening beast in question is on its last legs. Its chief priest died some two years or so since, and shortly after, the monster crawled out of Maiden Lane in the night, and for a time disappeared, so that its enemies began to indulge in the hope that he might have crossed the Strand and, blundering down some of the dark alleys there, tumbled into the river, and so an end of him. But he was not dead yet. Where he had lurked meanwhile, or on what he had been subsisting nobody knows, but one night he suddenly hung out his sign again. It is a queer sign that of Dragon Coal Hole. A shabby wretch, a sort of plucked and tame Solomon Eagle, carries the monster's insignia on his head, lit by a candle, covered by a sort of transparent hat. Yes, the dragon had come to life again, the sign on the man's head informed the public, and might be found jolly, hearty, and rollicking as ever in Leicester Square. Having the highest respect for Aunt Deborah, I had hitherto abstained from visiting the fascinating beast, but feeling curious and pleading the call of duty, last Monday night I paid it a visit.

Forearmed by the stories I had heard of the monster's art'fices to lure the unwary to destruction, while approaching its den I sternly resolved that neither the magnificence of its gilded saloons, the seductive flavour of its wines, the blandishment of its sirens, or the rich and racy humour of its great entertainment, called a "judge and jury," should move me to being anything else than a cool, calm, dispassionate observer, with his wits about him, and with a single glass of bitter ale before him just for appearance' sake. And with this steady determination I entered in at its portals.

The fee for admission was one shilling, which a man sitting in a little hutch on one side received, giving me in exchange a tin ticket, with the direction to go straight on. I went straight on towards a door covered with red cloth at the end of the passage, and pushed it open, prepared for the dazzling splendour that would immediately burst on me.

I was disappointed. The place in which I found myself was anything but dazzling or splendid. It was a smallish, odd-angled building, as though built over a back-yard atop of such walls as came handiest, and was a temporary, rickety-looking structure with a skylight ridge and furrow roof, and great stains all down the flashly-papered wainscotting where the rain had found its way through; while gas jets, depending from rough iron piping suspended across the joists overhead, gave out a dim and flickering light. To the left of the dragon's den as you entered was a nook where a wretched-looking waiter in greasy black, and with a dirty neckcloth, presided over an array of empty glasses, yawning hopelessly as he wiped out such as had been used with a cloth that might have been twin with that about his throat. Just inside the chamber there was an individual, palpably an Israelite, who performed the double duty of usher to the court (bearing in that capacity a long black rod, and wearing a scanty bedgown of black serge) and ticket collector. Fixed in rows were seats sparsely covered with the same sort of cloth as that on the door, with a strip of raw deal, about six inches wide, perched up in front, convenient to stand a pot on or knock the ashes out of a pipe. There was a select space covered with a drugget, and for its sake, rather than out of decency, provided with spittoons. This was where the "jury" sat, and strangers had the privilege of sitting with the jury on payment of two shillings instead of one. Just as I went in, although the case was proceeding, there were but five jurymen present, and one of them, rather than attending to his duties, was fiercely whispering in argument with the waiter, his grievance being that he had been charged sixpence for a glass of fourpenny ale.

Facing these "reserved seats" was the judicial bench, with his lordship sitting on it, flanked on the one side by two counsel for the plaintiff, and on the other by two counsel for the defendant. His lordship had some coloured liquid in a rummer before him, which, however, was suspiciously like ale, a glass of which sober beverage the counsel on either side had between them. Matters must have gone wrong with the dragon since the great Baron kept den for him. It seems that they will neither grant him a licence to sell beer or spirits, nor so much as trust him with sixpenn'orth of either, even for so short a time as it takes to deliver the same to a customer and receive payment. I asked for some ale. "I must have the money first," replied the dirty waiter, holding out his hand. I gave him it, and he shuffled off through a back door, and presently brought me about three-quarters of a pint of just the same opaque puddle as the juryman had complained of, and charged me sixpence for it, at the same time demanding a fee for his trouble.

The case his lordship was trying, for the sake of advertisement, hinged on the great Cornhill jewel robbery, but in reality had no more to do with it than with the distribution of the Indian prize-money. Mr. Caseley, however, was dragged into it, and there was a disgusting fellow dressed in female apparel in it, and a ruffian disguised as Mr. Stiggins, and a funny policeman with flaxen tow hanging down from his head over his shoulders, and his belly stuffed out with hay in a highly humorous manner. These, with the judge and the four counsel, were the whole of the performers.

It was not easy to follow the plot of the case, but there was of course a considerable deal about divorce and adultery in it, and, apart from the immensely comical acting of the stuffed policeman—who engaged in a sparring match with Mr. Caseley in the dock, and several times said, "O, crickey!" and inquired of the convict if his mother knew that he was out—all the fun consisted in Caseley calling the judge "old bloak" and the counsel "rummy codgers," and in the disgusting wretch in woman's attire, and who was supposed to be a native of Germany, importing filthy blunders into his broken English. Anything nastier, or drearier, or more completely deserving the contempt and reprobation of decent men it is scarcely possible to imagine. If the jokes had been merely of a sort to cause a man of decent mind to blush, under such circumstances they might perhaps be excused, but their effect was not such. Assisted by the judge and counsel, the man in the bonnet and petticoats would now and then utter a something that came at one as a rotten egg might, causing a shudder and a sensation of sickness at the stomach. Nobody except the usher and the waiter laughed, and then only by way of a lead, which I am glad to say was seldom or never followed, and which of course made the audacity of the whole business more apparent. I am quite convinced that nearly every spectator present had come there actuated much more by curiosity than vice, and prepared for a style of amusement broader and more reckless than might be found elsewhere, and finding himself "in" for the sort of thing that presented itself sat uneasy on his seat, waiting only for such a break in the performance as would enable him to escape from such a den without inconvenience to his neighbours.

There were several "breaks" in the performance, as was needful to enable the "case" to drag its unclean length through an entire evening. The German witness had a row with Mr. Vallantine, the counsel, and, coming down out of the box, scratched his face and, pulling off his wig, threw it in his face. Then the stuffed policeman fell down in a fit, and the business of the court was entirely suspended while he was brought to again. And during these intervals the first batch of visitors who had looked in out of curiosity, grown quite disgusted, went off, and a new batch of curious ones came in, so that during the whole evening the spectators were in number closely the same—that number being about thirty. Hilarity, or anything in the shape of it, never once appeared in the course of the whole entertainment. There was no drunkenness. Spirits as well as beer might be obtained somewhere out at the back door, but every one present was sober, even to melancholy. About ten o'clock a Chesterfield, clearly from Houndsditch, came in with rings on his fingers, a short stick, a rubicund countenance, and evidently "out on the spree." He was not a man of refined appetite, and tried very hard to enjoy himself; but as the case proceeded he grew sallow visibly, and by-and-by, draining up his brandy, walked out, favouring the usher, to whom he had rendered the ticket that had cost him a shilling, with the most savage of scowls.

It rather surprised me to find that as twelve o'clock approached the audience grew larger, and seemed more careful than hitherto in the selection of their seats. The reason presently became apparent. The trial being concluded—with a verdict for the defendant—the judge announced that from now till one o'clock all present would be charmed and delighted by an exhibition of *poses plastiques* of a very superior description. I had previously noticed that extending behind the judge's bench was a wide green curtain, and now I divined its purpose.

In the course of a quarter of an hour the gas was lowered till the room was nearly dark, and the usher (who, I should say, was the proprietor, from the over-seeing eye he cast on the entire entertainment) divested himself of the black bedgown, and took his seat by a chink in the back partition, with a little bell in his hand. Amid the breathless silence of the auditory he peeped through the chink, rang the bell, and the curtain rose, and, behold! there were four ordinary and elderly females attired in fleshings and kilts, hand in hand, and revolving on a pedestal, as though the machinery that moved them were a roasting-jack. There was no buzz of admiration or applause— a slight tittering, and that was all. They continued to revolve for a minute or more, and then the curtain was lowered. As though, however, the hall had thundered with plaudits, he rang the curtain up again, and the four middle-aged females performed another tedious revolution, with no more effect than that at first as regarded the spectators.

After a while the curtain rose once more, revealing the oldest of the ladies alone on the roasting-jack, attired as Diana. Still the audience were dumb, and the curtain was lowered and raised again. Then came "The Three Graces," but the audience remained unmoved. No wonder. Fancy a trio of bold-faced women, with noses snub, Roman, and shrewish, with wide mouths and eyes crowsfooted, having the impudence to represent the Graces! Mr. Moses, at the peep-hole, looked more ferocious than ever, and jerked the curtain down and jerked it up again, with such an if-you-don't-like-it-you-can-leaveit expression of countenance that it seemed unsafe to stay any longer, and I came away with at least this comforting reflection for my shilling—that an inane and nasty, though old-established, public exhibition was cutting its own throat with laudable expedition.

WITH A NIGHT CABMAN. TT was nearly one in the morning when I sought him, and the melancholy, drizzling rain that had set in with the preceding evening still continued, and there was a chilly wind blowing, and it was very dark. His was the only cab on the rank, and he was invisible. I knew where to find him, however. I tapped at the closed sash, and immediately ensued a rustling of straw and the sounds of a decidedly unamiable voice, crying " Hullo!" which I was sorry to hear, my business with him being of an unusual character, and one the revelation of which to a man roused from his sleep and savage might not be courteously entertained.

"Is it a job?" he demanded, in a muffled voice.

"Something in that way."

"Beg pardon, sir; thought p'r'aps it might be a lark. Where to, sir?"

I was glad to discover that he was a little man and gray-haired. Likewise that he was lame of a leg, as might be told by his crabbish way of shuffling out of the vehicle. It was possible that when I told him what it was I wanted he might regard it as a "lark," and demand immediate satisfaction.

"Whereto, sir?"

"Well, the fact is, I wish to go nowhere in particular. The case is this— It is my misfortune to"

"I knows all about it, sir," he interrupted; "'taint the first job of that sort I've had. Key of the street! Well, it *is* orkard. Never mind, sir; jump in. It ain't like the down beds and woolly blankets like what you've got at home, but the cushions is warm, and there's no draught to speak of. What time shall I wake you, sir? I'll put the mare down the road a mile or so, and perhaps that'll rock you off."

It is evident that he mistook me for an unlucky dog shut out of his legitimate lodgings and anxious to stow away for the remainder of the night at the rather expensive rate of two shillings an hour. He was considerably astonished when I told him it was my desire to sit outside the cab, and not inside—to keep him company, in fact, through the small hours, with a view to gratifying my curiosity as to the sort of business done in his peculiar line. It was some time before I could persuade him that I was in earnest, but, that difficulty overcome, no other presented itself.

I had a wicker-covered flask in my pocket; and presently John Barlow, badge 987,654, and myself were chatting together, as we sat on the driving-seat, as affably as though we lived in the same street, and had taken our licences out on the same day. It was some time, however, before we found a fare, and meanwhile the discourse turned on the two subjects nearest John Barlow's heart—the old brown mare in the shafts and his old woman at home. Concerning the former, he startled me with the information that, considering her age, and the fact of her having only three legs, she was a wonder. I looked down, and, finding that the mare apparently had four legs, asked him to explain.

"Ah! if you count that thing on the off side she's got four; but I don't call that a leg, it's only a swinger, and been nothing but a swinger this nine years, to my knowledge," said Mr. Barlow. "It's awfully agin her, that leg is."

"Something appears to be against her," I remarked. "Is it her appetite? She's rather bony, isn't she?''

"It's all owin' to that leg. Her appetite's all that can be desired, and a jolly sight more so than is conwenient sometimes," replied he; "but it's that leg that beats her. Oftentimes when we've had a run o' luck, I've got it in my 'art to stand a quartern of beans to the old gal, but I daresent; they'd get into them three sound legs of hers and make her so sarsy that she'd forget to be keerful of her lame pin, and lay herself up." "Is she your own?"

"No; I only drives her. I ain't my own master."

"I might have known that without asking. No man that was his own master would drive a night cab, I should think."

"You're right. I shouldn't, o'ny that I'm so awfully eat up with rheumatism."

"You are joking."

"Am I? Lord send I was!" And he shook his head in a manner more convincing than his words.

"You'll excuse my incredulity," said I; "but you must admit that being eat up with rheumatism is not commonly made grounds for preferring to pass the night out of doors rather than in one's warm bed at home."

"Well, it do seem strange to them as has the enjoyment of their limbs, I dessay. When you're brought to hate your bed, to cus it cos of its warmth, and you gets no more comfort out of sheets and blankets than if they was harsh and raspy as soleskins, it makes a difference. That's just my case. And my old woman, as I was speaking about just now, she works at a ropery up Bermondsey way—on her legs from morning till night, poor old creeter, and coming home as tired as a dawg. Well, nat'rally she wants sleep, and how's she goin' to get it with me alongside of her rilin' and groanin' with rheumatics? That's how the bed serves me; d'ye see, sir? Soon as I get warm it gets at my bones like rats a gnawing at a wainscot. She's agin my coming out, and takes on a bit; but it don't do to let a woman get the upper hand of you, so I sez, 'If you jaw till a blue moon it won't alter me. You go to bed and get your bit of rest like you ought to, and I'll go out, which rainin' pitchforks I'd as lief and liefer do than lay there being gnawed, and I'll have a spell in the day time when I've got the crib to myself, and ain't an annoyance to anybody.'"

And John Barlow, of that ruffianly, blackguardly, bullying race known as cabmen, shook his head determinedly, and put on as ferocious an expression of face as had doubtless accompanied his tyrannical speech to the old woman, who, it is to be hoped, was by this time asleep and resting her ropewalk-weary legs, while that rheumatic old hero her husband sat out in the dark and the cold. He was quite unconscious that he was a hero—(all real heroes should be, I suppose)—and had no idea of how uncomfortable he was making me, or perhaps he would not have talked so. Would it ever come into *my* selfish mind, supposing I was stricken with John Barlow's malady, to take my bed into the back kitchen, that my wife in an upper bedroom might enjoy undisturbed repose? It was quite a relief to me that at this moment a frantic voice calling "Cab I" was heard in our rear, immediately followed by the appearance of a young man, with his greatcoat buttoned awry and a comforter wrapped slovenly about his neck. With a chuckle, quite cheering to hear from a man so afflicted, John Barlow whispered in my ear, "Mrs. Gamp, I'll wager," and shuffled off his seat to attend to his customer.

"I knowed it was," said he, as, after receiving certain hasty instructions from his fare, he shuffled up to his seat again; "it's a extryornary thing that kids, twice out of three times, are born in the night; now, when I was a young man "Bang went the window.

"Can't you whip him up faster than that, cabby? Put the steam on, that's a good chap. What the does that fellow want on the box with you?"

"He's my reg'lar fare, and is letting you ride as a favour, sir; you ain't obliged to ride with him if you don't Hke," replied John Barlow, gruffly.

"Oh, I beg his pardon, I'm sure; he'd excuse me if he only knew. First to the right, cabman, and stop at the green lamp. Put him along, that's a good fellow."

Mr. Barlow shook his head compassionately, and gave the old brown mare a taste of whipcord.

"It's the first, I'll lay a farden," said he; "they takes it much easier when it come to five or six."

I think it must have been the young man's "first." Arrived at the green lamp, he sprang out like a cat at a mouse, and began hauling away at the brass-headed bell-pull, and never ceased to haul away at it till an upper window was opened, and a nightcapped head thrust out.

"Who's there?"

"44, Buskin Street, please; if you wouldn't mind being as quick as possible, doctor."

"Ay, ay, I'll be quick enough; don't wait." And the window was closed leisurely.

"Goin' any further, sir?" asked Mr. Barlow.

"I'm going to stop here a minute or two," replied the young man, with stem resolution in his tone, and evidently chafing under the doctor's cool treatment of his important mission. "Do you see a light in his window, cabman?"

"No; he's gone to bed agin, I think, sir," answered Mr. Barlow, with a malice that contrasted strangely with his tenderness for his old woman.

"That's pretty, upon my soul!" exclaimed the young man, excitedly, and once more he flew at the bell.

Again the window opened.

"My good man, I cannot come till I put my clothes on; I cannot, indeed," exclaimed the doctor, with a calmness that was wonderful under the circumstances.

"I should think it was all right now, cabman? Drive hard to 69, Jerusalem Street."

Jerusalem Street was not far from the doctor's, and we were there in a very few minutes. The young man didn't knock at the door, however; he felt for little stones in the road, and threw them up at the first-floor window. It was as though somebody within had been lying awake and expecting him. The window was raised, and a female head protruded.

"Is"that you, Joe?"

"All right, mother; come on."

"How is she? How long 'as she been bad, Joe?"

"It is all right; come along," answered Joseph, looking sheepishly towards us, and addressing his parent in a whisper, half persuasive, half remonstrative.

"Joseph, is Mary Ann's mother there? Because if so"

"Oh, bother! There's nobody there, I tell you; come on, if you're coming." And, to avoid further public interrogation, Joseph dived into the cab, and shut the door.

His mother, as a dresser, was swift. In less than five minutes she was heard unbolting the street door.

"Well, of all the strange things that ever happened," she began, as she closed the door, and continued on her way from the house steps to the vehicle—" of all the strange things that ever happened this bangs all. It was only last night that I said to your father, 'Something strikes me that Joe's wife will be bad to-night. I'll lay a shilling '"

The cab door shut in the remainder of the prophecy.

Relieved of its load at 44, Buskin Street (at the door of which, I am happy to tell, the doctor's gig was standing), our cab was once more for hire. It did not remain so long. Turning the corner of the street there was a merry party of four—two men and two women—who frankly informed Mr. Barlow that they had just come from a raffle, and had two miles to go, and would give him each sixpence if he would carry them that distance. Mr. Barlow was nothing averse, and the brown mare, warmed by her first job (and always considering that she had but three legs), did this stiffish piece of work in a very gallant manner.

i

After this there was a lull, and, jogging leisurely down the road, Mr. Barlow gave me some curious particulars concerning the cabbing interest. How that Hansoms (sho'fuls he called them) had to bring home—to their masters—fifteen shillings a day if they were "long-day men" (that is, if they came home in the afternoon and took a fresh horse, remaining out till twelve o'clock at night); all they "made" over that being their earnings. "Four-wheelers," he informed me, "took in twelve shillings for the same time, and night cabs from seven shillings to nine—the master holding the man's driving licence as security for the day's money..,

"I suppose it invariably happens that a man is able to earn at least his master's money?" I remarked.

"Does it! Lor' bless your soul, sir! why, in the winter time 'short money' is a common thing with us. Many a time have I had ten hours of it, and after all been 'bliged to pawn something for a couple of shillin's or half-a-crown to make up the gaffer's money—(he called his master "the gaffer")—without so much as a single oat for myself. I know dozens of men who have had to do the same."

"But, supposing that you take in only Jwhat you have earned?"

"Well, if it ain't up to the mark, 'cording to the contract, they sack you, and hold your licence till you pay up. I was chucked on my back on'y last Christmas time for three days, all through taking a bad half-sovereign."

"And how much do you count on earning as a night cabman?"

"Well, if I can tot up seventeen or eighteen shillings at the end of the week, I'm lucky."

At a quarter to three we got another fare. A woman, flashily dressed and drenched with rain, with a fashionable hat adorned with a wreath of green flowers, the colour of which was washing out and trickling down her face—not improving it, for it was a face pale with passion, and set with a pair of once beautiful eyes, glaring with gin and indignation.

"I want to go to Clerkenwell; how much?" she snapped out savagely.

"Only yourself?" D'ye see anybody else? Do you?"—and she turned fiercely to look in the direction she thought Mr. Barlow was looking— "Curse him! I wish I could see him, the shabby rascal! I'll mark him if ever I meet him again, sure as my name's Loo. How much to Clerkenwell?"

Mr. Barlow told her that the fare was eighteenpence, whereon she turned her back and counted her money by the light of a lamp.

"I shan't have a mag left for a glass of gin in the morning, if I give you eighteenpence," said she. "Won't you take fifteen?"

Instigated by me, Mr. Barlow said that he would. We set her down at the end of a decent street near the Angel.

"Hadn't I better take you to the door?" Mr. Barlow suggested.

"I think you had," replied she, with an ugly laugh; "that would be a good wind-up to the night's luck!" and away she scudded, and was presently out of sight.

Our next fare was not a pleasant one. He was seemingly standing by, but, as it afterwards proved, leaning against a lamppost when he hailed us; and when we drew up, without waiting for Mr. Barlow to get down, he slammed open the cab door and tumbled in. He was a tall, heavy fellow, and the springs of the night cab creaked as he flung himself down on the seat. Poor Mr. Barlow looked rueful as he descended to receive the commands of the big, tipsy man.

But he could make nothing of him. It seemed that he had recently come out of a row, in which his gentility had been called in question; for as soon as Mr. Barlow inquired where he wanted to go, with thick, drunken utterance he threatened to smash Mr. Barlow's head with his walking-stick if he dare say another word imputing that he wasn't a gentleman. Then he hung his head on his breast, and began to snore.

"Come, this won't do, you know," exclaimed Mr. Barlow j waxing indignant. "You'll have to get out, or tell me where to drive you."

"Drive to."

Mr. Barlow's wrath now exceeded his prudence. He placed his hand on the drunken man's collar, and the drunken man hit out at him with the knob end of his walking-stick, and crash it went through a window.

"If I were you I should drive him to a police station," I suggested.

"That's what I will do," said Mr. Barlow, shutting the drunken ruffian in, and mounting the driver's seat. But the crash of the glass and the mention of the police station revived the fellow a little, and, with his head out at the broken window, he protested against being treated in any way that was ungentlemanly, offering at the same time to pay the damage if he were driven to his residence in 'Slo Sreet, Shelse," which Mr. Barlow interpreted to mean Sloane Street, Chelsea—distant something over five miles from where we were—at the same time exhibiting a portemonnaie in proof of his ability to pay. I still inclined to the opinion that we had better drive him to the station-house; but my partner whispered that he thought it would be all right; so away we went.

Happily, it was growing towards daylight when we reached "Slo Street," as it enabled our fare, slowly recovering from his drunkenness, to make out certain landmarks, pointing to his residence. By-and-by he bundled out, and, still staggering, blundered up the steps of a house with his latch-key in his hand. He was cunning enough, however, to know how many miles he had ridden.

"How much?" he asked, once more taking out the portemonnaie.

Mr. Barlow's eyes twinkled with expectancy.

"Well, say four shillings the fare, sir, and another four for the glass—it's plate-glass, sir, and will cost all that," he replied, civilly.

Our fare looked up with a sneer on his very unhandsome countenance, and then, clapping a forefinger to the side of his nose, like the vulgar ruffian he undoubtedly was (I hope he may read this) exclaimed—

"What d'ye take me for? Five miles, at sixpence a mile, is half a crown. Here's the money. As for the broken window, summon for that, and be."

And with that he swung open his door and swung it to again with a bang in poor Mr. Barlow's distressed face. The outraged cabman did not knock at the door, as I am quite sure I should have done had I been in his place. Pocketing the shabby fellow's half-crown, he slowly mounted the box again.

"He's one of the blessings a night cabman meets, sir."

"But of course you will summon him?"

"Where's the use? I should only get my knuckles rapped for' carrying a drunken man. No, sir; I am all a shilling out by my gentleman, and I must swaller it."

Mr. Barlow's next job was to drive me home, and when he left me at half-past six a.m. he told me he was going to Euston Square to try and pick up an early train job. I hope he found one, and that afterwards he went home and rested his poor rheumatic bones, with his bed all to himself, and without being an annoyance to any one.

AT A DUSTMAN'S TEA-PARTY. JUST lately I received a polite invitation to be present at a public meeting on a grand scale, at which dustmen and their wives and children were to partake of a free tea, honoured by the company of "working men and their wives, ninepence a head," and visitors (the aristocracy of the neighbourhood) one shilling.

It was quite an experimental gathering. Society had already considered its sweeps and its scavengers, and its shoeblacks and its costermongers, and its street beggars and its workhouse outcasts; it had even condescended to hold out the hand of a brother to the thief, and to the female of his species whose misfortune it is to haunt the public highway at midnight; but somehow or other it had hitherto overlooked its dustmen. Day by day was heard their melodious call, and we gladly availed ourselves of their eminently useful services; but beyond ordering Jane to keep a sharp eye on them that nothing but dust-bin produce found its way into their baskets, we had troubled ourselves not at all in their concerns.

I accepted the invitation with great pleasure, for, as it happened, I was not altogether ignorant of the habits and customs of the dustman; and I knew that, when the committee invited that person's wife and family, they contracted a rather serious responsibility. If a man be a scavenger, or a sweep, it is more likely than not that beyond deriving sustenance from his avocation his family have no more to do with it: his boys may be shoemaking or bricklaying boys, and his girls maids of all work, or "something in the City": but with the dustman it is different. The young dustman's bride "takes his nature with his name," and their progeny is to ashes born. The wife must cut her own grass, as the vulgar saying is, and at the same time show her husband that, although a coalheaver's daughter, she does not look down on him for his lowly craft; and so she takes a place as "sifter" at the yard or wharf to and from which her husband plies, and earns her eighteenpence a day and her "perks," which is a handy abbreviation of "perquisites," and applies to anything shaped in metal she may discover in her sieve. Did the reader ever see dust-sifters at work? If so he has witnessed one of the most disgusting and degrading, if not the most disgusting and degrading application of female labour. As everybody knows, it is not dust alone that finds its way into the receptacles fixed for the purpose. All kinds of vegetable and animal offal is flung there, and accumulates to decay and putrefy until the dustman makes his call. Then the contents of the bin is carted away, and carried straight to the dustyard, where the sifters work. The sifters invariably are women and girls, and the "feeders"—those who shovel up the muck and pitch it into the sieve—are boys from ten to fifteen. The sifter is of picturesque appearance, wearing short petticoats, a bulky shawl about her throat and chest, and a bonnet of capacious dimensions, and which, in the case of the young and vain, apparently serves as a receptacle for all the gay flinders in the way of ribbons and artificial flowers that may turn up in the sieve. The sifter wears about her waist a leathern apron of about the same texture as her husband's "fan-tail." She stands in ashes to within a very short distance of her knees. Her sieve is a full-sized one, being three feet across and weighing about ten pounds. "Sarve I" she says to the feeder, and the feeder straightway delivers into her sieve an enormous shovelfuj from the reeking heap. She bumps the sieve with astonishing violence against her apron, and then proceeds to sort what will not pass through the meshes—her nose and mouth being within eighteen inches of the awful collection. She is surrounded by baskets for the "sortings"—the bones, the rags, the bits of bread, the old shoes, the big cinders and lumps of coal, and the bits of metal; and what then remains is pitched on to a heap of what is called "core," and is used in the foundation of new roads. The rags and bones are sold for manure and paper-making purposes, the coal and cinders go towards brickmaking, and the old shoes for making the fiercest of fires for colouring fine steel. As for the bread scraps, they are more valuable than any, being sold at the rate of eighteenpence the hundredweight to pig-breeders as fattening food. Only "metal" is regarded as legitimate "perks" by the yard foreman, except when it takes the form of money—all the money found (and the amount, as I am informed, in such yards as Messrs. Dodd's or Stroud's, who employ large gangs of sifters, is something very considerable in the course of a quarter) being saved and equally distributed at stated times. It not unfrequently happens that an entire family, including grandfather and grandmother, and sons and daughters, and grandsons and granddaughters, are in the same firm, and knowing this, and considering it in connexion with the liberal announcement of the committee that the entertainment was free to the dustmen and their wives and families, I was, as I said before, not a little curious as to how so ticklish an experiment would succeed. "Maybe," thought I, " they'll find themselves in some difficulty with a couple of hundred hungry dustmen attacking their thin bread-and-butter."

But, as a single glance round the room in which the tea meeting was to be presently held plainly showed, the individual who had taken the matter in hand knew his business very much better than I could have taught it him. It was a spacious room, or rather hall, and very prettily decorated. Flags waved from the oaken beams above, the walls were adorned with scriptural quotations more or less appropriate, and cut flowers, chiefly wallflowers, in profusion graced the long tables. The centre of the hall was apportioned to the guests of the evening, and on four tables extending the whole length of the building, and each capable of accommodating at least eighty persons, was an array of cups and saucers and lump sugar in glass basins, and new milk in jugs. To every four cups and saucers was allowanced a plate with a tremendous pile of bread-and-butter: none of your mincing shavings of bread hardly strong enough to bear the weight of the butter spread on them, but jolly, substantial inch-thick rounds of cottage bread, new and "crummy." Flanking these tables were the ninepenny ones set out for workmen and their wives. Except that the bread-and-butter was somewhat genteeler in bulk, and the quality of the cups somewhat superior to the others, there was nothing to distinguish the free tables from the ninepenny ones, and, with all respect to the management, I would, in prospect of a repetition of the festival, suggest that even this slight difference should be avoided. As guests the dustmen were entitled to at least as much consideration as those the value of whose company was estimated at ninepence a head. This may seem a small matter, but our worthy brethren of the fan-tail are just the fellows to resent such an invidious distinction. Besides, I am quite sure that the "workmen" were not of the sort who would appreciate such delicate attentions. It only tended to make them uncomfortable. It was different as regards the "visitors," it being perfectly understood (though why it should is not exactly clear) that these included gentry only. However, the platform was set aside for the accommodation of the latter, and the steps of the platform were tastefully ornamented with flowering shrubs and ever greens, and everything was as nice and pretty as hands could make it.

Five o'clock was announced as teatime, but it was not until a few minutes after the clock had struck that a body of dustmen put in an appearance. Finding that they were the first comers, this batch was shy, looking in at the door, and grinning and nudging each other as though they thought all along that it would be a "lark," and that now they were sure of it. But this was only make-believe. Just inside the door was a great table, and at work at it, under the direction of a pleasant little woman, with kind brown eyes, was a bevy of muscular damsels cutting up plum-cake at a tremendous rate. *This* wasn't a lark, anyhow, or, if it were, one of much too tempting a sort to be resisted; and when the brown-eyed little woman said cheerily, "Come along in, men; we are nearly ready for you!" in they went, biting the peaks of their caps, and took their seats in a row on the handiest forms, where they sat, wondering at the lump sugar in the glass basins, and eyeing the crummy breadand-butter critically; varying that occupation, when their bashfulness had somewhat subsided, by passing about one of the bunches of wallflowers, and sniffing it solemnly, and commenting in whispers on its market price.

It was comparatively easy for the next arrivals; for company's sake they were eagerly welcomed by the first comers, and took their seats as orderly as though to go to a public tea was an event of at least weekly occurrence with them. After this they flocked in in vast numbers—old dustmen, with their heads worn bald by friction of the fantail, and with decent smock frocks, with a flower at the button-hole, some of them; young bucks of dustmen, apeing heavy swelldom in their bulky flannel jackets, and their brilliant and bunchy "kingsman" (silk neckerchief) encircling their throats, and fastened in a holiday bow old dust wives, with the symbol of their life-long labour marking their wrinkles as plainly as though an artist had gone over them with his pencil, and with their fingers worn blunt and corny at the tips, through contact with the sieve-bars; blooming young dust wives, and sweethearts with gay handkerchiefs over their shoulders, and brilliant ornaments in their ears, and bran-new ankle-jacks upon their feet, and scores of boy "feeders," and girl odd hands and general assistants. How heartily the dustmen had responded to the invitation of their friends was signified by the fact that amongst their company was a blind man, one that was silly, and a poor invalid who was wheeled in in an invalid carriage.

As the number of dustmen increased I looked anxiously towards the master of the ceremonies, and was glad to see his blunt, honest face even more radiant than when I last looked at it. So I took no further concern in the matter, but found myself a seat between two nice old ladies with the corny fingertips before alluded to, and opposite a row of hearty, growing young dustmen, and waited for the tea urns.

I ought to have mentioned that instrumental music formed a feature of the entertainment. The police of the district had very kindly lent the band attached to their division, and there they were, a crew of smart young fellows, each with his instrument, posted at the end of the hall opposite to the platform. Presently the sound of trumpet and the martial roll of drums heralded the coming of the first tea-pot—or boiler it should rather be called, for its capacity was four gallons at the very least; and one after another came twenty of the same measures, smoking hot, and borne by lusty men. When these had been fairly distributed amongst dustmen and visitors, the cruel tantalizing endured during three-quarters of an hour was at an end, and a vigorous pounce made at the bread-and-butter piles by the males, while the women, with that self-sacrifice that ever distinguishes them, for the present restrained their appetite, and busied themselves in filling tea-cups from the big pots. The row of hearty young dustmen before me numbered nine, and I must confess that in a very few minutes my old fears as to the adequate provisioning of the garrison returned stronger than ever. To see these young men eat was terrible—awe-inspiring. The new and yielding rounds were easily divisible into four, and each quarter was but a mouthful. They ate silently, with downcast eyes, and their throats at ease in their voluminous wrappings. The only time when they evinced any emotion was when the musicians struck on an uncommonly lively key, and then they looked up with sudden pleasure in their eyes, and in the act apparently bolted half a slice without mastication— which, judging from their haste to return to deliberate and judicious eating, they regarded as a loss. I am quite within bounds when I say that in the course of half an hour of hard feeding those nine young fellows consumed at least nine half-quartern loaves. They didn't give their minds to tea very much. The new milk and lump sugar at first had its attractions; but tea-time has its limits, and it soon became manifest to them that they could not afford to dally with unsubstantialities.

But there was no stint. Soon as a plate was emptied a watchful waitress whisked it away, and replaced it by a full one. Byand-by the empty bread-and-butter plates were removed, and others full of cake placed in their stead. Then, for the first and only time during the evening, was a shade of discontent visible on the faces of my opposite neighbours. They were not angry with any one but themselves, however. They had been unwise. They had so filled themselves with bread-and-butter that to eat more than a couple of "chunks" of cake each was impossible! But they accepted defeat as men should, and with their expiring appetites fought the plummy enemy to the last extremity.

Without doubt the tea was a success. Three hundred dustmen and their kith and kin had taken tea in the presence of a couple of hundred highly respectable people, and there had not been a single fight, or so much as an unseemly or foul word heard;—which astonishing circumstance seemed to excite some wonder amongst certain ladies and gentlemen patronizing the feast. I must confess, however, that I saw nothing in it to provoke astonishment; but then, you see, I have mixed more with formidable creatures of the dustman breed than the generality, and happen to know that they are not inferior in intelligence to the brute creation, and that they really will express their gratitude when kindly treated. They will bark when they are teased, but seldom or never bite wantonly or maliciously.

So far the prime object of the gathering was realized. Silk and muslin had fraternized with cotton and gingham; superfine broadcloth had recognized dusty fustian ; and for the future our hitherto-despised guests are of us and with us: and all we ask of them is to set about improving their condition, and show themselves worthy of our condescension. And now we will clear away the tea-things, and spend the evening harmoniously.

And here began the blundering. While the management of the affair remained in the hands of its honest projector (who, be it known, is just a common greengrocer and lets vans for moving goods), all was as it should be; but now certain well-meaning but mistaken gentlemen on the platform took the reins, and, though they did no positive harm, they simply wasted their opportunity of doing good. It is an error to suppose that dustmen care for readings from Tennyson, or take interest in a milkand-water parody on the "Seven Ages of Man," in the form of the "Seven Ages of Woman." It is improbable that he will hasten his steps up the ladder of respectability when on the very first round the gray and knowing old dustman finds himself treated to pretty little two-syllable stories, with a moral to them.

However, all these little matters can be improved at the next dustman's tea party, at which I hope to be present.

AT A PUBLIC-HOUSE OF MOURNING. IVE miles without the City gates there is a cemetery of such prodigious dimensions as to provide constant employment for twenty grave-diggers. These men go to work as regularly as carpenters or stonemasons at six o'clock in the morning, and, excepting the customary half hour for breakfast and the hour for dinner allowed to all journeymen, work the live-long day at digging six-feet holes in the graveyard clay.

Nevertheless, in "busy seasons," the number of holes the diggers make never exceeds the demand for them, unless they work overtime. It has happened on a Sunday that more than seventy bodies have been brought there to be buried, and the average number passed through the cemetery gates on week days exceeds forty. It was an official attached to the buryingplace who kindly gave me this information. "And on an average, how many mourners attend each funeral, should you think?" I inquired. "Well, you might safely reckon 'em all round as five each," replied my informant—" But Sunday's the day for 'em. You never happened to drop in at the Jolly Sandboys on a Sunday afternoon, I suppose, sir? That's the Jolly Sandboys, the first 'public' you come to after turning out of the cemetery lane. The regular house-of-call for mourners that is. It is a sight to see, I can tell you, when the bar of every room is crammed, just like the scrouge at the door of a threepenny gallery at the theatre."

Between three and four o'clock, as I was advised, was the hour on a Sunday afternoon when the "scrouge" at the bar of the houseof-call for mourners might be expected to be at its height; but preferring to be in good time, the next Sunday I was on the road, and in the vicinity of the Jolly Sandboys, shortly after two. It was a lovely afternoon, and it was hard to believe that the quaint and modest little hostel in question could ever be anything but a house of cheerfulness and content. There is a broad space before the Sandboys, which lies back from the road, with lively flower-pots at the upper windows and a horse-trough in front of it, and wisps of hay about the ground, and matronly hens fussing over broods of unruly chicks, just under the palings, where the sun shines hottest. The only visible human being near the Sandboys is a lazy-looking man, who appears as though he had abandoned a seafaring life on the chance of one.day finding a horse to hold, and who sits on the stump of a post, with his head resting against the horse-trough, placidly puffing smoke from a short pipe, with his "sou'-wester" tipped over his eyes, so as to shade them from the sun, but not so far as to shut him out from a view of the chickens, who, as they nestle in the hot sand, plump and happy, and indifferent to the oats that lie within easy pecking distance, present to his sleepy mind's eye indeed a soothing picture, which leaves him nothing to desire— except to be a chicken.

But it was only while you stood with your back to the high road and restricted your vision to the strictly straightforward, shutting out what was to be seen to the left and to the right, that this, scene of tranquillity might be perfectly enjoyed. It is necessary to shut your ears as well as your eyes lest the rumbling of many wheels causes you to look about you, when the charm would be instantly broken for the wheels are those of black carriages—of hearses with dead men and women in them, and of coaches following close behind laden with those who bemoan the departed, and whose swollen eyes appear wofully at the windows as the hearse is heard to turn down the lane—the cemetery lane, which is a long lane, and for their dear dead has no turning. The Sandboys is close by, but it has no attractions for the bereaved ones, and even the hearse driver and the clusters of men in shabby black who hang on at the back of the sombre coaches pause not an instant in their cheerful chattering to glance aside. It seems very much as though my cemetery friend had hoaxed me. A crowd indeed! The tearful ones on their way to the buryingplace looked as little like pothouse "scrougers" as the Sandboys looked a likely place for scrouging in.

######

Four o'clock, and I once more approached the Sandboys, after an hour's stroll between the hedges, and lo! the scene is changed utterly. My cemetery friend was right; it is indeed a sight to see! Peace has been banished, and noise and confusion reign in its stead. The lazy man—he may be known by his nautical sou'-wester—has roused from the post stump, and is now an energetic ostler, divested of his coat and waistcoat, and, with his dirty shirt sleeves rolled above his elbows, rushing hither and thither, and bawling and swearing like a whipster at a horse market. There are other ostlers besides this one, three or four of them, as there had need be, for now within the square space before the tavern, where an hour since the chickens basked, fifteen hearses and black coaches find standing-room, and to every coach is attached a pair of big black horses, requiring refreshment after their load-drawing. The drivers and other attendants, too, they need refreshment, and they are taking it in the freest manner. There you may see them—the hearse drivers—in merry groups, lounging against the black wheels, with glasses of gin and pewter pots of beer in their hands, and short pipes in their mouths, cracking their jokes, and laughing, and funning for all the world as though they were on the road with pleasure-vans and a gay company bound for Epping Forest. Some of the undertaking people had white favours pinned in the crape swathing about their hats, denoting that they were concerned in the interment of some baby or poor little innocent maid; and queer it looked to see these symbolic hats all askew on their owner's head, and a pipe and a pot of beer in their owner's hands.

But where were the mourners? Where were the red-eyed ones whose woe was unquenchable, and who were suffering under such frightful outrage? Where were the males amongst them, who, with their indignation for the time grown stronger even than their sorrow, should have remonstrated with these indecent villains; and remonstrance failing, have plucked the scandalous pipes from their mouths, and spilled their abominable liquor in the gutter? Where were they?

Well, the astonishing fact is that they were engaged precisely as were the coffin-bearers and hearse-drivers, and giving countenance and encouragement to their sotting and pipe-smoking by doing likewise. Some were eating as well as drinking. Some, a shade more decent than their neighbours, or with a greater regard for appearances, declined to alight and enter the portals of the gin shop, and preferred to stay within the vehicles in which so recently their uncontrollable tears were shed and against the black cushions of which their heads, for ever bowed, had rested, and took biscuits and ale, and plates of cold beef, and brandy-and-water, and gin-and-water, while the master undertaker with one black kid glove off and his "weeper" trailing down his back, attended at the coach window to the orders of his customers like a tavern waiter—with this difference, that his customers, instead of giving him pennies for himself, pressed him to drink with them, and handed him liquor out of the coach window, which he drank with an expression of countenance beautifully indicative of the cheerful resign ion that upheld him in this trying hour.

This was outside the Sandboys; inside matters were not improved. My friend, the cemetery officer, had not exaggerated when he compared the crowding at the bar to the pressing for admittance at the gallery door of a theatre. The said bar, which is a very narrow and inconvenient one, is within a few feet of the entry door, and the door could not be shut, the rush was so great. Such a rush, too! Every one distinguished, though in never so modest a manner, by the trappings of woe— the men with black crape about their hats and caps, and with more black crape pinned on to their jacket sleeves where they were too poor to purchase black clothes; and the women with theii black gowns and their heads sheltered in the sombre hood that concealed their hair and left nothing but their pinched and ghastly faces visible; old women, newly made widows, young women, but a few minutes since parted from their dead fathers and brothers, jostling and elbowing within the narrow space, and clamouring with the money held up in their hands for halfpints of gin and pots of half-and-half, and short pipes, and screws of tobacco. Shut out the crowning horror of the hooded faces and the craped hats, and the uproar was just that to be met any Saturday night at a Whitecross Street gin-shop. Foul language and a disposition to "have a row" were elements not wanting. Two of the Sandboys' customers at least were in cue to provide against the last-mentioned deficiency. One of them was a costermonger seemingly, and wore about his hairy cap some crape wisped like a portion of a hay-band. "What did they mean by charging fippence a pot for beer?" "What sort o' game, his eyes, did they call it to charge fippence when fourpence was the reg'lar?" "It might do for sorre bloaks as come there and was too miserable to look arter their a'pence, but he'd see 'em all first before they fiddled him out of a farden." In vain his wife or his mother, or whatever she was, urged him to pay the other penny or give back the beer; not he, he would drink the beer without paying another mag, or he'd see who'd hinder; and as he spoke he shot from under the peak of his mourning cap dangerous glances at the slim young barman all very much to the amusement of four undertaker's men, who, a-straddle on a form, were regaling on a nice piece of cold pickled pork, brought down on the hearse with them.

Besides the standing room before the bar there was other accommodation for mourners, consisting of some large rooms and a sort of tea-garden in the rear. Before five o'clock every room was full, so much so that the limited accommodation in the way of hat pegs was exhausted, and there remained nothing— since the watchful eye of the undertaker, whose property the weepers were, was on them—but to pile the hats with the weepers attached in the centre of the tables where the gin measures and the pewter pots stood; but even here the precious streamers were not free from danger; it was impossible— especially after the fourth or fifth pot—to pour out the beer without spilling a little, and in this the badges of grief dabbled. To be sure, although the various parties at the tables patronized and obliged each other by pulling the bell and handing pipe lights, the conversation was not of a sort that might be termed cheerful, turning chiefly on the cattle plague, the high price and bad quality of liquor at these roadside houses, and the awful power of lightning—a subject suggested by a photograph hung up in the bar of two horses in a hay-cart struck down in a storm. Everybody drank deeply of the liquor, however indifferent it may have been—the women that, come what might, their crushing grief might be for the time forgotten, and the men as the handiest way back into the world in which, with a dead relative about their necks, as it were, they had found it inconvenient to mix of late.

The worst of it is that neither man nor woman can drink intoxicating liquids without becoming intoxicated—a fact that became painfully manifest as the evening advanced amongst the weakest of the mourners and those who were in the hands of the most unscrupulous of the master undertakers, who sat down with them and generously stood half-pints of gin out of the profits of the job. Gustave Dore might have met with a pretty picture or two out in that tea-garden. It was patronized by the women chiefly, the men affecting the rooms. I call it a tea-garden because there were settles and forms about it, and the trees and shrubs were of the common tea-garden type; but all the tea that was drank there might have been contained in a dram glass, or even a less capacious vessel. It was all gin. Rows of women— still with their cowls on—with gin measures or glasses in their hands—some desperately merry, some who had been so successful in drinking to forgetfulness of everything, that their matronly modesty was lost sight of; and some flooded back to weeping again, and wringing their hands, and letting their tears fall into their liquor, and refusing to be comforted, although a trio of their cowled companions stood round uttering "Cheer up" and "Come, come; don't take on so, that's a dear," and with more gin in their hands. It was about these maudlin groups that the ghouls in rusty black—the undertaker's men—were busiest, for there most gin was to be cadged: and they drank it with a grin and wink at their companions till their fishy eyes blinked, and their noses glowed on their cadaverous faces, and their white neckties went out of shape, and their professional hats inclined to the backs of their heads. It had never been my misfortune to see together so many assistants in the undertaking line before, and I may safely say that a more sottish, audacious, impudent set of ruffians it would be hard to find. It is through them or their masters that all this mischief is brought about. They bring away from the cemetery men and women worn out by long watching and anxiety and all manner of grief, depressed in spirits, and with no mind for battling against temptation or discovering the cunning designs of a rogue. How it is on week days I am unable to say, but without doubt Sunday is recognized by the undertaking fraternity as a day for boozing and drunkenness, and they rely on the "mourners" to provide the means. Their dodge is a very simple one. Turned out of the cemetery lane and approaching the Sandboys, "It is customary to bait the horses here—very comfortable house, I assure you, sir," says master undertaker, respectfully putting his head in at the coach window—" P'r'aps you'd like to get out and rest for a little while —p'r'aps the ladies would." That, in five cases out of six, is the way in which the weak-minded mourner—especially of the lower order—is trapped and betrayed into excess, and all in order that the coffin-carriers and the hearse-drivers may secure a skinful of gin and smoke their pipes for a couple of hours in a free and easy manner.

And yet, how may the evil be remedied? To shut up the Sandboys would be regarded as monstrous police tyranny, to found a training college for undertakers would be not unattended with difficulty. No Act of Parliament regulating the quantity of refreshment a mourner at a funeral should take would pass a second reading. Nevertheless, when one sees, as I saw, a company of bereaved ones in a hearse, setting out for home, the men smoking short pipes, the women giggling in semi-drunkenness, and for a driver, a hilarious person, likewise with a short pipe, and with the air of the ancient Jack Ketch driving a criminal to Tyburn, it really seems that something should be done.

"JOHNSON'S RETREAT.

« JOHNSON'S RETREAT" is eligible for the resting and J refreshment of those home-returning wayfarers who on Sundays and holidays patronize our end of the town for the sake of its hedge-skirted lanes and blossoming fields.

There is nothing of the flashy tavern tea-gardens visible about "The Retreat"—indeed, there is no tavern attached to it, and a glass of grog may not be obtained there for love nor money. Yet it is not strictly teetotal. Over by the stall where the ginger-beer and Banbury cakes are vended, you may procure, drawn from the barrel, a jug of ale. A jug, mind you, and not a dissipated bright public-house pewter— a vessel of brown glazed earthenware, such as farm-labourers and other rustics quaff their sober home-brewed from. The sort of pot it is impossible to sit and sot at. The influence of bright pewter measures on weak minds is a subject worthy the attention of our total abstinence chiefs. There never was so much drunkenness as since the invention of pewter pots.

In the old times, as our historical novelists have been at considerable pains to discover and make known, boozing and carousing occupied a large share of the leisure of such as could afford the luxurious pastime, but it is a remarkable fact that This place, which was situated in the Hornsey district of northern London, has happily been abolished since this article was written.
the tipplers and bibbers, from the humble retainer in the kitchen to the baron his master, who sat in the armour-hung hall of his ancestors, were invariably described as quaffing their potations out of flagons made of some lustrous metal or another; whereas, drinking to drunkenness out of delf, when delf was the universal material of the poor man's pot, was of such rare occurrence that the indefatigable Harrison Ainsworth himself has been unable to light upon a single instance sufficiently well authenticated to warrant its citation. How may this be explained? Are crockery and home—pottery and domestic felicity—so intimately associated that the brown jug, wherever it is met—even at the drinking shop—acts as a kindly remembrancer of wife and fireside, and ensures the happy balance of mirth and wisdom? If so, let us have an anti-pewter-pot association with all speed, whose aim shall be the total abolition of the more seductive measures and the substitution of brown jugs. At least, Parliament might be moved to make a law insisting that every publican shall hang up in his bar, and fair in view of his customers, the homely clay cup as a hint against inebriation and excess. Who knows the good that might follow the adoption of a plan so simple? There is a story told of a company of Californian gold-diggers, who for many months cut off from the wholesome influence of female society and left to their own devices, had grown to be as brutal and reckless a crew as can be well imagined. Well, one day this charming fellowship in the course of its wanderings in the desert came upon a woman's bonnet—a battered, tattered wreck of female finery, cast off and trodden into the mud. But there was enough in it to rouse tha better natures of the finders. Respectfully raising the discarded flinder they on the spot got up a feast in honour of it, giving it the post of honour at the head of their rough camp table. Sweethearts and wives were toasted, and home and old friends, long-forgotten fireside stories and songs were sung, and such fond memories of absent ones recalled, that every fellow of the company went to bed that night resolved to mend his ways, and, what is better, all stuck to the resolution more or less. Yet nothing is more common than for people to declare their disbelief in magic!

Johnson, of "The Retreat "—for the propriety of whose ways a hundred Sunday-school teachers and promoters of treats for little children are at this moment ready to vouch—affects earthenware drinking-pots, and out of them you must be content to take your liquor, supposing you should require refreshment of a more exhilarating nature than may be extracted from a ginger-beer bottle. You will be disappointed in expecting, because "Johnson's" is known as a tea-garden, to find the facilities for dancing afforded by the proprietor of "The Grotto" and similar disreputable places. "The Retreat" provides no German band, perched up aloft, no capacious platform. Such dainties may be very well where young men and women are concerned; but Johnson's customers are children merely, and if the frisking lambkins desire to indulge in saltatory exercise there is a nice patch of green, and it is hard but that they can caper to the music of their own sweet voices. The beer on tap is, of course, not for these innocents, but for their elders— their fathers and grown-up brothers—who, by way of a treat, bring them to this delightful old-fashioned place. There are swings here, and roundabouts, and pretty games of puss-in-thecorner, and kiss-in-the-ring, and the entrance gate stands wide open, and there is neither policeman nor money-taker. No wonder so worthy a place is well patronized and supported! No wonder, that Monday after Monday bands of schoolchildren, marshalled by benevolent gentlemen of clerical attire, with neat flags and banners bearing appropriate scriptural mottoes, are met in the green lanes on their way to "The Retreat." How the benevolent Johnson can afford to keep the place open is marvellous. All this great space of ground —all these arbours, and swings, and roundabouts, and no other profit except what arises from the sale of penny bottles of ginger-beer and a pint or so of ale, and the furnishing of substantial teas with thick bread and butter and watercresses at the rate of sixpence a head! Surely the concern must be a loss, and the proprietor of " The Retreat" no common tradesman but an eccentric gentleman of means, who, pitying the sad condition of little boys and girls dwelling in pent-up courts and alleys, devotes his time and his money in mitigating the evil, hoping for reward not here, but hereafter. May he find it!

It was as may be yesterday that, reflecting on the self-sacrificing of the amiable Johnson, we expressed this wish; and, as may be to-day, with our eyes opened to a totally different view of Mr. Johnson's character, we still say may he in some shape or way receive his due, and that speedily. That he may receive his due *here* and not hereafter is the very best his friends can wish for him, since, according as it is written in The Book, a man dying as he has lived may expect no mercy at the last assize. He is a man one would desire to be the exact reverse of. The creature whom in his ways he most resembles is now happily extinct in this country. No mother's baby was safe anywhere but at her own bosom while the ravenous monster was permitted to prowl at large, and even older children sent on errands were in danger from its cowardly cunning and ferocity—as witness the fate of little Red Riding Hood. What a shocking tragedy was that! Goodness knows how many centuries have elapsed since its perpetration; but ask any six-yearold child in the Queen's dominions and he is able to give you the fullest information on the subject, even to detailing the conversation that took place between the scraggy impostor and the affectionate little girl with the pot of butter. Long enduring as the English language is the legend of that wolfs infamy. The arch villain! Had he been content—he could not have been so very hungry—with devouring only grandmamma, his crime might possibly in time have been forgotten; but when we find him, with deliberate calculation and scheming, beguiling the sweet and unsuspecting little girl to a bloody and violent death, why then

Why then, since he gobbled her up body and bones at a single meal, his method of treatment was decidedly less cruel and much to be preferred to that adopted by modern wolves, in clothing fictitious and innocent-looking as"grandmamma's nightcap and bedgown, who lurk in dens of which "The Retreat" is an example, enticing little Red Riding Hoods by the score, and for the sake of a profit of twopence affording facilities for their descent to such terrible depths that from thence death is looked up to and cried for as a friend and deliverer. As already intimated, there is no bobbin to pull or latch to fly up at Mr. Johnson's gate. There it stands wide open. "How dark your garden is, Mr. Johnson!" "All the better for you and the stupid boy with you, my dear, that you may sit in one of my arbours and partake of the pint of beer he so manfully orders." "What great ears you've got, Mr. Johnson!" "All the better for you, my dear. The naughty things I am obliged to hear amongst my after-dark customers passes in at one and out at the other the more readily." "What little eyes you've got, Mr. Johnson!" "All the better for you, my child; otherwise I must see amongst my after-dark customers very much that is shocking and immoral, and turn you and your companions out and lock my gate."

Mr. Johnson does not eat the little girl all up, however. What he does do, and the fullest extent of his doing appears in the above imaginary little dialogue. It was on a Sunday night; just when the spring was advancing and the evenings growing longer, that " The Retreat" was visited, and a scene more disgraceful than that witnessed cannot be imagined. As regards the ordinary suburban tea-garden, the proprietor is obliged to observe a certain amount of decorum—he cannot admit little boys and girls, apparently under fourteen years of age say. Not that he objects on personal grounds. Oh, dear no. He has a family himself, and likes children as well as any man, and threepence *is* threepence by whomsoever tendered. Nor has he moral qualms worth speaking of on the subject. The matter stands thus:—Young men and women when they come out to enjoy themselves at a tea-garden like quiet. Without tranquillity sweethearting is the merest farce, and to preserve tranquillity where boys and girls are is simply impossible. They will romp and giggle and indulge their propensity for prying and peeping and poking their inquisitive little noses into just those places where they are least welcome. They—the sweethearting couples—won't stand it. They don't object to paying the rent of a box to the amount of several sixpences, taking ginand-water as a receipt; but they won't put up with intrusion. It is not likely. An Englishman's house is his castle all the world over, and whatever the place he rents, it may be fairly regarded as his house. Nor is the spirited proprietor.inclined to be hard with his renters. He is not the man to break a contract because it is insinuated, and not stated. When children of tender age seek admittance to his gardens he sternly refuses them, telling them that his is no place for brats, and that they had best be off home and get to bed.

And so, Heaven knows, they had better, and probably they would do so if no other gate were open to them. Mr. Johnson's is the other gate, and a walk of a mile or more is no obstacle to those flocking to it. Who and what are these juvenile teagarden customers? Errand boys as to the male portion—little boys engaged at shops or factories, and earning from 5s. to 8s. a week, and allowed 6d. out of it for pocket-money. Good boys enough in the main, in all probability, children of decent parents who see no harm in Bill and Dick staying out an hour after church-time on their only evening of leisure. Bill and Dick, aged respectively thirteen and fifteen, are not the youngsters they appear to be they would have you to understand. Wearing a tall hat is quite a matter of taste, and all young men have not got whiskers. If a young fellow chooses to wear a jacket and blucher boots, that is exclusively his business; like the tall hat, it is a matter of taste, maybe. Anyhow, he must be a pretty old boy who can take his swig at the beer when it comes to his turn, and who can smoke a cigar without betraying symptoms of illness; and there in the dark recesses of an arbour—("The Retreat" is absolutely dark, and without the slightest attempt at illumination)—may be made out Dick and his brother sitting along with Jemima Riggs and Betsy Trotter, puffing manfully at their penny cigars (though every puff produces an internal shudder worse even than that which attends a gulp of Epsom salts), and handing about the brown jug, and ejaculating "Damn," and "So help me" this, and "Strike me" t'other, with an earnestness and frequency calculated to impress the two young ladies that though young they are lads of mettle and knowing cards, up to snuff of every degree of strength and variety of flavour, and possessing a knowledge of the time of day to a fraction of a tick. It is wonderful the lengths these foolish little dogs will go— the serious sacrifices they will make in dread of "looking little " in the eyes of the shrewd old women of fourteen, their companions. They don't care a pin's head for beer, and, indeed, never take a drop of it through the working days, but beer is the drink of men—of young men as well as old. It would be ridiculous to think of smoking a cigar with gingerpop, or to "keep company " on sherbet or penny ices: so beer is the liquor in request, even though the purchase of a second pint of it sweeps away Dick's pocket-money to the last farthing.

And who are Jemima and Betsy? They are even younger than Bill and Dick, and though very forward and naughty children, have at present but a limited knowledge of vice. They are girls who are just launched in the world to learn a trade, or who mind children, or help mother who is a laundress, and very probably are absent from home on the same artful pretence as their "young men," and would as certainly as those worthies come in for a whipping if they were found out by their parents. If they are juvenile hands at factories they have constant opportunities for hearing the conversation of elder girls relative to their Sunday evening experiences of their flirtation, and their "sprees," and their sweetheart's generosity, until it becomes plain to Jemima—thirteen next birthday—that to have a "young man " is to possess all that is desirable on earth. That conclusion paves the way for the first step, which is to arrange with Betsy Trotter to "slip off" on Sunday evening and go for a walk. Then Dick and Bill are encountered, and four more customers are booked for "The Retreat."

There may not appear much in all this; it may even seem injudicious to discuss the morality of calf-love, and to drag before the public for its consideration the billings and cooings of Tommy and Sally. The records of our reformatories and penitentiaries, however, tell a different story. Nor is it necessary for any one who is curious on the subject to consult printed and published statistics. Let him any night, between the hours of nine and twelve, take a walk between the Angel at Islington and Highbury, or through Regent Street and the Haymarket, or along Westminster Road, from the bridge as far as the thoroughfare known as the New Cut. Let him count the number of painted, flaunting, poor little wretches, under fifteen years old, who, with the regularity of policemen on beat, there ply their terrible trade, and then say that no harm comes of calf-love of the sort described as indulged in under the auspices of a friendly Johnson all in the dark, and stimulated by a pint or so of that excellent tradesman's potent " sixpenny."

LITTLE BOB IN HOSPITAL.

'"THE circumstances attending my introduction to little Bob were scarcely promising of our better acquaintance.

It was an exceedingly muddy day, and the thoroughfare through which my way lay—never commonly decent, as the saying is, even at best of times—was now about as unfavourable to pedestrianism as can be well imagined. It is one of those old-fashioned streets that the increasing demand for broad highways flanked by palatial houses of business have bricked in, and buried alive, as it were. The houses of the streets are tall, gaunt, smoke-dried edifices, slatternly in decay, with the chimney-pot cowls all battered and blown awry as a dissipated beggar wears his hat, and with the doorsteps parted from the doorsill and trodden all aslant, like the heels of a tramp's boots. The windows of the houses, too, are peculiar, though I believe that they are in strict accordance with the notions of architectural beauty prevalent at the period when the buildings were erected. They are skimping little windows, set flush with the outer bricks, and have the naked and unnatural lock of eyes from which the lashes and brows have been shaven. The roadway is of the good old-fashioned cobble-stone pattern so favourable to the accumulation and retention of garbage and its essence, and the footway merely a more closely-woven selvage of the same material.

Heedless of the miry condition of the said selvage, it swarmed with children—whose home was the smoke-dried beggarly houses —engaged in the vigorous recreation afforded by shutdecock and battledore. There was one, however—a very small one—who appeared to prefer the delight of ease and contemplation. He had no boots on his feet, or socks; he wore no hat or cap, nor pinafore, nor. petticoats—indeed, unless some other garment had got tucked up and coiled about the higher regions of his body, one would be justified from the evidence of his senses in declaring that the three-year-old philosopher had on nothing in the world but a wofully dirty little shirt and a frock to match. As he did not move as I approached, and as he occupied the centre of the footpath, I paused.

"Hist him out o' the way, Sall, unless you wants your young 'un trod on," one old lady of ten or thereabouts, with her hair done up in a matronly knot behind, remarked to her companion.

"Can't he walk?" I asked.

"How can he when he's got the rickets?" replied the knowing female in tones that betokened her pity for my ignorance; "can't you step over him, stoopid? Bat up, Poll, keep the pot a-bilin'."

By this time the young gentleman, who during the conversation had sat with his shockingly thin white legs crossed tailorwise on the chill black pavement, mutely appealing out of his big heavy eyes to somebody to help him, proceeded to crawl out of the way as well as he could, which was not at all well. He had a monstrously great head, poor child, and a pot-belly, the two seemingly comprising a burden to which his puny strength was quite unequal. Besides, the clinging, slippery mud was against locomotion on the hands and knees. I took him up and sat him on the door-sill, an act of kindness that seemed to fill him with astonishment, judging from the look he gave me.

"What's your name, little boy?" I inquired. Now that his mite of a face was flushed through shyness, he was anything but an ill-looking child.

"Bob," said he.

"What else?"

"Bobby," said he, after some reflection.

"And what's the matter, Bobby?" (Poll was "batting up" to Sall's heart's content by this time, and at too great a distance to heed us). Bob didn't at first comprehend my question, so I amended it by inquiring whereabouts he ached.

"'Ickits. Don't ache. On'y nights." There was a pause between "Don't ache " and "On'y nights," and as the latter was uttered Bobby's babyish brown eyes in an instant grew dull and his dirty little pale face careworn, as though the nights of his life were indeed sad times with him. I beckoned Sall from her shuttlecock, and made a few further inquiries concerning Bobby. He was "three-and-a-half" she informed me, and she had threepence a day for minding him. That his mother worked at rag sorting over in the Borough, and that his father was a "drunken cove, as walloped her." Ever since he was a year old Bobby had been rickety, which Sall attributed to his obstinacy in sitting on paving stones and sulking with his victuals. "He ain't fit for a gentleman to see—he never is," said Sall, making a dash at Bobby, and straightening his little draggletail frock, and extemporizing a comb with the spread dirty fingers of her hand, and applying it to Bobby's hair with such vigour that the poor child was thrown off his unsteady balance, with his legs in the air. Such legs! The spectacle of their thinness was shocking when no higher than the knees was visible, but now the sight was one to make a Christian man cry out aloud. Scraggy and hollow-thighed, as those of a starved cat, they were deadly white, except for the mud and dirt that coated them, with the little knees black and corned almost as the hands of a coal-heaver.

"There!" exclaimed Sall, as she fetched him a spank for tumbling over. "You wouldn't think that I washed him all over this morning, would you, now?" To which I candidly replied that I really should not.

"What does the doctor say about him?" I asked.

"What doctor?"

"Does a doctor never see him?"

"What's the use, when it's rickets?" replied the little old woman; "he'll have to grow out of 'em. That's wot his young sister died of."

Next day I sought and obtained an interview with Bobby's mother, and within a week Bobby was accepted an indoor patient at the Hospital for Sick Children in Great Ormond Street. Being in the neighbourhood recently, I thought that I would look in and inquire how my little friend was getting on.) My acquaintance with hospitals is not extensive, and I knew the Great Ormond Street institution only by repute. Once or twice I had visited the sick-wards of Guy's and Bartholomew's, and once the accident ward at the Royal Free Hospital; and, though, no doubt, the very best under existing circumstances is done for all comers at these various noble establishments, the little children there, lying in close company with diseased and dying adults, furnished a feature inexpressibly painful to contemplate. I knew that the Hospital for Sick Children exclusively professed to remedy this serious objection, and was delighted to hear that its charitable founders had ample reasons for being satisfied with the success of their project but I never knew until I went to visit Bobby how complete that success was, and were I equal to the task of describing it—which, alas! I am painfully conscious that I am not—I am not sure but that I should hesitate to do so, lest the fond mothers of hundreds of ailing Bobbys and Pollys and Johnnys should joyfully hail the account as proclaiming the great barrier that has all along stood between them and the hospital removed, and they should flock there in a host that their darlings might be cured. Every mother knows what the barrier is. "To be sure, they might do more for him than I can," says poor mother, hugging her sick or crippled little one; "but how could I part from him? How could he part from me? God help my poor little fellow, I am his only comfort; he would pine to death in a strange hospital bed, amongst strangers."

At the risk of involving the Great Ormond Street authorities in the difficulty above hinted at, I make bold to declare to you, hesitating mothers all, that your fears as to the comfort and content of your ailing children are utterly and entirely without foundation. By what manner of magic the miracle is wrought I will not even attempt to guess, but there is the fact repeated seventy odd times in as many little beds—sick children afflicted in but too many cases with disease that is cruelly painful, lying there as cheerful and patient and pleasant as though they had thoroughly taken to heart the truth that they were there for their good, and that the best they can do is to be on their very best behaviour while they are being cured. I can only again repeat that it is marvellous, and this was still my impression even after I had made acquaintance with the magician in command. He is a young man, this magician—many a mother with a baby in her arms has a son as old—and his great gift is power to win the confidence of babies. He escorted me upstairs into the first ward, which is a ward for little girls. To tell of white floors and the neatest of beds is only to claim for it what is common to all hospital wards, with this difference: that instead of the dismal stump bedstead, each little patient here is provided with a pretty iron cot of a cheerful colour, surrounded at top by a rail on which slides a broad board at a convenient height for the patient to reach when it sits up, and on which is arranged its toys or picture-books. Everything is bright and light and pleasant looking, even to the nurses, who are not severe matrons, but neat young women, light-handed and cheery-looking, and with nothing but kind words for their helpless charges.

The first bed to which the magician introduced me contained a mite of a thing, aged about three years, and afflicted with dropsy. Wasted to mere skin and bone, the tiny creature was a sight to remember, as she lay with her great heavy head on the pillow, and her eyes half closed. But she brightened up as soon as the doctor touched her cheek and uttered her name. She couldn't speak, but she could smile, and this she did till her tiny goblin face was strangely puckered, and she kept her eyes fixed on him, as though it pleased her to do so, while we stood there and the magician gave me the particulars of her case.

Then we came to a bed out at the foot of which hung suspended a weight at the end of a chain, which told of a little sufferer from some disease of the hip which required that the leg should be kept still and straight—the other end of the weighted chain being attached to the foot. Again the same cheery greeting, with words of thankfulness this time, the patient being old enough. 'Well, little Polly, how do you feel, eh? Quite well! No, not *quite* well, Folly; all in good time. A very good little girl this, sir; a *very* good girl." Then came a case of amputation of the foot, the operation having taken place but three days before; but the patient, though pale and shakylooking, was quite cheerful and friendly with the magician, though tears came into her eyes when he said something about the poor little foot. Then a poor girl with such a wound in her throat as made me shudder to see, but who was now mending, as the doctor declared, and as the poor little thing herseli affirmed, when he asked her, by a motion of her eyes, for she was as yet unable to speak or move. There was a basin with water and a little sponge by the bed, and the way in which the good fellow applied the latter to the little girl's wound was a sight for her mother to see.

But it was the same story all through as we passed from ward to ward, where the cheerful fires were burning, and the kindfaced nurses moved hither and thither, and some of the sick ones sat up at work on their basins of bread-and-milk or beeftea, and othere were contentedly busy at their play-boards, hooking gay railway carriages one to the other, or giving the animals of Noah's Ark an airing, or, as yet unequal to such active employment, with quiet interest turning the leaves of a painted picture-book. No crying to go home, no fretting or pining; all as happy under the circumstances not only as might be expected reasonably, but twenty times more so. All glad to see the doctor—or magician, as I have called him—all grateful for his encouraging word, or a touch of his kind hand. All? No; let me keep strictly within the boundary of truth. Out of the seventy-five patients there is *one* sulky boy. He is known as *the* sulky boy, and is the exception that proves the happy rule. He is a delinquent of not gigantic proportions, being somewhere about two feet six in height, and five years of age; but he is getting well in a most ungrateful manner, and hangs his head when he is spoken to like a sturdy little bear being tamed against his will. He had a scratch on the side of his nose.

"How did you get your nose scratched, my dear?" I asked him. He was so nearly well, I should mention, as to be out of bed and dressed.

The rebel made no answer, but another patient exclaimed, "Please, sir, Bobby did it," at the same time pointing at the occupant of an adjacent bed.

This Bobby?—Bobby of the towzledhair and the holloweyes so eloquent of pain "o'nights!" Bobby, the mottled of dirt and pallor! This clean, bright, mischievous little urchin, Bobby! No other, the magician assured me. "It will take some time to set the young gentleman up, however," said he, patting Bob's head; and, really, when I reflected on what Bob was doomed to go home to, I was scarcely sorry to hear it.

And now, ladies and gentlemen, having given you, to the best of my poor ability, an inkling of what the hospital in Great Ormond Street is like, I make bold to recommend it to your charitable consideration. Nay, I beg of you to remember it, regarding it as no shame to beg even in behalf of suffering baby-boys and girls. The noble scheme is capable of vast extension; nay, in a country such as ours it demands extension. Here are learned heads, and kind hearts, and willing hands eager to engage in this blessed work if you will only give them opportunity. At present the institution has but seventy-five beds, and, it need not be added, they are all full. They are always full, and day after day the great men who so generously devote their time and skill to the comparatively few sufferers they have house-room for are pained to turn from their doors cases that in every respect are worthy of admission. There can be no doubt that this little hospital will in time grow—it *must* grow. Let it not be of slow growth. I heartily wish that the charitably-disposed could for themselves see what I have endeavoured to describe; they would need no further urging.

Since this paper"was written the Great Ormond Street Hospital has been considerably enlarged, and a handsome convalescent home in connection with the institution established at Highgate.

AT A "KNOCKING OUT.", TVT O. 44, in our row, where the late Mr, Tatters resided, was, one time o' day, the envy of the entire neighbourhood. The green railings enclosing the front garden were never allowed to appear in a coat of paint in the least degree shabby, the garden itself was a little paradise of red gravel rolled to the gloss and smoothness of ironed linen, and trim box borders and flowering plants of every sort and variety; the window curtains were matchless, the windows bright as a brook. As for Tatters' doorsteps, whether it was solely due to the superior skill of Tatters' housemaid or to a peculiar sort of hearthstone known only to a select few, certain it is that, whatever the state of the weather, they were a reproach to all others, left and right, and on the other side of the road.

What Mr. Tatters was, was not generally known. That he was something in the City was beyond a doubt, since precisely at half-past nine in the morning he appeared at his gate to await the coming of the Balham 'bus, the destination of which was the Bank, and precisely at half-past four in the afternoon Mrs. Tatters might be observed at the parlour window, confidently looking out for the return of her lord by the same vehicle. Mr. Tatters enjoyed the reputation of being very well-to-do. The fishmonger and poulterer, as well as the butcher, called every morning for orders, and the pastrycook's boy could have found his way to Laurel Cottage blindfold. Erard's people had been seen to deliver a harp there. Young Tatters rode out on a pony, and often of afternoons the same animal was attached to a basket phaeton to draw Mrs. Tatters and the two youngest girls round the country for an hour or so. About August the window-blinds would be lowered, to rise no more for the space of six weeks, during which time the Tatters family was at Ventnor or Broadstairs. These little matters had been maturely considered by the matrons of our row, together with the probable cost, and the conclusion arrived at was that Mr. Tatters' income was as near five hundred a year as possible.

Just after Christmas of the present year, however, there were evidences of something amiss at 44. Morning after morning half-past nine came round, and the Balham 'bus came down the hill and passed on innocent of Mr. Tatters. "What's come of the gent in the white 'at, Bill?" asked the driver of the conductor; "he ain't rid with us this fortnite. " "Ill, I shouldn't wonder; thought he looked shaky last time,I set him down. " "Oh! that's all right then, I was afraid the opposition had nailed him." And the driver, with his mind relieved, gives "the gent with the white 'at" no further thought.

The conductor was right. Poor Mr. Tatters is shaky indeed, The doctor's carriage is daily at the door of Laurel Cottage as punctually as the baker's cart, and the door-knocker wears a kid glove. This for two months or thereabouts, and then the doctor's carriage is seen at the door twice as often as the baker's cart. This for still a further two months, during which the knocker has worn out two pairs of gloves at least. Then comes a time when it would almost seem that the doctor had made a wager as to the number of times he can drive to and from between his own residence and Laurel Cottage from breakfast time till dusk—arriving at the close of the last heat with two other doctors in their carriages as though the waste of a moment would lose him his stake. Next morning the doctor does not call at all, and the blinds are down at all the front windows, just after the August fashion, and the neighbours know that the poor gentleman has gone out of town for good and all.

They buried him in so handsome a manner as to give grounds for the rumour that he had left his widow and five children very comfortable. But this was a mistake. On the contrary, he had left them exceedingly uncomfortable. He had been one of those easy-going, generous-minded men, content so that he grew grass enough for the present browsing of his little flock, and with no thought at all towards haymaking. He might have grown more thrifty and grudging by-and-by, but he was only thirty-seven when he died. That four months' long sickness had, on Dr. Balsam's account alone, exhausted the Tatters exchequer and butcher and baker, and tinker and tailor remained unpaid; and there were summonses in the house for poor's-rate and income tax, and thirty-one pounds ten due on the score of rent.

It was inevitable what would happen. All that poor Mrs. Tatters possessed in the world was the furniture of her house —(how the funeral expenses were met there were the pawnbroker's tickets for "two gold watches and chains, seven finger rings, twelve silver forks," &c. , &c., to prove)—and that the butcher and the baker and the house agent clamoured for. It was a very capital house of furniture, and first and last had cost the late Mr. Tatters more than seven hundred pounds. It might reasonably be expected that sold at auction property of this value would fetch at least two hundred pounds, which would leave the widow exactly sixty-five pounds, all debts paid, and with which modest surplus the butcher suggested that she might open a little school or something.

In a few days there was a breadth of stair-carpet drooping out of the second-floor window at No. 44, to which a placard was affixed announcing the sale; and knowing poor Tatters as a man of some taste, I procured a catalogue and marked a few articles that might be worth while bidding for.

There was no mistaking the house. Besides the Kidderminster banner floating from the window, there was drawn up in front of 44, and extending to 49 on one side and 38 on the other, a line of shabby trucks and carts, the horses in which had their nose-bags on, making it clear that they were destined to stay there some little time. The gate was open, as was the street door, and lounging on the miraculous steps, and within the neat hall, were groups of unclean men with battered hats and green baize aprons, who looked as though their sole feeding was mouldy corn, and their bedding the mildewing stalks of it. What their business at the sale was did not appear, since a threshing of their united pockets would not have yielded half-a-crown, but there they were, and at such places they are always to be found. The auctioneer's porters don't like them, and warn them off just as frequently as they encounter them, but they only turn tail for a yard or so, and then recluster in the passages and on the kitchen stairs.

The sale at Laurel Cottage took place in the parlour, with the folding doors thrown open. The auctioneer was perched with his pulpit atop of a table, and four or five other tables in a low formed a convenient platform for the display of the article at the moment "under the hammer." I found that many of poor Tatters' neighbours besides myself were present, and every one, I have no doubt, willing to give a reasonable price for such goods as suited them. But, alas for the widow and her five children! there were likewise present in mighty force a host of shabby wretches, with dirty shirts, and dirty faces, and dirty hands; and their business there was to conspire to bamboozle and deceive honest buyers, and to cheat Mrs. Tatters out of as much of the value of her furniture as possible. My knowledge of this gentry is not restricted to my opportunity for observing their practices that afternoon. I know them of old, at horse sales and wine sales, and sales of Custom House rummage, but it never before entered my head in my small way to expose the dodgers. Maybe I never met a case in which their machinations worked so cruelly.

Shabby and hungry as the members of the Jewish pack appear, they have money in their pockets. It is not very unlikely that they will want it, but they may, and it would not do to be without a pound or so. Their prime capital, however, is unscrupulous lying and impudence of so gross and disgusting a sort that decent people dare not face it, and prefer, from the same reason that they decline to touch pitch, to leave the company or remain silent. "Knockers out" these fellows are called, and they manage their business systematically. They do not group together, but distribute themselves amongst the *bona fide* bidders, pretending to act in a perfectly independent manner. The "knocker out" is very communicative to the people about him, rather boasting than otherwise of his acuteness as a dealer, and talking as Jewish as possible. There are some rare things going, he believes, but all that is worth buying will be bought by the trade. "Don't you see how it is? People who have got to pick up their living at sales take more trouble than private-buyers. It wasn't his luck to come yesterday and look through the house, but there is old Marks over there, and Hookey Barnet, and Phillips from Dog Row; they were here all day yesterday, and there isn't a stick nor a rag in the place that they haven't handled, and know the value of to a penny. There's one precious good job they are such close shavers that a man_,with any conscience at all can always bid a shilling or two over them!" This is Mr. Solomons who says this, and meanwhile Hookey Barnet over yonder is confiding the same yarn to his innocent neighbour, only that *he* is the unlucky man who couldn't get as far as Balham to the private view yesterday, and Solomons is one of the close shavers, who has valued every stick and rag; and so the pretty story goes round.

"Lot 28," says the auctioneer, "is an inlaid worktable and a velvet-covered settee; what shall I say for lot 28? Ten shillings, eleven, twelve, twelve, twelve, twelve! any advance upon twelve?" (Mr. Phillips' was the last bid.) "Why, gentlemen! the worktable is worth twice the money!" "Thirteen," exclaims a timid voice, whereon muffled voices in various parts of the room are heard to titter, and Mr. Phillips exclaims, "Knock it down, sir! let the gentleman have 'em; he'll have time to examine 'em when he gets 'em home." "Going for thirteen shillings!" cries Mr. Auctioneer. Mr. Solomons intimates another shilling by a nod imperceptible to any one but the keen man of the rostrum. "Fourteen! going at fourteen!" The timid bidder of thirteen shillings is glad to have escaped the threatened peril, and the lot is knocked down to Mr. Solomons.

Lot 20 is a feather bed and pillows. Next to blankets nothing has greater attractions for a furniture-dealer than a feather bed. Honestly the bed in question is well worth five pounds. As it is pitched down on to the platform Mr. Marks pinches up a great handful of it, and, shrugging his shoulders, turns away, muttering "Rubbish!" Mr. Barnet, on the other side, hooks his finger in at a seam, and tearing a rent, plunges in his fist and playfully remarks, "Oh, yes! they *is* feathers! Ain't there a shuttlecock maker here as vill bid for it?" "I shall give you a pound for it, and chance it," cries Mr. Marks. "Twenty-five," from Mr. Solomons. "Twenty-six," from Mr. Barnet. "More fool you," exclaims Mr. Davis, "it'll cost ten bob washin' and purifying before it can be used." "Only twenty-six shillings for a perfectly clean goose feather bed," says Mr. Auctioneer, "clean as a new bed, I assure you." But it is of no use; visions of small-pox and fever fill the minds of the majority present (they know there has recently been a burial from the house), and the feather bed is knocked down at twenty-six shillings.

Lots 30 and up to 35 are of a sort that the Jews have no fancy for, and these they willingly let strangers buy. Still nothing like a fair price is obtained. The Jews have, as it were, set the market, and the bids are ruinously low; but there is no reserve, and down goes the hammer. Then comes a lot that they, the Jews, will buy if they can get it next to nothing; if not, the buyer who dares come between them and their spoil shall suffer. Say it is a chimney clock of Swiss make, and not valuable. "Ten shillings," says Mr. Moses. "Twenty," says a stranger, attracted by the pretty brass works and handsome glass case. The bidder is a troublesome one, and more than once has nearly baulked the Jews of a bargain. The wink goes round—the stranger must be "run up." Mr. Abrahams examines the clock closely, and deliberately bids thirty shillings. "Thirtyfive," cries Mr. Marks. "Forty," promptly exclaims Abrahams. The stranger falls into the trap. Clearly the clock is worth more than he thought. "Forty-five," he bids. "Fifty," says Mr. Abrahams, with his hand eagerly laid on the clock, and his eye on the auctioneer, as though terribly anxious to secure the gem. The stranger hesitates; shall he lose it for the sake of half-a-crown?" Going for two pounds ten!" exclaims Mr. Auctioneer, raising his hammer. "Two twelve six/' says the stranger. "Going for two twelve six!" and down goes the hammer. The stranger is bit. A roar of laughter from the Israelites follows the fall of the hammer—of real mirth, and of a very different kind from affected make-believe sniggering; and the buyer sheepishly pays his money, and the transaction is a caution to all other strangers in the room. So the game is kept alive through the disposal of the hundred and forty lots that comprise Widow Tatters' household goods, and the entire proceeds realize a sum that, instead of sixty pounds, leaves her exactly eleven pounds fifteen "to open a little school or something" for the support of herself and her five orphans.

After the sale comes the "knock out." The parlour of the nearest public-house serves them as a meeting-place, and there they congregate. They are all dealers, but there is sure to be one richer and in a more extensive way of business than the rest amongst them. He takes the chair, with the catalogue of the sale and a pile of gold and silver money before him.

"The first lot, gentlemen," says he, " is the drawing-room suite, knocked down at seven pounds. I shall stand nine for it." "It's worth ten!" remarks one of the company. "Will you *give* ten, Barny?" inquires the chairman. "No, I don't want the lot." "Will anybody give more than nine pounds *T* Nobody will, and the chairman hands his eight brother conspirators each five shillings, and the lot becomes his.

So with the goose-feather bed—(there is no talk now about shuttlecocks or insinuations as to fever, the reader may depend) —and the carpets and the splendid mahogany tables, &c., poor Tatters took such pride in; and more or less the fatter from their picking of the bones of his widow and little ones, the vultures disperse.

A SHORT WAY TO NEWGATE. HERE is a plague that is striking its upas roots deeper and deeper into English soil—chiefly metropolitan—week by week, and flourishing broader and higher, and yielding great crops of fruit that quickly fall, rotten-ripe, strewing highway and by-way, tempting the ignorant and unwary, and breeding death and misery unspeakable. Were it possible to keep a record of the wreck and ruin the plague in question engenders, and to officially publish it as the cholera and cattle plague returns were published, a very considerable sensation would undoubtedly be the result; but since its baleful influence is—as is generally supposed—confined almost entirely to the vulgar ground it is indigenous to, and there is little fear of its spreading beyond certain well-defined and ascertained limits easy to avoid; since it is not, according to the popular acceptation of the term, "catching," and one need labour under no alarm lest it come on the wings of the wind in at our pleasant chamber window, and street cabs are not likely to be impregnated with it, nor omnibuses, nor theatres, nor halls of public assembly, why— why, there's an end of it.

It is, however, a plague not included in the ordinary category that is the subject of this paper—the plague of poisonous literature.

Before me I have twelve penny packets of the poison, gathered at random out of a choice of at least twice as many offered me at the little shop—one of a thousand—devoted to its propagation. It was not on account of their unpromising titles that the remaining pen'orths of poison were not secured. There was "The Boy Bandit," "The Black Monk's Curse," " Blueskin," "Claude Duval, the Dashing Highwayman," "The Vampire's Bride," "The Boy Jockey," "The Wild Boys of London," and many more, of the names of which I have not a distinct recollection. The dozen I received in return for my shilling are entitled, "The Boy King of the Highwaymen," "The Skeleton Crew," "Roving Jack, the Pirate Hunter," "Tyburn Dick," "Spring Heel'd Jack," "Admiral Tom, the King of the Boy Buccaneers," " Starlight Nell," " Hounslow Heath, or the Moonlight Riders," "Red Wolf, the Pirate," "The Knight of the Road," "The Adventures of an Actress," and "The Pretty Girls of London."

Nasty-feeling, nasty-looking packets are every one of them, and, considering the virulent nature of their contents, their most admirable feature is their extremely limited size. Satisfactory as this may be from one point of view, however, it is wofully significant of the irresistibly seductive nature of the bane with which each shabby little square of paper is spread. I have been at the pains to weigh them, and I find that the weight of each pen'orth is but a fraction more than *a quarter of an ounce.* The "Leisure Hour" weighs nearly eight times as much, so do the "Family Herald" and one or two other penny publications of a decent sort. It is the infinitesimal quantity of trash that may be palmed off for a penny that serves as the carrion bait to attract towards it the blow-flies of the book trade. They are enabled to hold out strong inducements to the needy shopkeepers of poor neighbourhoods. The ordinary discount to the trade on ordinary publications is 25 per cent., but the worthy publishers of "Alone in the Pirates' Lair" and "The Skeleton Crew" can afford to allow double that, and more. Wholesale you may buy the precious pen'orths at the rate of fivepence a dozen, and there is no risk to the dealer, since all unsold copies from last week are changed for a similar number of the day's date. This is the lure that tempts the tobacconist and the sweetstuff vender and the keeper of the small chandlery, and induces these worthy tradesmen to give to this pernicious, though profitable, class of goods all the publicity of which their shop window is capable. No doubt that many of these retailers engage in the business utterly unconscious of the sin and shame they are aiding and abetting. It was at a chandler's shop where I purchased *my* twelve pen'orth, and quite a wholesome, matronly woman, with a baby in her arms, served me.

"To be sure, sir," said she, "you are quite right. 'Tyburn Dick' and 'The Pretty Girls' just make the dozen;" and made up the parcel with as much indifference as though it were sugar or biscuits. She would have been mightily astonished, and not improbably indignant, had she been informed that this branch of her trade was as injurious to public morality as if she had kept a repository for stolen goods. It would have been no more than true had she been so informed, however; and if she and other sellers of poison for the minds of girls and boys should happen to read this, and take it to heart, why, so much the better.

A delectable company appears to be foremost of the gang whose profit is the dissemination of impure literature; but there are many rivals in the field—some bearing the printer's or publisher's name and address, others without either—and each vies with his neighbour in the decoction of the pen'orths of muck, endeavouring to outshine him. One and all of the poison packets are illustrated on the outside, and we will give a glance at each, both inside and out, as the fairest method of testing its quality. It may be mentioned that this may be done no less fairly by a weekly instalment of eight pages than by a review of the completed story. There is no such thing as "plot" in this sort of literature. Such an arrangement would only embarrass the publisher, whose sole and single aim is to go on supplying his public with "The Red Wolf" or the "The Skeleton Crew" just so long as they will swallow it. One pen'orth of my collection—" Black Bess; or, The Knights of the Road "—is *a hundred and eighty-four weeks old,* and is quite as vigorous now as at the first week of its birth.

"Spring Heel'd Jack, the Terror of London," is the first on the list. Picture: Jack—with the spring visible at his heels, punching savagely at a policeman's face, and dashing his head against the wall. Summary of contents: Jack indecently assaults a maiden lady, drags her about her bed-chamber by her bedgown, which is pulled over her head, and finally thrusts her into another bedroom to pass the night with an elderly bachelor gentleman. Somebody springs a rattle, neighbours rouse, bachelor's door forced, bachelor in night garment exposed, and maiden lady dragged nude from beneath bachelor's bed. Next chapter: the loves of a policeman and a maid-of-all-work, and a "spicy" scene of the pair in the shadow of a tomb in a churchyard at midnight.

"Says the policeman: 'You lets them catamarans (the girl's mistresses) frighten you from doing your duty, you does.' 'My duty?' 'Yes.' 'What duty?' 'What duty, Peggy? Can you look me in the face and ask the question?' 'I don't know what you mean.' 'You don't?' 'No.' 'I do.' 'What is it?' Bristles placed his hand beneath his belt, and heaved a deep sigh. 'Don't you tumble?' he asked. 'No.' 'Then you is green.' 'What do you mean, Mr. Bristles? asked the girl, in surprise. 'Mean? Oh! dull of comprehension!' 'I know I am.' 'You are.' 'But 'tain't my fault.' 'Not yours; no, no, not all; but part—but part,' said Bristles, shaking his head sadly. 'Oh! do explain,' said the girl, in a pleading and half terrified tone. 'What can I do? What do you want me to do? What do you ask?"'

And, in reply. Mr. Bristles, makes a joke disgusting enough to provoke the ghost of Lord Campbell, and so the story is left "to be continued in our next.''

"Tyburn Dick" is the next. Picture: A young gentleman, presumably the King of Highwaymen himself, with lace and ruffles, cocked hat, jack-boots, and a splendid jewelled star extending across his chest by way of denoting his rank, sword in hand, on a lonely heath at midnight, defiantly receiving the " warning of doom." (Doom being represented by a hideous spectre rising in flames out of the grass.) Summary of contents of part: "Dick in Newgate—The gaoler trapped into Dick's cell—" Give me the keys, or with my manacle, will I scatter your recreant brains against the slimy wall!"—Newgate on fire: the cell growing red-hot—" Give me the keys!" "Ha! ha! never!"

"Dick was exasperated to madness. Putting his two hands together, he grasped the long links, and, poising them straight and firm, dashed them into the gaoler's exultant face. The iron ring joining them struck him between the temples, the two long links dashed into his eyes. He uttered a fearful groan, and fell blind, stunned, and bleeding. 'It grows frightfully hot,' he muttered, as the hot beads of sweat rolled down his face. 'The cell is like an oven. There must be a furnace outside. Am I doomed to perish here? Confusion! why don't they batter down the walls? Ho, there! Help! help! I am here, chained to a wall, amidst the flames!'"

However, it is all right. A friend of Dick's has gone on a visit to the incarcerated highwayman's mother, who is a countess. There is a ball at the countess's, to which all the bloated aristocracy of the kingdom have been invited. However, hearing that she is wanted, the countess hastens down to the parlour, where Claude (the friend) is waiting, and is thus addressed by that gentleman

"' Be not alarmed! I am not come to taunt you with the wrongs you have done me, though they have seared my brain, I am come, unnatural and adulterous mother, to warn you of your persecution of that poor boy, against whom you have steeled your bosom—forgetting that he first drew his sustenance from it. You have hurled him from these halls, which are rightfully his, and have driven him to a life of roadside robbery, and even now have hounded him to a prison, whose walls he may only quit to go forth to a felon's doom. We shall free him this time, but I warn you, fair-faced devil!-cold, callous, unwomanly demon!—I warn you that if the bitter death you desire befals him—if a hangman's accursed hand crushes out his young life—you shall pay the penalty, and the penalty shall be death, though I myself tear your infamous heart from your unnatural breast!'"

And since, so far as the story goes, the lady shows no signs of relenting, the reader is justified in his expectation of getting a very fair pen'orth next week.

No. 3. "The Skeleton Crew." Picture: A pair of ghostly, bodyless legs advancing towards a cavalier who has an affrighted lady under his protection, and who, with hair on end, stands with his rapier advanced to receive the goblin remnant. Since the typographical part of the number makes no allusion to this mystery, it may be assumed that it was accounted for in the last pen'orth, or will be in the next. From what can be gathered in the eight pages, the "Skeleton Crew" are a band of decayed robbers risen from their tombs, and still continuing the nefarious pursuits that was their bent while in the flesh. They, however, retain an appetite for the substantials of life, and rob and murder wholesale and retail. Death-wing is the chief, and here is a specimen of his every-day employments:—

Old Redgill had two ships on their way from the Indies, laden with gold, spices, and silks. In consideration of receiving half of the cargo, Death-wing and his infamous crew resolved to waylay these two ships and attack them when about fifty miles from the Land's End. This was done. The crews of both ships were murdered in cold blood. This system of villany was repeated more than once, but as Philip's father's ships did not arrive in port except at intervals of many months, the villanous young man frequently found his money running short. "Bloodshed to him was quite a usual thing." So he murdered his father's cashier, and made merry with the money. However, the detectives are on his track, and unless his friends the skeletons assist him, he may look out for squalls. Humorous fellows are these fleshless ones, and the number is agreeably lightened by a droll account of how they hanged half a dozen innocent men in a belfry.

Pen'orth number four is entitled "Hounslow Heath." Picture: A poor wretch undergoing some frightful torture. He is extended on the ground, a waggon wheel is lying atop of him, and by his side are various instruments of torment, consisting in a knife, two flaming torches, a glue-pot, and a spokeshave. Gloating over his agony stand two ruffians with highwaymen's masks on. Dick Turpin figures in this story. Our number opens with an account of how he was hard beset by the officers of the law, how he blew out the brains of a Jew and sliced up others with his sword; but, overpowered by numbers, is about to yield, when in the nick of time he is rescued by some old friends who "suddenly appear on the scene." Then Dick stops a stage-coach single-handed, and robs the passengers in his customary polite and graceful manner. Further on, it seems that the band of which Mr. Turpin is the captain capture a person whom they suspect of planning to place them in the hands of justice. So they proceed to torture him as the picture on the front page faintly foretells.

"Firstly, they fastened him securely round the ankles with some stout cords. Then they passed two more ropes through these thongs, and dexterously enough hauled him up to the roof of the cave, where he was allowed to hang head downwards. In this unpleasant predicament they put him through such a course of novel tortures that a tribe of North American Indians might have picked up a wrinkle there. And they made merry while he was in the greatest agony. The more he shrieked with pain, the louder grew their shrieks of laughter. They probed him with their swords and burnt the tip of his nose with a red-hot poker, while one of his torturers held back his arms. A huge, square block of-stone was brought and tied across with stout cords, the ends of which were made into a noose, and slung around Toby Marks's neck. No rack ever known could create such awful torture as this."

After a while, however, they released the victim from the weight of the stone. "Toby Marks dangled now a dead weight by his legs; the two robbers saw the thick and deep-coloured blood roll sluggishly from his nostrils. Then it burst in a torrent from his ears and mouth, and soon his face presented a horrible spectacle to look upon. The blood had completely saturated his hair, until he looked as though he had been newly scalped. The torture was over. The traitorous wretch could bear no more in safety, and so they cut him down. And thus did they avenge the sad end of the gallant Tom King!"

"The Pretty Girls of London" has, as its title was doubtlessly calculated to imply, more to do with the tender passions than with the bravery of masculine adventure. The illustration on the outer page depicts a hideous lady administering the Russian knout to three young women, who are naked to the waist and gracefully writhing in agony. A young lady named May would appear to be the heroine of the tale, and we find her immured in a convent over which the Rev. Mr. Blinker has authority. An interview between this person and May occupies considerable portion of the part.

'"I tell you I want to be your friend; come with me quietly,' says the Rev. Mr. Blinker. 'And if I don't?' 'I shall take you by. force.' May shuddered. 'Come along then,"' As he spoke he gently drew her a few steps. She followed hiin mechanically out of the room door and into the passage. What did his conduct mean? She trembled and recoiled from him in terror. He held her hand tighter and drew her into a room, the door of which was locked when May tried it. He seated her on a couch and himself beside her. 'Listen to me,' he said in a thick whisper, while his eyes had a strange wolfish glare in them which made May shiver and flush deeply beneath his devouring gaze, 'I do not wish to harm you or get you into trouble. Will you leave this house with me quietly, or stay till your persecutor returns? you know your doom if you stay.' 'I will not go with you,' said May firmly. 'Then I shall take you.' She gave a violent start, although his words were more than half expected by her. She endeavoured to disengage herself from the encircling arm which he stole round her waist. She pushed back the hideous face which he thrust close to hers. She was like a child in his arms; her struggles were without avail. With loosened hair, flushed face, and disordered apparel, she struggled madly in the monster's arms. His hot and hateful breath upon her face, his dry lips glued to hers so red and moist. She felt her last remaining strength fast failing away, and soon nothing could save her from the clutches of this odious ruffian. But in her desperate striving to free herself from this monster's embraces, her hand fell upon some hard substance in her pocket; she recollected a little knife she always carried about her. With a desperate effort she tore herself from his arms, and to open the knife was the work of a moment. She plunged the tiny weapon into the man's face. He started back from her with a sharp cry of agony, and staggered away a yard or two, the blood streaming down from his wound."

The pestilence in question is old enough to be gray—as one of its earliest promoters is alive to attest. It is now nearly a quarter of a century since the "Mysteries of the Court" and similar works from the same talented pen appeared to poison the minds of boys and girls; and at the present writing I have before me a "penny number," by the author of the "Mysteries of the Court," and I am bound to state that a cursory glance through it convinces me that it lacks none of the ancient fire— and brimstone. It is, therefore, quite a mistake to suppose that the literary ape is an animal of recent birth—a mistake the less excusable, because for a very long time past he has been at no pains to conceal his existence. Any day within the past ten years he may have been seen in his most hideous complexion staring bold-eyed from a hundred shop windows in and about London, alluring the unwary by means of pictures so revoltingly disgusting and indecent that modest eyes unexpectedly encountering them tingled in shame, and of which as much of the text pertaining as was exposed to view was the faithful echo. Possibly this ape, turned romancist—this "old man in the cloak"—has grown bolder of late. It is not unlikely that by dint of patient wallowing and groping in muck he has contrived to scrape together a considerable sum of money, and his terrors of a sentence of fine or imprisonment have consequently decreased, while it has enabled him to push the sale of his contagious trash by means of millions of handbills and advertisements in the few nasty newspapers remaining open to him. Anyway, it is certain that for a shameful length of time he has dared to bring his wares to the public market openly and unblushingly, and with the cool assurance of an honest man; and it is not a little curious that the lynx-eyed guardians of public morality have not ere this joined hands to catch and crush him.

It is always better, if possible, to show what a thing is in its own shape and colour than to endeavour to describe it. Half the abuses and miseries that, as a civilized nation, disgrace us, might be cured if the public could be brought to view them with its own eyes instead of trusting to the evidence of those of other folk. Undoubtedly it is very convenient to rely on hearsay, but there can be no question that it fosters dilatoriness and a neglect of individual duty, and should therefore be discouraged as far as possible. People believe only half what they hear, and. though it may concern never so grave a grievance, are content to do no more than join in the general lukewarm cry of condemnation, leaving the vigorous application of a remedy to those who have inquired into what is amiss, and who are therefore in a position to know all about it. It is so with this iniquitous boy literature and the sudden outcry against it. Everybody believes it to be odious and abominable because everybody says so: and so the dog, and most deservedly, gets a bad name—but he is *not* hanged; he is simply avoided. Because he is such a mangy, ill-looking cur, offensive alike to the nose and to the touch, all decent people shrink away from him. But he would much rather have their room than their company, and grins to himself as they give him the path, and permit him to continue his career of ravening and rending. He must be discovered in the act of mauling one of our little ones before we are moved to take hold of the brute and strangle him.

Now, it may be fearlessly asserted that there never lived an animal of prey of uglier type than this two-legged creature, who poisons the minds of little children to make his bread. Never a more dangerous one, for his manginess is hidden under a sleek and glossy coat, and lips of seeming innocence conceal his cruel teeth. His subtlety, too, is more than canine. He is gifted with a devilish power of beguiling boys and girls to take to him and nourish him in secret. Beware of him, O careful parents of little lads! He is as cunning as the fabled vampire. Already he may have bitten your little rosy-cheeked son Jack. He may be lurking at this very moment in that young gentleman's private chamber, little as you suspect it, polluting his mind and smoothing the way that leads to swift destruction. You may scout the idea with indignation, knowing your Jack to be a boy of honest mind, and one least of all likely to conceal matters of this kind from you; but, my dear sir, pray bear it in mind that nine-tenths of the parents of England are as ready as yourself to stand forward and vouch for the purity of *their* Jacks and Jills: but for all that, it is estimated that *upwards of a million* of these weekly pen'orths of abomination find customers.

I find, on looking through my "weekly numbers," that one "plot serves for the construction of the whole. It is a simple and at the same time comprehensive plot, and may be briefly summarized as a mocking and laughing to scorn of the full number of the Ten Commandments. The main arguments are, that there is no creature so noble as the thief, and that the noblest fellow's primest reward consists in boundless debauchery, in which intoxicating liquors and the loveliest of her sex, of course, figure most conspicuously. Here is a little ditty that may more clearly express my meaning. It is extracted from No. 5 of a stirring romance entitled "Tyburn Tree":—

"Let the asses who choose drive the plough or the spade,
Let the noodles of commerce get guineas by trade,
Let the sailor for wealth skim the wild raging sea,
I envy not either—the high road for me!

"Brave fellows who, scorning to flinch or to falter,
Defy full-wigged beaks, and don't care for the halter;
Who taxes alike spendthrift, miser, and churl,
Then is off with light heart to his crib and his girl.

" And if, boys, at Tyburn, our exit we make,
A curse on the sneak who shall peach, or shall shake;
Let's swear to be faithM, if such our end be,
And manfully drop, like ripe fruit, from the tree."

The talented author, however, does not seem to regard this wind-up of the convicted ruffian's existence as a *sine qua non,* for at page 40 of his story he feelingly remarks: "Thank God! the torture of the Inquisition is now abolished, as we trust that the gallows will be before long. *But we must not moralize"* Well, to be sure it does seem a little out of place, considering that a little further on our author puts into the mouth of one of his most famous characters such a sentence as the following:—

"Who the devil would be chained to a dull shop, to plod for paltry shillings, when he could jump on the back of his good steed, cry ' Stand and deliver' to the first he meets, and return to his girl and his glass with golden-lined pockets?"

There is always a banding together by means of some terrible oath amongst the ruffians and murderers of penny romance. Wretched little London errand boys, following to the best of their ability in the footsteps of their heroes, not uncommonly imitate them in this respect. To be sure they cannot hope just at present to get up so imposing a ceremony as the "Tyburn Tree" band engaged in, but no doubt it has furnished them many valuable hints.

"A large goblet nearly filled with red wine was brought and placed on a low stool; on either side of this were laid a dagger, a phial of deadly poison, a halter, a loaded pistol, and a hideous-looking human skull from which the hair had not yet all fallen away, and which had an earthy and charnel-like odour.

"All the lights in the hall excepting the one which hung immediately over the low stool, and the fearful things placed thereupon, were then extinguished, and the red light now glaring on the instruments of death and on the grinning skull produced a fearful effect!

"One of the gang, who had a rude lancet in his hand, then commanded Hawkins to bare his left arm. This having been done, he was made to kneel down, and the lancet having made an incision into one of the small veins at the bend of the elbow, the blood which streamed from the orifice was suffered to fall into the wine goblet, and when about the sixth part of a pint had issued, the flow was stopped and the slight wound bandaged up.

"' Lieutenant, administer the oath!' commanded Captain Fury.

"Fresnean now requested Hawkins to repeat after him—

"' I hereby, in the presence of God, man, and devil, bind myself to serve as a freetrader in this gang; to obey my captain in all his commands, whether at the peril of my life or otherwise; to keep faithfully all his secrets, and never to betray those with whom I am associated. Also to guard against all treachery; in the performance of my duties to spare neither friend nor foe—young or old—man, woman, or child; and if guilty of traitorhood, to agree to take my choice of halter, poison, or dagger, and never until death to quit the Black Gang.'

"As soon as Hawkins repeated the words of this oath, the goblet of mixed wine and blood was handed to him, and he was ordered to drink to the dregs the fearful mixture. The cord, the poison, and the dagger were then handed to him, the halter being dropped over his neck, the poison phial placed to his lips, and the dagger's point placed to his breast. His hands also, during the speaking of these words, were placed on the hideous relic of mortality.

"It was the head of a former member of the gang. Pointing to it, Captain Fury informed Hawkins that the crime of which the man to whom it once belonged had been guilty, had been a violation of his oath, and that his skull would be so used should he be guilty of a similar offence."

And so, having bound himself in the eyes of " God, man, and devil," the new member of the villanous brotherhood was entitled to participate in the manifold advantages the high distinction confers. Chief among these is the companionship of " female beauty." It is in this branch of his profession that the cankercr of young minds shines brightest. His tactics are invariable. Awaiting the return of every "highwayman," or "burglar," or "burker" of his collection is a "lovely young female," who as soon as he takes his seat perches herself on his knee, and enfolds his neck with her "soft, plump arms, white as alabaster."

But further to select from the ugly batch of seventeen would be to suggest the possibility that in only a few instances were they so very bad. This would be conveying a false impression. Undoubtedly, some of the weekly numbers contain more of obscenity and flagrant indecency than others; but of the ingredients indicated they are one and all composed, and differ only in proportion and mixing. In every one of the "romances" in question there is a highwayman, or a burglar, or a footpad, who is wonderfully successful in all he undertakes, and with whom guineas are as common as nuts in a squirrel's nest. In every instance there exists the fiercest hatred between the "hero " and the law, and it is the author's aim to show constantly what a purblind, weak-minded affair the law is; and considering how very little a "daring spirit " has to encounter in defying it, and how that same defying it means every luxury that can be desired without the mean, degrading drudgery of working for it, what a wonder it is that there are so many "asses who drive the plough or the spade," and so few valiant ones "who defy full-wigged beaks, and don't care for the halter." This is the theme never-ending—this and the other deadly pernicious ingredient, the "lovely wanton," in a description of whose "charms," from her eyes to her heels, the author wallows with evident great personal gratification.

What more remains to be said, except once again to apologize to my readers for so boldly uncovering the unsavoury stew and clapping it so immediately under their nostrils? It is a most unthankful task to do so; but the effect will be salutary, I hope and believe. It is hard to credit that fathers of families would so long have endured the existence of the "Boy Highwayman," or the "Boy Burglar," or "Tyburn Dick," if they really knew the monsters each and every one of these worthies were.

GOING TO THE DOGS. COME few years ago it entered the heads of a few sensible and kind-hearted individuals that it would be a good thing to establish a sort of temporary asylum for dogs inadvertently lost, and for whose restoration the owners would thankfully pay recompense, and for sick, starving, and discarded dogs that nobody owned, and who were eking out a wretched existence, kicked from door to door, and made cruel sport of by those merciless little human savages that infest London streets. This small community of charitable ones convened a meeting at which the proposition for founding a "Home for Lost and Starving Dogs" was put and carried, and certain moneys told down at once to set the scheme afloat; and immediately afterwards advertisements appeared in the newspapers inviting the benevolent to contribute towards the good aim.

If I rightly remember, however, the idea was not received by the public at large with that degree of enthusiasm the committee might reasonably have anticipated. People shook their heads and sneeringly demanded to be informed whether the very last little boy or girl had been fished out of the kennel to which the vice or poverty of its parents had consigned it— whether it had been set on its little legs, and cleansed and clothed, and sent to school, and permanently provided for—that these humanitarians felt at liberty to extend a succouring hand to mangy little puppy dogs and prowling curs generally, orphaned and in distress. The funny periodicals of the day had their fling at the scheme, and drew a ludicrous picture of that soft-hearted creature, Violet Poudar, Esq., hugging beneath the breast-flaps of his dandy coat a forlorn little whelp recently rescued from the gutter, while at the end of his cambric handkerchief, converted for the nonce into a dog-collar and cord in one, he hauled along a gaunt, ill-favoured tyke, who resented this interference with his liberty in a manner that threatened the speedy destruction of V. P.'s trousers, one leg of which was already rent by the indignant and unwilling captive's teeth.

One way and another such an abundance of ridicule and cold water was cast on the project and its promoters, that had the latter been actuated by any sordid motive, instead of the pure and simple one of benefiting creatures that could in no way express their gratitude except by wagging their tails, it is extremely probable that the institution would never have known existence but the kind of persons who devote their lives to charities of this description, in their wrestlings with obstinacy and apathy and stupid-headed ridicule, rather enjoy than otherwise a contested battle; and having attained certain ground they stuck to it, and fought manfully for more.

Foot by foot they have gained it. Their success is not enormous, but sufficiently so to save the national credit, and release us from the stigma of being mere wordy hypocrites as regards our intelligent and honest four-footed *ally camsfamiliaris*. We never tire of lauding the respectable qualities of the dog. We have all stories to tell of him, either derived from personal observation or from sources the truthfulness of which is beyond doubt. We acknowledge him to be brave as the lion, gentle as the lamb, patient as the camel, enduring in his affection, and of a fidelity that is staunch to Death's door. Books about dogs may be reckoned by the score. Poets have sung of the dog; painters have delighted to do him honour. Soon even as we in childhood have mastered the letters of the alphabet, and are promoted to one-syllable stories, we read that "The—dog—is —both—kind—and—brave; he—will—face—death—to—save —the—man—who— owns—and—feeds —him; gold—nor—rich —meats—will—buy—his—love,—he—gives—it—free— to— such—as—are—kind—to—him." A very ugly continuation of this easy lesson would be "So—when—he—grows—old,—or—too—sick—to— be —of—any—use—he— is—put —out—to— starve—or—be—beat—to—death—by—bad—boys. Once— on—a—time— there—were—good—men—who —would —aid —the—sick—dog—who—had—no—home—and—take—him —and—feed—and—cure—him,—but—some—made—fun—of —these—and —cried—them—down,—so— the—good —work —was—not—done."

But the good work is done—or, at least, commenced, and, as far as it has gone, to the entire satisfaction of all parties concerned. It is situated at Battersea.

Never in my life did such a Babel of sound greet my ears as when I came in sight of the troop of prisoners playfully disporting, or cozily coiled up for a doze, or soberly sauntering in pairs and threes in friendly confabulation. A mongrel with a goodish dash of terrier breed in his veins seemingly gave the alarm, and instantly there was a pattering of feet and a rush to the rails, and fifty voices—there must have been more than fifty, I think— were raised against me.

Nevertheless, it was good to observe the clamouring pack, and how clean and decent-looking they were. I had nearly written "how contented," but although this might apply to the majority, who joined with the others, and barked's for barking sake, and because it was the rule of the moment, very many there were—and these the first and most eager to rush to the bars—who barked with a purpose. These, no doubt, were the really bereaved dogs—the animals who somehow or another had Jpst sight of a well-beloved master in the street, and after searching miles and miles, and all round about to find him again, were discovered muddy and miserable, and with worn and bleeding feet, and conveyed unresisting to the home. But it is not a question of paunch and kennel with this kind of dog. Other dogs, contemptible curs, all teeth and belly, may endeavour to persuade these honest creatures that nothing can be more foolish than to thrust themselves forward to be owned out of such snug quarters, retired from the cares and anxieties of the world, and nothing to do but eat and sleep; but the really faithful tyke turns a deaf ear to all such pernicious counsel. He wants his master. He has pined for him night and day ever since he has been an inmate of the refuge, and whenever he hears the outer gate slam, his heart is in his mouth. If one had a clever ear for dog language, he might note the various emotions that disturb the poor brutes by the various tones in which he utters his "bow-wows." "Bow-wow-wow! I hear him, I verily believe! It isn't his footstep exactly, but perhaps he has come out in his slippers! Bow-wo-ow! Ah, no! it isn't him, nor anybody I ever recollect seeing with him. Bow-wo-o-ow! will he never come and fetch me out of this?"

Oddly enough, there are dogs within the enclosure that one would no more expect to find there than their missing masters. Two sheep dogs, to wit. The idea of a sheep dog being guilty of the weakness of losing itself! If there exists a more astonishing fact, it is that both animals had been at the home over a fortnight, and no application had been made for their recovery. I inquired of the keeper whether dogs ever came of their own accord, but he had no recollection of such an instance; otherwise a key to the mystery might have been sought in the speculation, had the two poor brutes, provoked beyond further endurance by the ruffianly behaviour of the drovers their masters, consented to run away together and stow here on the chance of finding a more comfortable home. To be sure, they sat apart and acted as entire strangers to each other; but if they were artful enough for the perpetration of the main trick, this small matter of dissembling is no more than might be expected.

Another dog of the incongruous pack was a great brown dog, curly and handsome, just such a creature as a man would trudge twenty miles to reclaim. Here he had resided for several months, as I was informed. Of dogs that are so continually losing themselves, and which must be held in high respect by petty printers on account of the large business in the handbill line they secure to them, there was no lack. Bandy-legged, long-bellied little dogs these, with a monstrous shock of hair overhanging their weak eyes. How on earth can a dog help "losing himself," when fashion suspends a thick fringe of tow before his optics? These are the sort of dogs, however, that are more profitable than any others to the institution, there being a demand for them; and their owners very willingly paying round little sums for their recovery; or if not, at the end of fourteen days they are at the disposal of the home authorities to dispose of to any customer, the bargain being subject to this important condition: that should the original owner afterwards claim the animal, its then possessor must part with it—the home authorities *not* guaranteeing the return of the purchase of deposit money, as I suppose it would be called.

The dog most commonly to be met with on the society's premises is the ordinary mongrel with a dash of better breed in him, enough, perhaps, to perch him higher on his legs than other mongrels, or give to his coat an inclination to curl, and turn his honest head from his proper jog-trot concerns, and set him hankering and wondering after improprieties of the vicious town. If there is one of these misguided dogs here there are twenty at least—intelligent, bright-eyed brutes, both little and big, and which I beg to recommend "to parties in want of a dog" to guard a house or a garden, being quite convinced by their sorrowful and penitent air that they sincerely regret the error of their ways, and if they are once again vouchsafed a trial they are steadfastly resolved to give satisfaction.

The dog that does *not* put in an appearance at the institution is the out-and-out gutter-bred street cur. The-keeper remarked this, and evidently saw something singular in the fact; so do not I. I know that dog, and can answer for him that he is the artfullest villain that walks on four legs. I will not go the length of expressing my belief that he may have made himself acquainted with that clause of the society's regulations in which it is so significantly intimated "that the public may rely that a dog once housed at the Home *will never again be set at liberty* with no better prospect than starvation before it," but I have not the slightest hesitation in declaring that the out-and-out street cur is least of all living dogs liable to starve while he keeps his shrewd head sound on his shoulders, and a stout set of legs to carry him swiftly out of danger, incurred through his dishonest practices. This is the dog that has his regular beat and attends it with ten times the diligence and punctuality of any policeman of the force. He has his coffee-shop, where working men go to breakfast early in the morning; he has his public-house tap-room, where working men dine, to investigate at noon; and come the dusk of evening, he finds leisurely and profitable employment in "snatching" from unguarded butchers' boards and laxly-watched tripe-shops. His worst time is of nights, since, being a marked character in the neighbourhood he haunts, lodgings he has none. Oh, he is an accomplished cadger! Are you out at midnight, hurrying home muffled from the cold, you hear a soft pattering of feet behind you, and looking, behold a poor dog—a forlorn, limp-tailed animal, with downcast eyes and wofully puckered mouth—who stands still as you gaze on him, and humbly awaits sentence. Sentence deferred. You go on again quicker than before, not caring to be bothered by dogs, and once again the pattering, and again you turn on him with "Hish! go home!" on your lips, but this time he raises his eyes, that you may read in them by the light of the street-lamp a beggar confessed; but ah! if you only knew under what extenuating circumstances!" Poor old boy P say you, and that night he reposes on your door-mat. Next morning he is off, and is only impatient to get away ere some treacherous friend has forestalled him in the coffee-shop round, and appropriated all the bacon rinds and crusts of bread.

Well, since he is independent of the aid the Dogs' Home affords, let him stay out of it and welcome. He can be very well spared as long as he can pick up a living for himself, but should he fall ill one day there is the hospital in question open to him, and he may rely on careful physicking and clean straw to lie on. This is the portion of all sick dogs taken to Battersea, while plentiful and wholesome food takes the place of physic in the case of lost healthy dogs. It is marvellous how a place providing accommodation for so many dogs can be kept so sweet and clean, and without doubt its condition reflects the highest credit on the keeper, who is a very civil person, cheerful and ready to give you any information concerning the home and its management. The most unsatisfactory item he furnished me with was that the money came in very slow indeed just now, and he hoped that matters might soon mend in this direction. So hope I.

THE COMFORTS OF HOME. HEN the wintry winds blow, when chilly rain descends, or choking fogs prevail—when the roads reek, and the pavements wear an overcoat of mud, then culminates an Englishman's love of "home." Through the summer months and the pleasant autumn time, when London highways are tolerable and the meadows skirting the city are green and sunny, his great aim and desire is to get away, his sweet dream by night and day is of that glorious moment when, with his luggage comfortably stowed on the cab-roof, and his hands washed clean of "business" that shall not sully them for a month to come—fancy! for full one-and-thirty lovely bright summerdays!— he skips into the vehicle, and bids the driver make haste to the station at London Bridge. But if in the December time of year, with the leisure and money to spare, a friend proposed to him a trip to Jersey, or even to Hastings or Brighton, he would beg to be excused. "The country and the sea-side are very well in their season; but a man cannot get on without *home,* and a goodly share of it too." "But what do you mean by 'home?' Does the term, as used by you, simply comprehend a cheery room, happy faces, cosy hearthrug, tea-and-toast, and that sort of thing?" "By no means, my good sir. I should hold myself but a selfish man if my ideas of home were clipped so narrow. Home surroundings and associations are not to be forgotten. Abroad, I may procure an apartment, as commodious as this, with coals that glow as cheerily, crumpets as well toasted and buttered, tea as invigorating, and the identical feet with whose tread I am familiar participating with mine own in the cosiness of the lodging-house hearthrug; but beyond that point the comparison fails. I need not go far to discover that I am not at ' home' in the true and happy acceptation of the term. I go no farther than my window. Where are the familiar faces, and sights, and sounds that tend to the perfection of that tranquillity and repose expressed in that magic little word of four letters? Until it comes to careful scrutiny one is altogether unaware of the seeming trifles that go to the production of the comfortable whole. So small a matter as the clink of a milk-can may have to do with it, and its harmony may be marred by the absence of the muffinbell. That bent-backed old fellow whom we now see looming in the evening twilight (and sober and punctual man that he is, he invariably *is* seen looming at this time), is not a picturesque object, and his shrill harsh voice as he shrieks 'Wa-ter kree-eses' is decidedly owlish; but, grown accustomed to it, the mind undisturbed and methodical has it in expectation, and would miss it and grow uneasy at its failing."

"Exactly *f* but since your liberal ideas of home embrace the muffin man, as well as his muffins; and the water-cress man, as well as his cresses, pray what of the latter or of the former? What of that muddy boy, with his straight red hair sprouting like early crocuses through his tattered cap, and who blithely carols "Hop light, Loo," as he trudges home with a stumpy birch-broom on his shoulder? You need not inform me that he is the boy who sweeps the crossing in the High Street, and that the labours of the day at an end, he invariably selects this as his homeward route. I already know all about it; but what of him? You are familiar with his appearance—he is a recognized object in your "home" picture; tell us something about him. There is the little lad with the evening paper ringing at your gate; surely he, with his ruddy face and his red comforter, and his manly little voice, which seems to bespeak the importance of the news he is the bearer of, is included within the limits of your home circle; what of him? Who is he? Splashing through the mud, and bawling "Pa—per" are not the prime objects of his life; what are?

You don't know. You make it a point to give the crossingboy a halfpenny when you avail yourself of his industry and happen to have coppers with you. Your evening paper is paid for, and if you knew your servant to stand higgling with the man of the green baize and bell over an odd muffin you would be extremely angry. Still, your sympathy with the muffin-man extends not beyond his wares and the tinkling of his bell. He is as complete a stranger to you as the old woman with the handkerchief over her head and clattering wooden shoes who came crying sweet cakes under your window when you were in France. You know more of the history of the hippopotamus than of the crossing-sweeping boy, for you have read about it, and you have paid a shilling for the privilege of seeing it flounder about in its grimy bath at the Zoological Gardens. Where does your evening paper come from?—where your morning paper? By what sort of enchantment is Ruddy-face enabled to come chirping with it at your gate before daylight these late mornings? You don't know; you don't inquire concerning these things. You take them as they come, and they all help to make "home," and you are quite contented and happy in that condition of life to which it has pleased God to call you.

Which in the main is right and proper enough, still you are not absolved of the charge of selfishness. In reality your house is your world, and your sympathies are bound by the four walls of it. The familiar faces and things visible from the loopholes of your castle may conduce to your enjoyment of home as the sight of falling snow or accumulated ice enhances the worth of a glowing gratefull of Wallsend coals; but as far as your real knowledge of the passers to and fro is concerned, you might as well look out on a desert.

And this is a pity, because with the lacking knowledge would come increased satisfaction, and a more thorough enjoyment of home and its comforts. Imperfectly, the knowledge in question is mine, though rather out of business pursuits than by Christian and virtuous seeking. I can tell you all about that old water-cress man. He is seventy-six next birthday, and has been a soldier. Rheumatism is a more malignant foe of the old fellow's than ever were the king's enemies against whom it has been his duty to strike steel or speed bullet. He has a wretched home, but he won't go to the workhouse: he will sooner die first. He told me so. I saw him one morning in November down at the water-cress beds near Hackney. It wanted fully three hours of daylight, and while I talked with him we stood on the frosty planks stretched over the bleak oozy "bed" where the cresses grew, and from which a man was gathering them by torchlight. I did not feel the cold, for I had already partaken of a good breakfast, and was well wrapped from the weather; but the old water-cress man, without so much as a neckerchief, and his shirt collar wanting a button, winced before the bleak wind that blew his white hair about and visibly increased the blueness of his poor old nose.

"You would be better in the workhouse," said I.

"Better in my grave, where I shall be afore long, God willing," answered the old soldier; "but no workhouse for me, thanky."

"Why don't you buy your cresses in the market?"

"Because it's cheaper to buy 'em first hand. You'd be astonished how much cheaper. Why, it makes as much difference as *threepence* or *fourpence* in a day's stock!"

Beside the old man, there were women and girls—a dozen of them, at least—all braving the field fog and the early darkness—coming, in some instances, three or four miles to brave it—to save threepence or fourpence in a day's stock I Think of this next time you buy water-cresses in winter time, my friend, and bid your servant not grumble over-much at the smallness of the bunches.

Muffins, again. For all the jolly jingle of his rhyming call and the merry tinkle of his bell, the business of the muffin-seller is of but shabby account. It is not as though he was his own master, as the saying is; if it were so, things would be better with him He is only a commission agent. If you meet him at Highgate his headquarters are as far off as Shoreditch. A tradesman lives there who does the most extensive muffin business in the kingdom. During the summer months he devotes his attention exclusively to ginger-beer; but come September (the seventh I believe it is, or the ninth—anyhow there is a fixed date for the opening of the season, like as for the Lord Mayor's show or the oyster season), he goes in with tremendous vigour for muffins. His bakehouse is an extensive place, and goodness knows how many sacks of flour he consumes weekly. It is his boast, I am told (based on information derived from his little boy, who is the cock of his school for arithmetic), that since he has set up he has made and sold muffins and crumpets enough to pave the whole world, mountains and all, two deep. He must be making vast sums of money this muffin-man, but his "lads" are anything but rich. They have to find their own white-sleeves, apron, and "blanket" (to keep the tender muffins warm), and bell; and the commission they are allowed is threepence in the shilling. When they have disposed of five shillings' worth their earnings amount to fifteen pence, and five shillings' worth of the article is a tolerable board-load. Usually it is about tea-time when the muffin-man's bell is heard, and—especially if it should happen to be in the suburbs, to reach which he has trudged four or five miles—it is not at all difficult to imagine what a delicious surprise it is for the poor fellow when, on a dark, nipping afternoon, some good-natured buyer says, "If you like to step inside for a minute I will give you a cup of hot tea." It is said that by so doing a singularly delicious flavour is imparted to the crummy discs when they are toasted. I can't answer for the truth of this, but it is an inexpensive experiment and certainly worth trying.

THE DETESTABLE BOOTS. (A TEMPERANCE STORY.) ND this is our museum," remarked the good-natured in-spector in charge, and, so saying, he selected a key from the bunch and unlocked a door that ranged with the celldoors, and looked like one of them. The interior disclosed showed the cupboard to be of considerable capacity. Affixed to the walls were shelves and books, on and about which were bestowed as miscellaneous a lot of goods as one can well imagine. "This is where we keep our waifs and strays," said Mr. Inspector; "we have a clear-out every three months, and judging from our stock, I should think the time can't be far off." Articles of wearing apparel chiefly were the waifs and strays in question. There were women's shawls and mantles, in many cases torn and ruined in the brawl that possibly cost the late proprietress her liberty, and with the mud baked hard and dry on them; there were bonnets and hats with falls and feathers attached, and parasols more or less sound and fashion able. There was an elaborately "worked" petticoat once white, which Mr. Inspector informed me one of his men had strangely enough discovered suspended across the rail of a street lamp-post. Of male attire, the collection was scarcely as large and various, and was, indeed, mainly confined to hats and coats, and travelling wraps and shawls. But beside these, there was an extensive assortment of baskets and carpet and leather bags and walking-sticks, and umbrellas, besides several just such bundles as a thief might drop in the heat of the chase, glad enough to escape on such easy terms. But what chiefly attracted my attention was a pair of great clumsy boots, such as a "navvy" wears, but utterly worn out, with heels aslant and with holes fretted in their upper parts, blue as bilberries with mildew, against which the russet rust of the battered nail heads showed to advantage.

"These articles look as though they had lain here considerably longer than three months," I remarked to Mr. Inspector.

"Ay, indeed, it must be nigher fifteen months than three since they were last thrown in here," he replied, taking up one of the ancient ankle-jacks by its mouldy tongue, and regarding it with evident interest.

"Why were they not turned out at the last clearing?"

Mr. Inspector smiled. "They are uncommon boots—privileged boots, sir," said he. "I much question if the price of the handsomest pair of Wellingtons that ever were made would buy these old jacks out of the hands of the man who sets such store by them."

"I should like to be informed in what respect they are valuable," I remarked.

"Take them in your hands, sir, and see if you can find out for yourself."

But I could make nothing of them except that they were worn out quite, fit only to be thrown on a dunghill.

"Then I will explain to you in what the essence of their value consists, sir," said Mr. Inspector. "They were once the property of a murderer."

"Of a murderer!"

"Of the man who was hanged at for the murder of his grandfather," continued Mr. Inspector, stooping to recover the boot that in my momentary horror I had dropped. "You recollect the case, sir, I dare say. About as cruel a murder as ever was' done, I think, that was. All through drink." "But why are they the more valuable for the reason you assign? The wax-work people in Baker Street might be excused for taking that view, but really"

"If you will come and sit by the fire I'll tell you how they came to be accounted worth preserving," Mr. Inspector obligingly remarked.

"As perhaps you may recollect," he began, "the poor wretch I allude to was apprehended hereabouts, though the murder was done far down in the country; and the way in which he came to leave his boots here was simply this. From the time of his committing the crime till he made his way to London he got no rest, but tramped on and on, day and night, more miles than I should like to say, speaking from memory. He tramped until his feet were blistered and swollen, and when he came into the office—into this office—one night between eleven and twelve, saying to me, 'Is this a place where a murderer may give himself up for punishment?' he was barefoot, and carried his boots—these boots—slung by their thongs at the end of the stick with his little bundle.

"But it isn't about *him* that I have anything to tell. All I need say is that his feet being too bad to admit of his being able to get his heavy old boots on them, an easier pair were found for him, and I believe he was hanged in them. Anyhow, his old ones were left here, and thrown into that cupboard.

"Well, there they lay for over two months. And now I must tell you that two years ago the most troublesome customer this not over-polished or genteel neighbourhood furnished us was a drunken farrier—a middle-aged man, a big, broad-chested fellow, who could drink a pailful of beer, as the saying is. When he chose to work, there was no one of his craft more clever and dexterous, so that any time in three days he could earn as much as a plodding man could earn in a week. The consequence was that he never worked more than these three days, and gave up the rest of his time to drinking and bragging of his ability.

"You would never have guessed that he earned good wages, judging from his appearance. Nothing but rags covered him, and he had never a pair of decent shoes to his feet, so that when he went to work his master was obliged to place him at the back of the shop for shame's sake. Saturday was his grand day, and almost certain as the night came he would be brought here to lodge, drunk and incapable for anything but holloaing and swearing. His wife, Sunday after Sunday—a decent little woman enough—used to bring him a bit of dinner, and we used to let them sit together while he ate it in his cell, thinking that it might make him feel his degradation, and tend to his mending.

"But it was all of no use; there seemed no more chance of mending him than there is of making a rotten apple sound. He grew worse and worse. One Monday morning, in the depth of winter, just as they were turning him out (we never took him before the magistrates, if we could avoid it), I noticed that he was without the tattered old shoes he generally wore; so I bethought me of the old ankle-jacks lying idle in the cupboard, and, calling him, got them out.

"' See if you can squeeze your feet into these,' I said. 'If you don't sell them for gin, they may carry you along for a month or so.'

"'No fear; cuss the gin!' he replied, as he squatted down on that stool there to pull the boots on.

"' I tell you what it is, Bill Herd,' I says to him; 'if you don't alter your course these boots will last quite long enough to carry you to a madhouse; or, worse still, perhaps, to the place where they left their last owner.'

"'And where might that be?' he asked. He had got one boot on, and the other was in his hand.

"' At the gallows. They are Thomas Patten's old boots. You know the man I mean?'

"My dear sir, it was a sight to see him then, I assure you. He started up with a yell, and held out the foot with the boot on it as though something within it was stinging him and causing him frightful pain, while his staring eyes were bloodshot, and his limbs trembled as though shaken by palsy. Then he commenced tearing at the laces without saying a word, and got the boot off, and standing with his naked feet on the cold stones, he seemed changed from a drunken brute to a sober man.

"' I'd rather walk my bones bare than wear 'em,' said he; 'I'm bad enough, the Lord knows—no better than a brute beast; but I ain't glad as yet to wear a murderer's boots. Thanky for the lesson, however. My feet shall have a scrubbing to-day if they never did before.'

"Well, the story served to amuse us awhile, and the boots were flung back into the cupboard again. We made no doubt that the 'lesson' he had received would wash out with the first quart of beer he drank, and that as usual we should have to provide him lodgings on Saturday night. When we found that he did not trouble us, we set it down in our minds that he was ill—that lie had drank himself down to a bed of sickness at last. Two, three weeks passed, and then one day, when I was sitting here all alone, Bill Herd made his appearance. For the moment I did not observe that he was unaccompanied.

"' Here again, then?' said I, reaching up for the charge book; and then I noticed that he was not only alone, but that he was perfectly sober, and much better dressed than I had hitherto seen him.

"' What do you want? Who brought you here?' I asked him.

"'Nobody, master,' he replied. 'I haven't been drunk— haven't touched so much as a pint of beer or a glass of gin since you last saw me. It is because I fear that I am just on the brink of breaking out again that I have ventured here to ask of you a favour.'

"'What is it?'

"' I want you to give me or sell me the boots that belonged to—to—never mind who—*you* know, sir.'

"' What! Pattens' boots! Surely you don't mean those?'

"' No others, sir. It isn't because I haven't got a pair (and as he spoke he held up one of a very good pair), but because I feel like fading out of my fright, and want another dose to hold me quiet.'

"'You may have them, and welcome, Bill,' said I, and I couldn't forbear laughing at the recollection; 'you stripped 'em off pretty quick the last time you had them on; however, you shall have them if you fancy them.'

"' There you're wrong, sir,' he replied, with an earnestness that was startling. 'It is no fancy. It is because I hate 'em, that I want 'em, and, what is more, I want 'em to wear. Nothing weaker than them is strong enough to hold me back from the drink. Good resolutions won't do it—all that my wife can beg and pray is not equal to it. I've kept off it for three weeks now, but you don't know what I've suffered. It is worse than hungering for bread is thirsting for gin when once you let it get tight hold on you. It haunts you. Itpeeps out at you in brimming measures and in tempting wide-mouthed glasses from the dark corners of the workshop. I sweat of it the harder I work, and its trickling down my face drives me mad almost. I go to bed o' nights only to dream of it. For the Lord's sake let me have the boots. I shall never be able to make a strong stand against the temptation until I have 'em on.'"

"Of course, you had no hesitation in giving him what he desired after such an appeal?" I remarked.

"Of course; I got them out for him at once. 'There you are, my lad,' said I; 'if they only do you half as much good as you imagine, they would be cheap at a hundred pounds.'

"So he took them, thanking me heartily, and away he went. No one knew of the farrier's strange fancy but myself, and I resolved to say nothing about it. 'If I'm not mistaken,' I thought to myself, 'the whole town will hear of it soon enough for after he was gone it occurred to me, and caused me no little uneasinesss, that unhinged as the man's mind evidently was, this wearing of the murderer' boots would provide the finishing stroke, and presently we should hear of drunken Bill Herd as an inmate of a lunatic asylum.

"But I am glad to tell you that I was mistaken—altogether mistaken. His hunger for drink was so violent, and his dread of its effects so torturing,?that the remedyhe chose against it proved not a bit too strong. Feeling uneasy, I kept my eye on him and saw that he stuck to his purpose manfully. I met him as though by accident the very next day as he was returning from work, and he touched his cap cheerfully, at the same time glancing down at his feet, which were encased in *the* boots. I saw him many a day after that, through six months, till one Monday morning, a healthy-looking and respectable man, he made his appearance here with a parcel in his hand..

"' I thought that I should find you alone, sir,' said he. 'I hoped so. I've brought back the boots. I can do without 'em at last, I do hope and believe.' And then he went on to tell me of the struggles he had endured, and in which, aided by the doughty boots, he had contrived to come off victorious. 'Once,' said he, 'that was three weeks after you were so kind as to let me have 'em— I had worn them every day, and felt so strong in my mind that I thought I would give my feet a holiday, so I brushed my other boots and put them on and went off to work. But somehow I couldn't settle down to the tools. As I stooped to the shoeing the boots that I had so nearly slipped in seemed to mock me and to say, "You'll be at it again before nightfall." And so I believe that I should, had I not, as it were, taken the devil that was tempting me neck and crop and bundled him out. I didn't hesitate a minute, but putting my tools aside, I ran home every step and got into my ugly make-sure boots again. But that's a long time ago, and I think that I'm all right now.'

"' Don't make too sure, Bill,' said I.

"' I don't mean to, sir, else I should have burnt my makesures or thrown 'em away; as it is, I bring 'em back for you to mind for me, if you will be so kind. At the same time hoping and praying that I may never want 'em.'

"And I don't suppose that he ever will," remarked Mr. Inspector, in conclusion, "for it's over a year ago since he pulled them off, and now he is a rising man, with a farriery of his own."

GOING HOPPING. ROM the coal-heaver, who with the back of his dirty --hand brushes the grime from his lips ere they are allowed to salute the chaste rim of the shining pewter measure that contains his "heavy wet"—(and no one ever yet saw a coal-heaver engage at his pot without this preliminary) —to the wing-whiskered swell who imbibes Bass's or Allsopp's beer—calling it "bittah beeah," we are nine-tenths of us interested in the subject of hops. As is popularly supposed, hops and malt enter equally into the concoction of the national beverage; but the welfare of the latter ingredient is not nearly so much an object of anxiety and solicitude as is the former. This comes of undeviating faithfulness. Our barley we are sure of. The crop may be light, lightish, or heavy, and the price may vary a few shillings in the price of a "quarter" of it, but that is a matter to be settled between farming folks and brewers. It does not, or it seems not to, affect the public at large. Dear wheat means dear bread. If Mark Lane puts the screw on to-day, by to-morrow evening every baker in London is charging an extra penny per quartern for his loaves; but there are no such fluctuations in the retail price of beer. The working man gets his quart of it for fourpence, sixpenny ale is never sixpence-half-penny, and the price of "bittah" is as fixed as the corks that secure the creamy nectar. So long as barley is true to us we are sure of malt and of beer in abundance; its quality is another matter, and for this" the fickle hop, and not the patient barley, is held responsible.

Never sprang there from the brown bosom of Mother Earth a plant so "inconstant, insincere." It is a wonder of wonders that hop-growers live to be such jolly, ruddy, prosperous old gentlemen as we discover them. Their trials and afflictions are enormous and increasing. From the moment when the unfortunate little emblem of bitterness thrusts its weak head into the world, its miseries and the tribulations of its grower begin, and the grower, unselfish in his grief, allows the public to share it with him. Surely as the autumn comes may be read in the newspapers frequent bulletins of the health and growth of the bantling, and invariably are they hopeless, and melancholy, and dejected. Painful indeed must be the existence of the growing hop! Before it is a month old there is a horrible whisper of "mildew" abroad, and should it be nipped in its infancy it would surprise nobody. Then we are startled by an alarm that the little hop is drowning—that the long-continued rains have drenched and overwhelmed it, and that it is as good as gone—nothing can save it but a long, long continuance of hot, sunshiny weather. Then comes the sunshiny weather, but, alas! as it never rains but it pours, so the sun never warms but it scorches; and here is the hop, the suffering hop, that is but weakly, having outgrown its strength during the rainy season, having its innocent head baked on its shoulders, and that while it is a mere husk, and empty as an egg-shell. Now it is mysteriously blighted, and in a manner that the oldest grower in Kent never before saw the like of, and cannot make out at all. Now. gloomy rumours cf smut prevail; and barely is *Hvmuhts Capulus* so far recovered as to appear with a clean and cheerful face after the last-mentioned unpleasant visitation, than is issued a startling statement of a plague of flies! Flies have seized on the persecuted plant, they are eating its head out, and nothing, as we are informed, can preserve our darling—our tall, graceful, young queen of beer, from a premature and horrible death.

Then ensues the very natural consequence—the unfortunate hop-growers are ruined, or very nearly, and to enable them to exist at all the hard-hearted and exacting Government must remit part of the hop duty—or, at least, extend the time allowed for paying it. Deputations of growers wait on the Chancellor of the Exchequer to this end as regularly as the postman waits on his customers for a Christmas-box, and until the faces of the poor petitioners must have become quite familiar to him. Several of these unhappy tillers of the soil he must remember when he was last in office, and as he listens to their tale of long-suffering and distress, he must feel increased pride in his countrymen when he sees them bearing their burdens on such broad backs and with jolly countenances.

Whether it arises from its inability to read newspapers, or from any other cause, is not ascertained; but it is certain that there is, at least, one class of persons whose confidence in a tolerably good crop of hops is undeviating. Where the individuals comprising this class spring from it is hard even to guess, but all through the latter part of the month of September, and even for a week or so in October, they may be seen on a Monday morning at London Bridge Railway Station waiting for the train specially set apart for their cheap conveyance to the distant hop-gardens.

Not knowing their purpose, the early traveller on the line in question must be considerably astonished at the strange spectacle. It is as though the vilest stews of the metropolis had been skimmed, and that here was the skimming. At a glance it is evident that the stews in question must have been Irish stews. To say nothing of the characteristic type of rags, especially of hats and bonnets, and the unmistakable physiognomy and brogue, no company of tatterdemalions but an Irish company would have exhibited such an amount of good humour at six o'clock of a damp and chilly October morning, breakfastless, and with no better sitting or standing for their naked feet than the cold paving-stones. Not that the majority of them were without shoes, but it is not the economy of the Irish tramp to wear his shoes under such circumstances. The saving of shoe leather entered into his calculations when he resolved to ride to Maidstone; and since shoes are only good for walking in, why should his feet be cumbered with them when for many a mile he has no walking before him? So he carries them slung across his shoulder, along with a few items of bedding, and perhaps a second "slop " and pair of breeches, done into'a sizable bundle, and tied in an old patchwork counterpane; while his wife—if he is a family man—is laden with, in addition to the baby, a stock of cheap London grocery and bacon; the biggest boy carrying the cooking kettle, the barelyclosed lid of which reveals the shoes and boots of the small fry, securely packed within, and only to be worn when stern necessity requires.

The fare charged to Maidstone for these hop-pickers is the very reasonable one of two shillings; "children under twelve half-price "—a piece of liberality which seemed to cause considerable trouble and vexation to the unlucky official ruling at the turnstile that led to the departure platform. It was this individual's duty to examine the tickets the pickers had received in exchange for their money, and certainly the barefaced attempts to pass off marriageable young men and women as "under twelve" was enough to provoke a man whose duty is inexorably regulated by railway time. "D'ye mean to tell me that she isn't more than twelve?" exclaimed the bewildered ticket examiner of the mother of a strapping wench of seventeen at least, and who, with an air of charming, childlike simplicity, held out a half ticket for the officer's inspection— "Why, she's big and strong enough to carry a sack of coals." "Big, collicther, dear, but not shthrong," explained the littlegirl's mother, coaxingly—" she's outgrowed her strinth, poor soul, and a feather ind 'ud knock her down." "Then what is she going down for if she is too weak to work?" The 'cute collector thought he had the old lady there, but she had done battle in the same suit before to-day. "Shure, collicther, dear, you are no family man, or ye wouldn't ax the quistion; did yer niver hear that the bitter ov the hop was strinthenin' to invilades? But it isn't the dirthy shillin' that shall baulk the baby," continued the old lady, perceiving that the officer was not to be convinced—" I'd rather be the t'other half iv her out of pocket;" and with a knowing wink at the "baby," away she went to buy the other half ticket.

And so, after countless skirmishes of a like character, the whole number pass on their way to the train; and I see no more of them—(I can hear them plainly enough, though the carriage I occupy is a long distance from them—I can hear them chanting ditties, both comic and sentimental, and laughing and "chaffing," as though bound on a holiday instead of to a bout of hard drudgery)—until Maidstone is reached, and they troop out at the station gate and take the road like folks who are not at a loss for the right way to go. This way undoubtedly was the way towards the hop fields, so I, too, took the road, expecting merry, if not select, company all the way along.

But in this I was mistaken. I speedily discovered that it Was only when herding together, with nobody to look and nothing to be made by dissimulation, that they indulged in a natural flow of spirits. Soon as they were on the highway they broke up into gangs of three or four—some loitering, while others went ahead, so as to divide the chances of the road fairly amongst them; and became halting, whining beggars, imploring of every passer-by the "laste thrifle in the wurrld, yer honner, for the blessed God's sake," to save them from "dhroppin' down," they having tramped it all the way from London. And really they were enabled to put on an appearance so fagged and wobegone—an air so eloquent of dustiness and footsoreness, that I have little doubt that in a walk of a mile or so they were able to cadge at least half their passage money.

Did the reader ever see a hop garden? It is a curiously pretty sight. I never saw a vineyard, but should imagine that a hop garden was its exact counterpart. A great level plain that at a distance looks completely and thickly covered by slender flowing pillars, all green and gold, but which on closer inspection prove to be a succession of fruitful walls, with a path about six feet in width between each. These are the hops on the straight ranks of poles, each one planted in a little mound about a foot round and a foot high. In each mound three roots are planted, and under favourable circumstances flourish and make such a grand display of foliage, and twine and bind one pole's covering with that of its next neighbour, that it is like a weaving of leaves and fruit through the entire length of the row, and, with the sun shining through the interstices, throws odd-shaped, quivering patches of light across the shadowy path, making a picture not easily forgotten.

There are many different kinds of hops, differing much in price. There are "Goldings" (the best), and "white bines," and "grapes," and "Joneses," and "Colgates," the last-named the most prolific, but accounted the rankest. The picking is "piece work." Part of,the hop-grower's stock-in-trade consists in a vast number of enormous wicker baskets, and these you see in the rows where the pickers are" at work. They work in gangs, and to each gang is attached a "pole-puller," whose business it is to cut the plants close off at the roots, and then, pulling up the pole, convey the lot bodily ta the "bin" or basket, where the pickers are at work. The price paid depends on the leanness or fatness of the crop. At a plentiful harvest "nine a shilling" is the prevailing tariff—that is, nine bushels a shilling; but in bad, "thin " seasons work at such a price would be little better than starvation for the poor picker, and as much as sixpence a bushel has, as I was informed, been paid. Some growers allow perquisites in the shape of prematurely ripe and weakly flowers, which are known as "blowers," and are used in the brewing of small beer. Several times in the course of the day the "measurers" come round with their great bags and bushels, and the produce of the picking deposited in the "bin," round which the gang squat, is "told." This is a part of the proceedings watched jealously by the pickers. It seems that there are two sorts of measurers, known respectively as "duff" handed and "feather" handed, and the picker very much prefers the latter. The "duff" (heavy) handed measurer is generally a "master's man,"—that is to say, he studies his master's interests, even to the extent of cheating the ragged labourers; and in teeming the flowers from the bin to the bushel, will dexterously lay so heavy a hand on them that they are crushed down and flattened; whereas a "feather" handed measurer will pile them in fairly and lightly, topping off with a flat strike, heaped-up measures being against the laws that regulate hop-picking. Very few single men or women, or even married couples without children, are to be met amongst the pickers. It is the family man that makes good harvesting. Any baby of three years old is clever enough to strip the flowers from a hop bunch, and there you may see them, too little to reach the "bin," squatting round a big open cotton umbrella, playing at pork, and making fine fun of it, and all the while they are putting a penny in mamma's pocket. An industrious family of seven or eight in a fair season will earn as much as eight or nine shillings a day.

Out of this, all they have to provide is food. Firing for cooking purposes is yielded by the neighbouring woods and hedges, and the labourers are lodged at the cost of the growers, And this is the worst part of the whole business. The place they are housed in is generally a barn or shed, used in the winter for sheltering fattening bullocks. Sometimes the floor is boarded, sometimes bricked. Beds there are none, nor even straw, except of the lodger's own lucky finding. If the pickers do not bring a blanket with them, they lie bare, except for the rags on their backs; and there they herd, little children, grown boys and girls, married and single, higgledy-piggledy, without even a lantern light, till morning and the stick of the "foreman picker" hammering at the barn door rouses them.

A ROUND OF THE PARISH "STONE-YARDS."

TOES the reader know what a parish "stone-yard" is? It is the scene of the "labour test" sanctioned by Act of Parliament. The sorely distressed mechanic or labourer, unable to obtain work, and with too much manliness as yet remaining in him to beg, having sold and pawned every available article of wearing apparel and household furniture, and borrowed of friends and relatives to the extremity of their means or their patience, as a last resort applies to the workhouse authorities. Not as a pauper. He is told that if he is willing to work he may even yet obtain food for his family, and avoid the shame of pauperism. He is willing to work. Show him the job that he will not undertake, provided it is possible for him to accomplish it. Nothing is more easy of accomplishment he is assured; a born fool would find it not at all difficult to do the work suggested in a satisfactory manner; it is merely to take a hammer in hand, and with it to convert big stones into little stones, or to shred into fine threads short lengths of old tarred rope. "What are the wages?" the eager applicant inquires But there is no fixed rule; in some parishes the stone-breaker receives so much a day, in others "as much as he is able to earn." These last terms best suit the desperate out o' work. To be sure, he has heard and read of the idle riff-raff of the casual ward rebelling against the severity of the task of stonebreaking, imposed on them as an equivalent for their bread and lodging, but that is nothing to the purpose. He is a man of different mettle. Hard work won't daunt *him,* since it is piecework!—and he spits on his palm, itching to grasp the bread-winning hammer. Knowing something of this beforehand, I selected the "stone-yard" as a place before all others where "the truly destitute and unfortunate" might be discovered; not without the hope that while I fulfilled the charitable mission entrusted to me, I might be able to pick up sundry scraps of information useful to my friend the reader. How far I have been successful in this last-mentioned respect what here follows will show. 1 selected the stone-yard of St. Mary's, Islington, as being the first in my route from home. I applied at the workhouse where the "board" was sitting, and the chairman of that august body granted the favour asked with a magnanimity that impressed me favourably. He courteously directed the master to instruct a decent old fellow, who sat in the hall attired in a suit of corduroy, to show me the way.

St. Mary's stone-yard is about a quarter of a mile from the workhouse, and nestles amongst the cattle lairs in the Liverpool Road. On the road my civil guide informed me that the destitution in the parish had been " something awful," so much so that a few days since a hundred and forty men of the district had sought work at stone-breaking. Matters, however, had mended a little since the frost broke, and he did not think that more than a hundred men were employed in the yard at present. He escorted me to the office of the labour superintendent, which was in the stone-yard. "You had better have a pair of shades before you go round, sir," said the superintendent, "you may chance to get your eye cut out else;" but as he spoke there entered in at the door a tall, thin gentleman, of pale complexion, who had "been the round," I suppose, and was then wearing the shades—two monstrous protuberances of woven wire covering his eyes and the greater part of his nose, and secured by strings of broad black tape tied over his ears, and rendering him such a frightful object to behold that I hesitated to avail myself of the superintendent's obliging offer. "Do all the men at work wear the shades?" I inquired. "Oh! no; very few of them. " "Then, I think I will take my chance," said I, much relieved.

The "yard" is an open space, containing several huge mounds of granite broken small enough for road-making purposes, and dotted here and there were sheds in which the men worked. They were not enclosed sheds—merely slanted roofs perched on upright beams, and quite open to the snow and rain, the prevalence of which is one of the main reasons why men seek employment there. The majority of the men were busy under these shelters, but a dozen or so were out in the open air engaged at the arduous task of reducing, by means of sledge-hammers, great lumps of granite to sizable pieces for the breakers with the little hammers.

I should judge that my informant was rather above than under the mark when he guessed the number of men at work to-day as numbering a hundred. Possibly there were eighty, and a glance was sufficient to convince the observer of the kind of men they are. Every craft has its livery. The stonemason, by the white dust that still lurks in the crevices of his dirty trousers and jacket; the sawyer, by the handkerchief about his waist to support his unmentionables in lieu of braces, and by the curious bagginess of the fore part of the lastmentioned article of raiment (he "pads" when at work, to save himself from injury by an accidental slip of the big saw);and the worker in iron, by his blue shirt and the greasy blackness of the sides of his fustian trousers and by his "rule pocket." There were men of these trades present, besides bricklayers and plasterers, and such other trades as effect the cap and jacket, while not a few, even in their present strait, stuck to the tall hat and the black coat—out at elbows, and frayed, and darned, and threadbare, but still a black coat, and a badge distinguishing them from the horny-handed out-of-door operalive—and which, together with the tall hat, made the wearers look preposterously out of place, squatting on the ground smashing stones. Under other conditions, I believe that the rough-reasoning men in caps and jackets would have resented this affectation of gentility in men seeking work with them; but, poor fellows, there did not appear to be in them any spirit for anything beyond brooding silently over their heaps and banging away at a particular stone, as though viciously actuated against it, and with their hats and caps pulled far down over their eyes to protect them from flying fragments. I began to wish that I had accepted the wire shades. Before I had been in the yard five minutes I received a stinging blow from a spiteful chip that caused my eye to smart throughout the remainder of the day, and, besides this, I saw one man with a lump on his forehead as big as a pigeon's egg and another with a gash extending right across his ear and trickling freely.

I entered into conversation with several of the stone-breakers, and made myself acquainted with the system here adopted by the parochial authorities of St. Mary's, Islington. I found that the rate of pay for "willing workers" was three-halfpence per bushel for the stones broken, until a shilling was so earned, and a *penny* a bushel afterwards, and, in addition, one loaf a week for every child the man may have. "I 'spose they think that the stones get softer after eight bushel have been broke," an out-of-work engine stoker remarked ruefully. I learnt, however, that it was not until a man had had some experience—a month, at least—that he could break as much as eight bushels a day. "Some of them," said the stoker, who was an intelligent young fellow, out of work since March last, and having a wife and six children—" some of them, when they first try it, can't break two bushel a day. They get a stone, and they nibble and nibble at it with the hammer, knocking it as round as an apple, and doing no good at all. Many and many of them leave of at the end of the day with fourpence-halfpenny to take. A goodish many come and have a try at it, and lose heart before they've broke a hatful. That's one of 'em, I reckon; I haven't seen him since about eleven o'clock." As he spoke he pointed to a tiny heap of broken stones, about a peck, perhaps, with a block of wood used as a seat, and a hammer idly lying. On the centre of the small heap was a jagged stone, the size of a Bath brick, all dented and spotted, showing where it had been ineffectually hammered. While we were yet speaking, the stoker remarked, "Oh, here he comes back again /' and, turning about, I saw a young man of the tall hat and black coat order, pale looking and wofully dejected, and with his right hand bound round with a bit of rag. "What cheer, mate? you're come back _to it, then?" said the stoker. "No, I haven't," replied the young man; "I can't go on with it. I've got a great blister on my hand through trying, and it's broke. Can't you give me something for what I've done, and put it with your heap?" "Not I." "Can't you give me a halfpenny? it's worth that. Come!" "It's against the laws, old boy," returned the stoker, going on with his work, while the disconsolate one walked slowly away. He was a grocer's assistant, he told me, and had a wife and two children. He was unable to get a job because of his shabby clothes, and was still weak through lying several weeks at St. Mark's Hospital. The good lady whose almoner I was would like to have seen the expression of his white face as he received one of her half-crowns.

Amongst the stone-breakers I found very few grumblers— concerning the rate of pay, that is to say. What they chiefly complained of was the bitter cold—for, work never so hard, it is difficult to keep the blood in brisk circulation squatting in an open shed, with a nor'-east wind blowing, and the fact that they were not allowed to work after about half-past two o'clock in the day. The stoker had been at the work for about three weeks, and by this time was able to earn about tenpence in the day. When he first tried it he earned three and fourpence halfpenny in a week. He thought that ninepence a day was more than was earned on an average—not reckoning the bread, of course. I asked him why he did not, after a lapse of three weeks, have another look round after a proper job of work. "Well, so I will, is what I say every night when I get home," said he; "and so say many working chaps that have come here, but you see, sir, the missus has got used to the few regular halfpence at night and the loaf, though it's only a half a one, in a manner of speaking, may be depended on, and I'm loath to throw it away on the small chance of getting a job at stoking. That's the case with dozens of fellows working here."

From St. Mary's I went to St. Luke's Workhouse, in the City Road, and to the stone-yard, which is in the rear of the main building. I had thought that nothing could be much worse than the condition of the industrious poor fellows at the Islington yard, but I was sorely mistaken. I found that, although a stone-yard, the labour of breaking granite for roadmaking had been for some time suspended at this establishment, oakum-picking taking its place. I have no doubt that St. Luke's is a poorer parish than St. Mary's, including as it does Whitecross Street, and Golden

Lane, and the squalid neighbourhood surrounding the parish church. If I had any doubts on the matter they were set at rest the moment I entered at the heavy wooden gate of the labour-yard.

Extending along a wall, to a length of a hundred and fifty Improvements have been made at the establishment in question since this article was written.
feet I should judge, was a long shed, fairly open on its outer side, and no loftier than the height of a tall man. Employed beneath this open shed, huddling and crowding together, were about a hundred individuals picking oakum. In the midst of some of the groups there was a bit of a coke fire in an old saucepan, or some similar vessel, at which it seemed the oakum pickers took it in turns to warm their benumbed fingers. Even in a casual ward I think I never saw such a crew of hopelessly poverty-stricken ones. Their clothes were, as a rule, tattered and dirty, their faces bristling with neglected beard, while their unstockinged feet peeped out of their broken and worn-out boots. There was a mildewy look about the wretched company such as I never before witnessed, a mildewy look about their faces as well as their clothes, and an effluvia sickening to think of, as though the forlorn hundred had that morning crawled out of a damp cellar in which they had long been incarcerated. Every one of the hundred had his bunch of oakum, over which he employed his dull fingers, melancholy as men working for their death rather than their living.

There had been no stone-breaking, they told me, since a month before Christmas, and when I inquired did they not find it easier to sit down by the fire and pick oakum, the universally expressed opinion was that they did not, "because it gave one the horrors sitting still a-thinking." As to the fires, they, I was informed, were their own, several men contributing halfpence, and bringing in the coke in their pockets. "It seems to me that if you were to move your fingers a little quicker you would be all the warmer," I ventured to remark. "What's the good of doing that, sir, and sitting still half the day?" was the reply; and this was the explanation given. The guardians of St. Luke's Workhouse have a fixed rate of pay for everybody expressing himself able and willing to work. This rate is *sixpence a day* for men and *threepence* for lads, with the same weekly allowance of bread as at St. Mary's. As for the work they perform—that is a minor consideration. It would be possible for the hands to pick five pounds of oakum daily, but so long as a couple of pounds are picked properly, and that without fuss and bother, nobody grumbles. This at first sight might pass as kindness, but that it arises from sheer dilatoriness and a shirking of trouble is sufficiently shown in the fact that a worker is expected to be the whole day—from nine o'clock till dark—over his little job; and even though he executed it by dinner-time, as often he might, he would be compelled to stay with the rest or forfeit his pay. The willing men, and I found very many here, as at St. Mary's, complain loudly of this. They say if sixpence is the worth of picking two pounds of oakum, why not pay them when the work is done, and let them out on the chance of finding a job, or give them four pounds to pick and a shilling for picking it?

Amongst the poor fellows here I discovered many decent mechanics accustomed to earn five and six shillings a day when there was work to be got, and not a few costermongers and hawkers who had lost their "stock money" through sickness and otherwise, and who might be started as free and independent men again at a cost of ten or twelve shillings. There was one unfortunate man, an engineer, who had lost an eye through an accident, and could hardly see out of the other eye. He served his last master fourteen years, and up to the time of his accident. He has six children, and for some time has vainly solicited the guardians to grant him about thirty shillings, so that he may buy a few tools and go to rough ironworking, such as butchers' hooks, &c., which he might be able to sell about the streets. There is another man (well spoken of by the superintendent), with three children and a wife, long an outpatient at the Cancer Hospital, who feels sure that he could get a job if he had something more respectable to wear than the poor rags that now envelop him. But, for that matter, I have a list recording at least twenty such cases from this one "stone-yard " alone.

The labour-yard pertaining to the great parish of Marylebone is situate in the vicinity of the Harrow Road, and is a most extensive establishment. I am happy to make known that it possesses features that contrast favourably with many other stone-yards of the metropolis it has been my business to inspect.

The boundaries of the Marylebone yard embrace three-anda-half acres of land, and three sides of it are fitted with conveniences for stone-breaking and oakum-picking. At St. Mary's, Islington, and elsewhere, as I have already noticed, the stonebreakers work for the most part in confused groups in an open shed, every man squatting down where he pleases, and without in the least consulting the convenience or comfort of his neighbour; whereas at Marylebone each labourer has a compartment to himself, like a "stall" of a stable, in which he may perform his task, "keeping himself to himself;" which must be an advantage of no little importance in the case of poor fellows who resort to the parish yard only after every stone in the outer world has been turned to no purpose. This may seem a fastidious view of the matter. Hardheaded, matter-of-fact people may urge that a man should throw overboard everything in the shape of squeamishness when he is compelled to bring his labour to the stone-yard, as being the best market presenting; that he should abolish from his thoughts all sentimental regrets, and regard himself for the nonce merely as a machine useful to smash stones. With all respect, I beg to differ from matter-of-fact people who propound such opinions. I have a tender feeling even for those infatuated individuals who so tenaciously assert their right to wear, even in a stone-yard, those badges of respectability, the tall hat and the black coat, although the said articles of raiment mock the baseless pretension, and laugh it to scorn, out of a hundred rents and tears. There is hope for him just as long as he thinks there is. Let him retain every grain of that repugnance to stone-breaking that possessed him when first the grim suggestion presented itself to his desperate mind and would take no denial. His squeamishness and sentimental regrets are the salt that keeps his manhood sweet, and they are as such to be respected and encouraged as much as possible. The adversity that merely causes a man to bend his neck does him no great harm; his conviction that it is only a temporary embarrassment will, more than anything, tend presently to his relief from his load; and to-morrow or the day after you may meet him with his head erect as the best; but contrive to instil into his mind that he is altogether past better things, and that nothing remains for him but to face his miserably-altered circumstances, and accommodate himself to them, and for evermore he will have no more power to raise his head than a dead man.

It may appear but a very insignificant help towards enabling a man to preserve his self-respect, this system of providing him work'by himself in a stoneyard, but I feel sure that if the matter were discussed with the unlucky workers themselves, their opinion on it would be very decided. You see, in the eyes of a man who hopes to get back into the world again in a little while, who really and sincerely believes that he shall so get back and be "all right" once more, there is all the difference between doing a job at stone-breaking in a quiet sort of way and making one of a recognized stone-breaking gang.

In the Marylebone labour-yard there is every convenience for the kind of work transacted there. The tools are good, material easy to get at, officers kindly disposed and obliging; but the occupation itself is as objectionable as ever. It seems impossible to elevate this monstrous "labour-test" an inch above the false and treacherous ground on which it is based, however perfect the machinery used for the purpose. Here, as elsewhere, is revealed the wearying spectacle of the sturdy villain—the parish rover and vagabond by profession—earning with ease enough at least to buy him bread to eat, and beer to drink, and tobacco to smoke, while the hundred times more deserving, but weak-bodied and soft-handed out-o'-work tailor, or baker, or clerk is sweating under the rags of his old respectability, and straining his unused muscles that he may carry home a dry loaf to his children.

"And what do you pay?" I inquired of the civil foreman.

"We pay them at the rate of five farthings a bushel, and they are allowed to earn as much as fifteenpence if they are able."

"Do many of them earn so much?"

"The old hands, those who have had years of experience, do it easily. The new hands make a sad mess of it at times; sometimes they will thump away here all day long and earn threepence or fourpence, *sometimes no more than three-half-pence."* "Do you give them bread as well? A loaf a week for each child is the rule, I believe?" "They get no bread here." "Do you see the same faces day after day?" "In many cases, yes, they are the old and knowing hands, who not unfrequently earn their fifteenpence by dinner-time. A great many of the men new to the work get an order from the house and come here, and give it up as a bad job by breakfast-time, and walk off and never come back again."

Can anything more clearly demonstrate the folly and iniquity of the stone-breaking "labour-test?" It is all of a piece with Mr. Bumble's management of his "casuals." It is firmly fixed in the narrow ways of his small comprehension that the terms " destitution" and "crime" are synonymous, and that poverty is only to be checked by harsh dealing and the infliction of punishment. He sets his "test" at his workhousegate as a man sets a mastiff to guard his warehouse, and he cries to all comers "Come in—if you dare!" It is his idea that a man should be tested as gold is—with this difference; that having assured himself that the man is sterling, he does not hasten to relieve him of the biting acid that has proved him—he insists on his remaining steeped therein until its corrosive teeth gnaw his bones bare.

Part of the range of worksheds in the Marylebone yard are devoted to the use of oakum-pickers, and here, as in the stone-yard, the arrangements contrast favourably with those of other parishes, notably with St. Luke's. At Marylebone the pitiful spectacle of a herd of famished ragged men and lads, shivering over their oakum-picking in a shed open to the wind and snow and rain, is spared the visitor. Each shed is built to accommodate about twenty men, and is snugly shut in and has windows. There are benches round the shed, and a block of wood in the centre for banging the oakum against, so as to render it easier to shred. Does the reader know what oakum is, or rather what is the material from which oakum is derived? It is the worn-out cordage of ships, saturated with tar, and rendered hard as wood almost by long exposure to the weather. It is chopped into nine-inch lengths. Some of it is as thick as one's wrist, and some no thicker than the little finger; and I observed that, in weighing out the stuff to the pickers, the taskmaster gave to new and inexperienced hands a liberal share of the thicker bits, while the knowing ones got a preponderance of "thin," which they received with scowls instead of thanks, much to my surprise, for the " thin" appeared to me softer-looking, and easier by far to pick to pieces than the "thick." It was not so, however, as I was informed; the thin stuff being composed of finer material, and more tightly twisted and completely soaked in tar. Twopence per pound is the price paid to the pickers, and they are permitted to earn a shilling a day—if they can. They are allowed a long day to work in, from half-past six in the morning till five in the afternoon, so that by steadfast diligence even a "green" hand may earn as much as eightpence or ninepence. It is not a nice sight to see oakum-pickers at work, even under conditions more than ordinarily favourable. Every man has a hook strapped above his right knee to assist him in tearing the rope asunder, and he sits with that knee crossed over the other, all huddled up, and with his back bent over his work. In almost every case the hook strap causes the right trouser to recede up, exposing a foot or so of dirty naked leg, which has not a pretty effect when viewed in conjunction with the rags of the workers and their dull hopeless faces as they pick and rend and tear at their valueless and distasteful work. Monstrously valueless. For every pound of oakum picked in a parish yard the price received by the guardians is little more than a *farthing*. That is the real value of the work (which could be done ten times better by machinery), and the parish authorities *lose* seven farthings by every pound of oakum produced by the labour test. At St. Luke's they lose *twopence three-farthings* a pound by their oakum; but, as before stated, they allow the pickers to produce no more than two pounds.

Paddington labour-yard is not a great distance from that of Marylebone. I don't know what is the population of Paddington, or what are its proportions of rich and poor. The limited extent of its labour-yard would bespeak it a well-to-do parish, and one but little afflicted by out-o'-works and tramps. It is healthily situated on the banks of the canal, to which its entire length is open. On the day of my visit there, expecting after my Marylebone experience to discover a swarm of desperately poverty-stricken men seeking to get bread out of stones, I was singularly disappointed. As I entered the yard, which is only an acre and a quarter extent, all was silent as a graveyard, but presently I made out a sound of stone-chipping in the distance, and, following it, found one man at work with his hammer, while close by was another man mending a stone-sieve. I could scarcely believe that this was the parish stoneyard, but both men assured me that it was, and while I was speaking with them up came the superintendent of labour, a shrewd-looking, hard-faced man, brief of speech. What he said, however, was to the purpose, and at once accounted for the strange slackness of the business under the hard-faced man's control.

I remarked to him that he did not appear to be very busy, to which he replied that he was quite busy enough. I ventured to observe that it was very different at Marylebone.

"We are busy here sometimes," he answered; "not often. It ain't the sort of work that suits them. Many of them come and have a try at it, but they give in as often as not."

"I suppose that your system is like that of other yards?"

"What *is* the system at other yards?'

"To pay so much a bushel, or so much a day, for the stones broken."

"That ain't the system here; we don't bother over bushels; it's half a yard, or none at all.",

"I don't quite understand what you mean by that."

"I mean that I don't measure less than half a yard—nine bushel that is."

"If a man breaks less than nine bushel, then you guess at the quantity, and pay him to the best of your judgment?"

"I don't guess at all. I don't trouble at all about it. I never pay for less than half a yard."

"But suppose a poor fellow comes here, and is unable to break more than four or five bushels, say?"

"That's his look-out."

"But surely he will get something for his labour?"

"He will if he can get one of the others to take the stones off his hands; not without."

"And if they consent to do so, at what rate will they pay hiin?" "I don't know. They settle it between them somehow, I suppose; they know it's no good calling on me to measure less than half a yard. Bless you, there are fellows who can break a yard—eighteen bushels—in a day, as easy as winking."

"And others who find it difficult to break six."

"More of that sort than the other, a precious sight."

"And they are obliged to make the best terms they can with another stone-breaker?"

"That's it."

"And if nobody will buy their broken stones they must go away at night no richer than they came in the morning?"

"That's it. But that don't happen often, I should think. There is always somebody ready to buy of 'em at a figure."

And that, good reader, is the delightful shape that the "labour-test" takes at Paddington.

There" is a stone-yard at St. Pancras. Seeing that it is a poorer, larger, and more densely populated parish than Marylebone, I expected to find that here the labour-test would be afforded plenty of elbow-room. It is not so, however. I was informed that the stone-yard was attached to the workhouse premises, and I made my way there, thanks to the guidance of the labour-master. I found, however, that this was not the labour-test yard, but simply the place where the casuals who had to work out the value of their lodging and gruel exercised their skill. It being now some hours past the time for discharging the casual host, the stone-yard was untenanted save for half-a-dozen or so of incorrigible young scamps, inmates of the house, who were set to break five bushels of stone a day as a punishment, but who endeavoured to bear up against the crushing penalty by means of a game at "cock-shy," at which pastime the stern task-master and myself surprised them. On three sides of this yard—a small and gloomy place enough— there were wooden hovels for the men to work in, and at one end a shed about the size of the back kitchen of a sevenroomed house.

"This is the oakum shed," explained the labour-master; "this is where the casuals who are not set at stone-breaking perform their work." "Then you don't do much in the way of oakum-picking I presume," I remarked. "Oh, they sit pretty close." "But sit as close as they may, such a little place can hold but few; not more than twenty." "Oh, yes, sir, twenty-four; if you count them you will find that there are four-and-twenty nails driven in round the walls. They are the nails the men tear the oakum on." "Well, twenty-four is not a large number of oakum-picking casuals. I know of workhouses where they so employ fifty daily, and occasionally more than that." "Fifty! why we more often have sixty or eighty," remarked the foreman, smiling at my innocence. "My dear sir, you mustn't imagine that the nails represent our average number of casuals." "Then you have another oakum-picking shed?" "No, only this one." But supposing that you have as large a number to find work for as you just now mentioned—sixty or eighty?" "Then all over four-and-twenty must do their work out here." "What, in the open air, whatever the weather is?" "I can't do more than the best I can, sir." "But have they nowhere to sit; no hook to assist them in tearing up the hard rope? Do you mean to say that the man who cannot find room in the shed must stand out here in the cold, or sit on a stone and so pick his two pounds of oakum?" "That is just so, sir."

Gentlemen of the Board of Guardians of St. Pancras, are you aware of this uncomfortable condition of affairs as regards your oakum shed? Is space so very precious with you that you cannot avoid a continuance of the present plan? Just reflect on this, come the next chill and nipping morning, when you have comforted your inner man with the roll and the bacon rasher, and the soothing cup of coffee, and the unlucky " casual," whom you have harboured for a night, has finished his regaling off six ounces of dry bread and a pint of "skilly." Before he may quit your premises, to try his desperate best to find a job that shall save him from another night of the "ward "—he must shred two pounds weight of hard ship rope till it is as fine as loose flax. Picture to yourselves how difficult this must be even under the shelter of a shed roof, and with a hook to aid in rending asunder the tough tarry wisps, and how unjustly that difficulty must be increased-if the poor devil of a picker has to stand or sit out in the freezing air, with his feet in the mud, and with only the nails of his benumbed hands to accomplish the job. Think of this, good gentlemen, and grant your oakum-picking "casuals" a little more shed-room for mercy sake.

The St. Pancr,as labour-test yard is situate a long way from the workhouse, a mile and a half the stone-breakers told me, which, however I should think was a slight exaggeration. But if it is no more/than a mile, it is too far, considering the small amount of a stone-breaker's earnings. Gillies Street, Kentish Town, is the site of the yard—a mean and inconvenient little place, not/half large enough for the requirements of so extensive a parish. I may here remark that at these places the superintendent in charge is almost invariably found to be a civil and comrriunicative person, ready to open his books for a visitor's inspection, and to frankly and freely assist him to a view of the picture from all points. The St. Pancras task-master will be gratified to learn that he is not classed with the exceptions. He informed me that the accommodation for the stone-breakers under his charge was very deficient; that he had room but for *twenty-nine,* and that if a large number came he was obliged to turn them away. That morning he had been compelled to write "No room" on the back of the relieving officer's order presented by five applicants. He did not know what the disappointed ones got for their trouble of walking between two and three miles—an order for the next day, he' imagined. The breakers were paid five farthings a bushel, and the majority of the men at present employed were habitual workers there—men who could break eighteen bushels "comfortably," and earn one and tenpence-halfpenny a day. I made inquiries of several of the men at work, and they confessed to working there " pretty constant," as well as to earning about eighteenpence. I asked on what principle the men were taken on, and was answered, "Come first, first served." No doubt these "regular hands" were always in good time, every nne of them usurping the place of a poor fellow for whose benefit (') the test was instituted. What business had men who have settled down to a contented earning of one and tenpence-halfpenny a day, and who regard it as their regular employment—what business had such fellows in a test-yard while there is waiting without one de-cent man temporarily shut out from his regular employment, and willing rather than beg to take the stone-hammer in hand for a day or so? Scores of lads and young men would flock to London, leaving their ill-paid work in the agricultural districts, if they could make sure of earning eleven and ninepence a week at breaking stones, and undoubtedly they would earn as much after a few months' practice. But it is but one of Mr. Bumble's thousand blunders. Mr. B. considerately finds eye-shades for his stone-breakers, but they are of such peculiar construction that only young men of powerful sight could see through them; the weak-visioned old fellows, who have need to take the greatest care of their fading optics, are obliged to work without them, blinking and winking in terror of the flying splinters.

Mention was made at the commencement of this paper of a workhouse at the south of London whose labour-test consisted of "crank-work." This is Lambeth workhouse. It is now some considerable time since I applied at that stapled knocker and traversed the chaste hall so scrupulously hearthstoned and bematted. Then it was night; now it was noon; but I verily believe I could have found my way from that front door to the one at back that opened on to the yard had I been blindfold. There was the memorable crank shed—there was the identical crank at which for three weary hours I had turned and turned—there was the little bell up high at the ceiling, and even as I gazed on it, it came to life and tinkled as once before I had heard it. There were the terribly dirty and filth-encrusted stones, and I could have walked up to and set foot on the particular one on which my hay-bag lay (I hope hay-bags are no longer allowed to be laid on them). There was the iron pillar where stood the horse-pail at which my nude and thirsty fellowlodgers rose from their lairs to take a drink.

But there was *not* the miller whose instant suspension from a sour apple-tree was demanded by the insolent majority of corngrinders. That long-suffering and patient man is long since dead, a perky and dandified young miller filling the office. There was no one else but the perky young miller to answer my questions, which I was rather sorry for, because, having ascertained my name, he appeared to regard it as his duty to his masters to treat my trespass as unwarranted, and to baulk my purpose, whatever it might be. But the fact I had come in search of was too broad in its bareness for his screening. There it was before me. This was the Lambeth test— this and roadmending. Here was a shed so dark that it was impossible to discern a man's features at half the length of it, and within it eighty men were packed at the crank handles closely as they could stand. There they were, the dissolute with the decent, the hard-working with the inveterately idle, seemingly working together. Seemingly, for such really was not the case by a very long way. Of all descriptions of test labour it would be impossible to show one more monstrously unfair to the *bona-fide* working man than this crank-work exhibits. It amounts simply to this, that the man willing to work is compelled to work *twice* as hard as he should, while the lazy rascal works not at all. Here is an iron bar to be grasped by six men, and by their united labour to be raised and lowered with a circular motion. All that the lazy ones do is to lay their hands on the bar, and let their arms swing with it, while the industrious ones—the poor fellows who are anxious to get the task accomplished, grasp the bar, and bend their backs with a will, dearly enough earning their scanty reward. It is impossible/for the keenest overlooker to detect the cheat, and the men who are imposed on can only convict the rascals by suddenly withdrawing their hands, when of a surety the bar comes to a standstill. But there is no use in complaining; the cheats are liars as well, and ready to take any number of oaths of any strength that they have all along been working like niggers. Besides, it is not the miller's business to examine into individual complaints; so long as the work is done—and done it must be—it makes no difference to him who does it.

So much for the nature of the test-work at Lambeth; now as to the pay. No worker gets money; he gets bread, and nothing else. A single man working at the crank all day long gets a *two-pound loaf fox* his pains. If he is married he gets a four-pound loaf. If he has children he receives two pounds of bread per diem for each. So that if he has six children, he may carry home the enormous quantity of *sixteen* pounds of bread, not a penny for coals or candle or a bit of sugar—only sixteen pounds of bread. And why, one would be glad to know? Why not eight pounds of bread and a shilling in money, or even sixpence? What is the inevitable result in the case of a man who has sixteen pounds of bread and nothing else given him for his famished family? He sells part of it for as much as he can get, and buys other necessaries with the money. Again, why should a man's labour be valued according to the number of his children; and the man with no family at all, who is probably the most able man of the two, receive of the value of *fourpence* for his day's work, while the man with a family receives of the value of *two and eightpente?* To be sure, the family man may be more in want of two and eightpence than the single man, but to what extent ought this consideration enter into the question of a labour-test? Why, again, should the lazy vagabond be permitted to find harbourage in the crank shed, doing no more than such an amount of mischief as presents for his idle hands to do, and at the close of the day receive the same amount of pay as the painstaking and industrious out-o'-work? It is devoutly to be desired that when reform of the existing "labour-test" is attempted, the reformers will commence at the crank end of that crying evil.

It is but fair to say that the foregoing descriptions were written some three or four years ago, and that for all I know to the contrary some amendment may have taken place in the systems pursued at the various establishments.—J. G.

OVER THE HOUSE-TOPS. 1V OW has the season of long evenings and gas-light set in, and all the showmen of the town are busy as bees preparing the street walls and banging their gongs and shouting to the public through speaking-trumpets made out of newspaper advertisement-sheets concerning the surpassing excellence of the entertainment provided at their various establishments. A man might be possessed of as many legs as a centipede, and still be unable to accept half the invitations to "walk up " that assail him on every side. Theatrical managers have new plays and old actors, and new actors and old plays for him. Gal- leries of Illustration open their doors to him, ventriloquists and conjurors and magicians beg his patronage, and he has his choice of " Readings" from a penny upwards. Those delightful and still improving places of amusement, the music halls, are not behindhand. Neddy Bray, the inimitable Neddy, has a bran-new song with a hee-haw chorus (copyright), in which the audience are permitted to join, and Rummy little Ramsbottom promises to convulse his admirers with something original and spicy, entitled " Julia's Crinoline." If, however, good reader, you will for this one evening be guided by me I will undertake to introduce you to an entertainment the like of which may not be seen elsewhere in London, and the cost of it shall not exceed sixpence. If you are desirous of knowing its nature, I can only tell you that it is something in the way of a gallanty show. But you would never understand the sort of exhibition it is from mere description, and as it is growing dusk if you wish to see it to-night we had best start at once.

We must take train for conveyance to the show-place. We must mount the many stairs at Fenchurch Street Railway Station and procure passage to Shadwell. "What! is it at that shady quarter of the town where the said exhibition is?" you ask. To which I reply, "Not at all; the gallanty show I promised you is to be seen as we travel along. On the Great Eastern line all trains are slow, but it is on this occasion to our advantage to take the slowest, and that which stops most frequently. This is the "Parliamentary;" let us take our seats. Now that we have advanced so far, and have a spare minute or two before us, in order that you may be spared puzzling as to the show's invention and contrivance, I will explain the matter to you.

You see, a railway fully armed with Parliamentary powers is the most tyrannical monster under the sun—a big, blusterous bully, who will take the wall for no man. Resolved on a certain road, "obstacle" is a word erased from its vocabulary. If a hill opposes, it must be cleft; if a mountain, it must be bored; as for a few mere streets of houses, down they go before a flick of the monster's finger and thumb. It made up its mind, did the monster, that a proper way to extend its snaky length was from Fenchurch Street to Shadwell, a district crowded with tumble-down tenements of the most poverty-stricken kind, and straightway it carved itself a passage without more concern for the creatures it disturbed and deprived of housing than a gardener digging a trench considers the worms that his spade dispossesses. Low lying ground is that on which the oldfashioned over-crowded houses stand, so that the railway, starting from a superior elevation, could not, here arrived, stoop, but maintained its original level perched on arches so tall that the engine panting and whistling on its way frequently overtopped the surrounding chimney-pots. Again, the said groundi although at present so shabbily covered, possessed a prospective value so enormous that the railway was glad to pare its requirements to an inch, buying nothing to waste to the right or left; the consequence is that the tenements remaining abut so closely on the iron way, that in many cases the stoker at his post might tap at the windows with the aid of a mop-handle, and in any case could easily hold whispered conversation with the inhabitants of the upper chambers of the houses, supposing that the latter at any time were so disposed. Passing along the railway route in question at noonday these windows, bare and naked, or scantily curtained with drooping rags, affording a view more or less distant of the strange interior, is an odd spectacle to behold, but it is not until the evening, when the candle is lighted, and such makeshift blinds as may be are drawn across the grimy panes that the panorama of poverty attaips perfection. Then commences our gallanty show.

In well-ordered and ordinarily decent neighbourhoods the upper rooms of the houses are invariably devoted to sleeping purposes, but, hereabouts, small and inconvenient as are the tenements, not in one case in ten can any apartment pretend to be a bed-chamber and nothing else. The inhabitants cannot afford it. Dilapidated and wretched as are these shallow and narrow houses, with their patched roofs and little windows and door-sills all aslant with age and decay, the rent demanded and eagerly paid for them in many instances exceeds that of the roomy and convenient suburban villa residence. Any mite of a chamber in this district of squalor will realize a rental of at least three shillings a week, and how can a poor toiler for farthings and halfpence afford to pay more? Besides, sleep is a luxury in which these hardly beset ones grudgingly indulge under any circumstances. If nature were not so exacting with them; if they might enjoy immunity from weariness, and never feel sleepy, they might earn perhaps twelve shillings in a week where now they can earn but seven. What a fine thing it would be if some Houndsditch genius, a merchant tailor he should be, could invent a precious ointment which applied to the eyelids would ensure perpetual wide-awakeness! If, in addition to this invaluable property it possessed another—that of endowing the anointed optics with the cat-like capability of seeing in the dark, the boon to poor needlewomen and sweating tailors would be perfect. Just imagine the joy with which such an invention would be hailed. No candle to buy, no time wasted in profitless sleep, no work bungled and ill-stitched in the weary small hours of morning, when gapes and nods will assert their sway in spite of all manner of preventives resorted to, such as sipping hot tea without milk or sugar, or sitting with the feet in cold water, or eating salt that the pangs of thirst may goad and keep flagging nature in a lively condition (all of which mysteries of slop needle-craft and many more are, notwithstanding the innocent reader's incredulity, nightly practised within sound of Big Ben of our Parliament Houses). Why, by a free use of the precious ointment the poor stitcher would be enabled within five years to lay down the implements of his craft and retire into the country—to Ilford or Woking. There is no burying in towns now, thank heaven; no conveying a wretched tailor from the miserable garret where he stitched himself into a parish shroud to just over the way to the prison churchyard adjoining the market High Street, with all its Saturday night's roar and rattle and its costermongers' clamour, and its flare of gas and naphtha. Acts of Parliament now forbid such indecency, and the defunct tailor must be carried out into the country to sleep his last sleep, though, through all his tedious life, his knowledge of grass was confined to seeing it in its manufactured state of hay in the Whitechapel market. A most excellent alteration this, but one which has not altogether escaped censure at the hands of those unconscionable mortals who are never satisfied. Say they, "It is very well, as far as it goes, this new and improved state of things; but how would the system work if it were exactly reversed—if you packed your *live* poor into the country, instead of the dead, and brought the latter for interment to the town?" But, of course, such an argument is too absurd to occupy the mind of a sober citizen for so long as a single minute.

But we have got quite away from our gallanty show, though indeed, for that, the subject of the digression is responsible; it was all through observing the figure of a hard-working tailor reflected on a makeshift blind made out of an old newspaper hung behind a top floor window. He is a quarter of a mile away by this time, but he is still present to the mind's eye. He must have worn a shade over his eyes I think—a peaky shade that cast a reflection shaped like an enormous beak. How else is it to be accounted for that the shadow on the blind was like nothing so much as a bird of the dodo species, lame of a wing and stuck in the mud, and exerting itself might and main to effect its extrication? Poor man; it is doubtful if he ever heard tell of a dodo. Anyhow, his experience of the hawks and vultures of the human tribe is much more extensive. At present he is engaged at work provided him by one of the latter, Abrahams by name, and the wing-like action of his swift right arm is accounted for by anxiety to earn fifteenpence a day by making soldiers' trowsers at fivepence a pair.

The next scene, ladies and gentlemen, of our gallanty show is of so puzzling a nature that it is a fortunate circumstance our train slackens its speed, giving us a fairer opportunity of observing it. This time it is a coloured counterpane that serves as a window blind. When the hour for roosting at length arrives, and the roost is far advanced, the candle will be extinguished, and the perverted counterpane restored to its proper office. The colours and the patches of the blind make the shadows on it harder to understand. Evidently there are several people little and big employed in the room, and judging from all the evidence visible they are one and all engaged in teasing and torturing flat fish, of the plaice sort, in a manner frightful to behold. Each operator has a fish by its tail, which he is clawing and squeezing until in its agony the poor creature presently emits from its mouth a monstrous bubble larger than one's double fists, and which the torturers snip away from it with a pair of scissors, and immediately begin again their cruel handling of its tail. You might, my worthy companion, contemplate the odd spectacle long enough before you guessed what it meant, but as it happens I have witnessed the operation in substance as well as in shadow, and know all about it. The occupants of that apartment are not a family of fish torturers— they are manufacturers of "air balls "—those coloured balloons so popular of late years with the little ones. What appears to be a flat fish is in reality a pair of bellows, and the bubble or bladder is derived by fastening the bit of skin over the nozzle of the bellows and inflating it by working at the handles. When the bladder is full its mouth is secured with a bit of thread and snipped off, to make way for a fresh one. When this ingenious little toy was first invented thousands were sold in the streets at sixpence each; now they are made and sold by these Bethnal Green toilers at the rate of three shillings and sixpence for a gross of a hundred and forty-four.

Jerking us a little way forward, the engine answers the purpose of pulling the bobbin, and we have a change of scenery. This time the window is bare, and we have grim reality in place of fantastic shadow. Here you observe a party at tea. A party at prayers it appears like at first sight, since with the exception of the woman, all the members of it are down on their knees. They are small members every one, and they are ragged and towzle-haired. The woman is the mother. Hasty, flaring sticks have made the kettle boil, and by their fading glow what is going on may be distinctly seen. Mother, with her bonnet on as though but recently home from work, has a loaf on her lap and a knife in her hand, and fast as her experience enables her to cut slices, she is evidently unequal to the demand. Cups and saucers, or a teapot, are luxuries unknown in that family. There is a big yellow jug, containing something that smokes, and in the interval of devouring slices the members of the teaparty take up the vessel and have a swig. Just as we are losing sight of this window mother has the bottom crust of the loaf elevated on her knife, as though she was asking "Who will?'' "Who would!" Seven pairs of hands, eager and open as the beaks of young blackbirds, are ready to answer her. Send the widow a bigger loaf, good Lord!

Here is a picture on the blind of a group of slipper makers, as may be known from the pile of the leather and carpet luxuries set on the window sill to dry. This is another tailor, who with his wife are squatted down, plucking pain and trouble from their breasts, and flinging it away at the rate of sixty strokes an hour. So the shadow will have it at last. Here is an old gentleman, a dirty old gentleman with bare hairy arms and a long beard (there is no blind at this window) amusing himself with a popgun. That is to say the thing in his hands as at first seen in the distance and by a feeble light looks like a popgun. He has lots of popguns lying on a table and hanging against the wall, and apparently he is engaged in testing the one he has now in hand, ramming a pellet into it with a stick. Alas! poor man. Such trivial amusement is not in his line. He is a maker of German sausages, and that heap of brown stuff on the old tea-tray is not material for popgun pellets, but wholesome sausage stuffing. All night his evening's work will dry in the smoke of the sausage-maker's chimney, and to-morrow he will be found on his beat from public-house to publichouse, vending his foreign produce to taproom customers at the rate of sixpence a pound. It is said that this person does an immense trade, the flavour of his goods being peculiarly spicy and agreeable. It is to be hoped (in the event of the sanitary authorities not discovering it beforehand) that the sausage merchant will not depart this life with his secret unrevealed.

THE MYSTERIOUS "PELL'S OWL: ATELY there died on the premises of the Royal Zoologi —' cal Society, in the Regent's Park, the great Pell's owl, deeply regretted by all who knew him and enjoyed the advantages of his amiable and beneficent society. *Requiescat in face.*
Hush! laugh not—smile not, dear reader; this is no joke, but a grave fact, and one that should be recognized as such. "What! the death of an owl a grave fact! a common, stupid owl! preposterous." Once more, gentle reader, hush, for goodness sake. 'Tis true that the Pell's owl is defunct—that his carcass has passed into the hands of the stuffer, and passed out of them again; that eyes of glass supplant those living orbs so dreadful to contemplate; that the skull wherein once throbbed that mysteriously brooding brain is now empty; that innocent tow fills out the feathery shape from head to tail still who knows? Ah!

who knows? Even as I write the ghost of the Pell's owl may be fluttering on the top rail of my chair, and peeping over my shoulder to read what it is that I dare to say about him.

First of all, I must say this much, that there never is a greater mistake made than when the great Pell's owl is styled a *mere* owl —a common owl. Did he look like a common owl? I appeal to any lady or gentleman who ever saw him while alive, did he? No, he did not. He looked exactly what he was, ana what he proved himself to be, to the society's cost and confusion, a Fetish bird. I am not a superstitious man, and what I just now said as to the probability of the ghost of Pell's owl peeping over my shoulder was all nonsense, of course ; still as a mere matter of delicacy and politeness towards a creature against whose character *nothing has beat positively and absolutely proved,* I hesitate to render into English what is our equivalent for the word Fetish. Let it suffice that our equivalent for the word is *not* "heavenly." He is dead and gone now, poor fellow, but it must be admitted that he never was regarded as an angel—of the upper regions, that is to say.

It was very wrong from the first to meddle with him; a foolhardy, daredev- I should say, daring business, and if mischief came of it, as unquestionably it did, the meddlers had no one but themselves to blame. They should have listened to what the natives of the owl's country had to say on the subject. Who should know so much concerning Fetish as the Fetish worshipper?

It was not as though the peculiarities of this particular owl were not sufficiently understood. Everybody, even to the lisping savage of half a dozen summers, could have enlightened the inquirer as to the terrible mystery that attached to the strange bird. Throughout the length and breadth of its native land it is looked on as the epitome of bad luck—in all respects save one—and, under ordinary circumstances, it is regarded as a dire misfortune to catch sight of one of these owls roosting or flying, and if a native found one perched on the thatch of his hut, he would promptly turn out, though he and his family slept on the grass. As for housing one of the mystic things, a native would as soon thing of harbouring a lioness. There is blight in its breath, and death and destruction lurks in the glances of its eyes. It is good for nothing as a captive—but one thing, as above hinted.

This is what it is good for: it confers on its possessor the power of subduing womankind. No matter how proud and haughty the damsel, or how low and insignificant the suitor, she is lost, provided he has the courage to trap and cage a Fetish owl. If he be ugly as sin, and she the pearl of her tribe, that will not save her; with his owl captive he has but to beckon with his finger, and she will instantly respond, or find some cunning means of doing so presently, should the males of her kin for the time hold her back. Of course this is very terrible. As, for instance, the reader has possibly observed in his walks about London a lantern-jawed, ragged, squint-eyed wretch, who exhibits three owls nestled in a basket, and on the strength of the interesting spectacle, solicits halfpence. Well, just suppose for a moment that these owls were not of the common sort, but Fetish, and gave to that young man power to win the heart of any lady on whom he preferred to squint. Just imagine the consternation there would be, if, one day in Regent Street or Pall Mall, was presented the strange sight of a young Mayfair beauty drawn out of her brougham by the fascination of the young fellow with the three owls, and following him, despite all that could be urged to the contrary, towards St. Martin's church, and down Long Acre, to his home in Seven Dials!

This being the nature of the Fetish, and as revealed by the natives to certain African explorers, nothing would do but that a specimen of this most curious of the *Strigidce* family must be trapped and carried to England alive. "Why not? Fetish was nothing but heathen bosh. How could it affect men, white, civilized, and educated? Ha! ha! The idea was absurd!" And so they secured a Fetish owl and brought it home with them. I fancy I see that sage and mysterious bird wagging its head, and winking one of its round eyes, as, confident of their impregnability to Fetish, the knowing ones packed him in a basket and sent him aboard ship!

It is not recorded that anything *very* serious occurred on board the vessel that brought the Fetish owl over; still, it does not follow that nothing uncommon *did* occur; at that time the owl's dire influence was not even suspected. It was not until the Fetish owl reached this country that he commenced the exercise of his peculiar talent, and to make for himself a reputation. He was presented to A, who speedily discovered his true character, and kindly transferred him to B, who shortly afterwards made him over to C, who, with difficulty disguising his fright, blandly presented the rare bird to the Royal Zoological Society.

Alas, woful was the day when the great Pell's owl entered in at that menagerie gate! Could the creatures there assembled have known who and what it was that was approaching to settle amongst them, such a chorus of roars and howls and shrieks would have greeted him as might have warned the custodians of the Pell's owl of the' rash thing they were doing. But, to be sure, it was too much to expect from dumb brutes a display of sense superior to that exhibited by their biped keepers; and in the Fetish owl was carried and duly installed.

Then began the mischief. Within a month it was observed that animals attached to the society's collection, and previously hale and hearty, began to pine and sicken. Those even of most frolicsome disposition were not exempt from the mysterious blight, and it was remarked amongst the visitors that all the curl had gone from the opossum's tail, and that the countenance of the azure-faced baboon was bluer and longer than ever. Then a few deaths occurred, of minor importance, certainly, but under such extraordinary circumstances as should have alarmed the directors as to the future. But they would pay no attention to the mild warning.

The animals had died from natural causes, there could be no doubt of that. The great owl was in no way responsible for the strange mortality. Pshaw! could anything be more ridiculous? "Hoo! Hoo-o! hooted the African Fetish that same night; "Hoo! Hoo-o! here's sport! my *masters* these fellows call themselves! I have but one master, and he doesn't live here, but I'll do my duty by him." And next morning it was discovered that the big polar bear was ill, and was not likely to live five hours longer.

The bear died, and a *post-mortem* examination revealed the existence of several little iron hooks attached to a piece of cloth bedded in its maw, and the authorities gravely gave out that this was the cause of the creature's death. Doubtless it was so, but *who caused the hooks to be administered to the seabear?* Was it the work of Fetish? Go, if you dare, and look the great owl in the face, and ask him the question,

After the sea-bear's demise the creatures one and all, furred as well as feathered, and even those that were scaled and lived in thin glass tanks in the serpent-rooms, grew ailing, and drooped day by day. The hyena moped and loathed his meat, and could not be wrought beyond a sardonic grin, poke him up as the keeper might. The wolves shed their coat and became lamb-like, the brown bears of the pit did nothing but whimper and wring their paws dolefully, the lions and tigers languished and shuddered visibly if the least bit of fat was offered them at dinner-time, and the elephant seemed to be attacked by a sort of mildew that caused the hair to rub off easily from his skin, leaving him bald and mangy-looking. At the end of each month quite a large sum had to be handed to the man who at dusk of evening came with his cart to remove the dead. Meanwhile one creature remained bright as a daisy, and grew daily sleeker and brighter-eyed and jolly-looking. It was the Fetish owl.

It was very extraordinary, everybody said—of course there was nothing in it, hjw was it possible? Still it was a strange coincidence that heathen superstitions should be so heavily backed by downright fact. So strange was it that a certain artist suggested to the manager of a certain highly popular illustrated journal that it might be interesting to the public if a portrait and a brief sketch of the career and peculiar attributes of the Fetish owl were published; but the proprietor sensibly declined, shrewdly remarking that it was impossible to say how superstitious the bulk of his patrons were, and he did not think that it would be worth while. And this is quite true, and pleased indeed am I to be able thus publicly to compliment the gentleman in question on the soundness and breadth of his views on such a subject.

If matters had continued so, there can be but little doubt that in twelve months the Pell's owl would have polished off every bird and beast in the place, but *somehow* (I say somehow, as undoubtedly it must have been—I make no insinuation) somehow the Fetish owl himself took ill and died. A day or so previous the dromedary, under the bird's evil influence, gave up the ghost; and it may have happened that grief for that worthy animal's death overwhelmed the attendants, and they were betrayed into neglecting the prime prize and pet of the gardens—the Pell's owl. Perhaps, blinded by his tears, some faithful feeder could not for the moment discriminate between substances pernicious and those that were wholesome, and the great owl's death was the result of accident.

Anyway, die it did, and "strangely enough," as say the wilfully blind and unbelieving; but as a matter of course, as must be plainly apparent to folks of common sense, as sooii as the breath had left the Fetish owl's body, the whole collection of birds, beasts, and fish began instantly to revive, and by this time their health is completely restored.

I have an idea that the next Pell's owl offered to the Royal Zoological society will be declined.

P.S. Now, is it not strange that what I hinted at the beginning of this paper as to the possibility of "Fetish" still lingering about the owl's carcass, should have become verified? I mentioned that the creature was entrusted for preservation to the gentleman who usually undertakes the bird-stuffing of the establishment. I am credibly informed that from the time of the dead Pell's owl's reception to that of its completion and packing off, other business was absolutely at a standstill on his premises—not a single customer presenting himself, but that immediately on the creature's departure the old and satisfactory condition of affairs was at once restored.

AT A GAOL DELIVERY.

"C XACTLY opposite the prison great gates there is a public'house, and it is a long-established custom with the prisoners, on their discharge from the former, to make for the latter straightway. One might reasonably suppose that they would be anxious to escape with all speed from the neighbourhood of the sombre building that had so tediously held them; but it is not so, and for a very substantial reason. It is an understood thing amongst the fraternity that when this particular gaol is delivered of one of them, he shall at once repair to the hotel in question, in certain prospect of there finding a faithful friend or acquaintance, rich enough at least to "stand" comfort for the emancipated to the extent of a pot of beer and a pipe of tobacco.

I cannot explain how it happens, but as a rule these gaol deliveries are more numerous on a Monday morning than any other of the week. Perhaps there is a rule against the discharge of a prisoner on a Sunday, even though the term of his sentence then expires, and it is the overdue batch that swells the number: anyhow, so it is. On a Monday morning you are sure to find some of the faithful, male and female, drinking at the bar and engaged in whispered converse (and oh, so civil to Mr. Landlord!) or shyly peeping through the windows towards "over the way,"

Not many Mondays since it was my fortune to be thereabouts just at the right time, and I saw emerge from the sullen wicket three young men, an old man, two women, and a small boy. The women, who were scarcely so in years, but who in vice were aged almost to decrepitude, burst out laughing as soon as they were on the free side of the threshold, one of them turning and making an impudent gesture at the grim gate-keeper with his keys. The old man, who was dressed in seedy black, was evidently not one of the hardened sort, for he pulled his hat over his eyes in shame, and hung his head lest honest people should see and recognize him, and, buttoning his thread-bare coat, shuffled off at a half trot. As for the three young men, "petty thief" was written unmistakably in every line of their features, in every movement of their lithe limbs. It is doubtful if they had ever seen each other before or exchanged so much as a nod of greeting, but coming out at the gate they flocked together instinctively, as do all birds of a feather, looking neither pleased nor sorry nor more ashamed than if oakum-picking were ordinary journeyman's labour and they were journeymen coming from the workshop and going over the way to drink a half-pint of beer for lunch. It is much more difficult to describe how looked and behaved the last prisoner of the batch—the small boy. He was wretchedly clad, and the morning air was keen; but he had a clean face, and such good looks as he possessed appeared to advantage. He was a sharp-eyed, keen-looking boy, not with a ill-shapen head, as might easily be judged since his brown hair was cropped close, and he wore no cap to speak of. I should guess his age to be about fourteen, but it is difficult in such cases to judge of years from physiognomy—a hard-faced boy, with a thin-lipped, resolute-looking mouth. As he emerged from the prison, coming after the three young men before mentioned, he was evidently at a loss. The three young men walked slowly, and the small boy seemed of a mind to join them, at the same time being painfully conscious that his extreme youth was against him, and that to attempt to do so might be regarded as an act of presumption, and be so resented. So in the twinkling of an eye the small boy clapped two years on his age. He shifted the peak of his old cap so that it tilted with a rakish and devil-may-care hang over his left ear, and plunging both his hands into the pockets of his monstrously too big trowsers, he quickened his pace and came up with the veteran trio. He did not speak—he merely kept step with them, and looked as though he wanted to be sociable. Presently one of the three made a little joke, and his friends laughed, as did the small boy. This brought matters to a climax. The youngest of the companionship, with a close cropped carroty head and a most villanous countenance, paused in his laughter, and regarded the poor cringing little beggar sternly. "You can hook it," said he, which, rendered into polite language, is equivalent to "Go away; we don't want you." It was just outside the prison boundary where this heartless cut was given, and there was nothing to be done but for the snubbed and rejected small boy to sneak off, while the three young men crossed over to the public-house, followingTin the wake of the two impudent young women.

Two other" young women, brazen-faced, sluttish wenches, were in readiness to receive their female friends—nay, soon as the impudent ones'were descried stepping out at the gate'opposite a half-pint of gin was called /or, and two brimming glasses of it poured out for the released prisoners. Why it appeared strange, almost startling, that these four women should kiss each other, is hard to explain. That they should toss down their glasses of gin with the dexterity of drunken cobblers seemed not nearly so unnatural. "And how have you been doin'?" asked one of the recently liberated 01 she who had paid for the gin. "Rubbin' on; much about the old style," was the reply, accompanied by a significant shrug of the shoulders. The old style was a very deplorable one, if it might be judged by the speaker's personal appearance. Compared with it, that of the two women just set free was far preferable; for whereas the one was dirty and famished and ginsodded, the others were sleek and plump and wholesomelooking—which is, of course, incontestible proof of the salutary working of the law, and should be an inducement to irresolute folks not to stand shilly-shally between crime and honesty, but to embrace the former at once and so ensure those rewards that the friendly, though seemingly severe, hand of the law holds out.

The three young men in the adjoining compartment facing the bar were not friendless. Succour for them appeared in shape of three male friends and one elderly female, who was shedding tears of rejoicing on the shoulder of the carrotyhaired individual before mentioned. An unnatural brute! "That's twice I got a light for my pipe, and you've made it go out; why the 'ell can't yer leave a cove alone?" was his ungrateful response to the old lady's third demonstration of grandmotherly affection. It was singular to watch the avidity with which all three of them fell to smoking tobacco. Even the beer measure was neglected for it, and the wrapt enjoyment with which each of the young men took long and steady pulls at their pipes was denoted by their lazily blinking eyes. It is always so, I was informed. A deprivation of spirits and beer a prisoner may grow resigned to, and have no great yearning for when he obtains his liberty; but his passion for smoking is unconquerable, and towards gratifying it his ingenuity is boundless. The friends of prisoners who have visited them, although rigorously searched before they are permitted to approach the gate through which the conversation must be held, have been known to evade the prison rules by carrying in their mouth a neatly rolled "quid," and deftly shooting it through the bars should the warder's attention be for an instant withdrawn. Tobacco so obtained, a prisoner, having somehow become master of a lucifer match, has been discovered smoking as a cigarette, a bit of paper or rag forming the envelope—having first of all, with infinite pains and no little peril, climbed up to the ventilator in his cell, so that the tell-tale smoke might not lead to his detection. A more extraordinary instance than this of a prisoner's passion for tobacco was given me by an officer attached to Portland Prison. Somehow a bit of tobacco and a pipe were smuggled in in a manner that made it the joint-stock property of three of the convicts, and it was treasured until there transpired a fair opportunity for its enjoyment. At last the longlooked for time for the treat arrived, and then came the question how was the luxury to be fairly shared. One suggested six whiffs each till the pipe was exhausted, but he was a stronglunged villain, and his device was at once seen through—it was clear that he could " pull" as much smoke in his six whiffs as could the others in ten. It was a nice point to decide, but presently one of the party, whose ingenuity somewhat exceeded his delicacy, hit on the exact thing. Two straws were procured, and possession of the precious pipe was tossed for. This preliminary settled, the trio sat down, and the pipe was lit, the holder of it taking in his lips one of the straws as well as the pipe-stem. The other end of this straw the second man took in his mouth, as well as a tip of the third straw, at the further extremity of which sat the third man. Then the "treat" began. The man with the pipe took a whiff, enjoyed the mouthful of smoke awhile, and then carefully blew it through the straw into the mouth of the second man, who, after taking toll of it, passed it on through the straw to the third man, who, in consideration of what virtue the tobacco might have lost, coming to him, as it did, at third hand, was permitted *to swallow it* —a precaution rendered necessary lest the warder should get scent of the prohibited indulgence. To return, however, to my uncaged gaol-birds. Having disposed of their half-pint of gin, and of a quartern more, the four women went their way, and the hunger of the three young men for tobacco becoming somewhat assuaged, they went in for beer-drinking, all excepting the grandmother, who, finding her tender regards repulsed, was silently weeping in a quartern of rum, which for her consolation she had ordered; so, foreseeing that matters were in a groove in which they were likely for some time to remain, I took my departure. Having gained the street, however, the first object that my eyes encountered was the disconsolate small boy, whom the young men had so unfeelingly slighted. Round about the prison are posts connected by hanging chains, and on one of these latter he was sitting, idly swinging his feet.

"What are you doing here? Why don't you go away?" I asked him.

"Why don't I go away to where?" he replied, eyeing me suspiciously.

"Home; you've got a hoine, I imagine. What were you doing before you were sent to prison?"

"I warn't a doin' no harm to you, anyways, afore I were sent to prison," he answered, after a considerable pause; "what call have you got to ask? I can get off these yer chains if they're yourn. " And so saying he disdainfully swung down.

"It is no business of mine where you sit or why you are waiting," I remarked; "but if you will take my advice you will avoid the company of those fellows you parted from when they went into the public-house. It is easy enough to see what they are."

He laughed. "What am I then, mister, since you are so good at seein'?" he asked.

"I can't tell you what you have been, but I can tell you what you now are."

"Tell us."

"A boy free to be honest if he chooses and to learn to forget what the inside of a prison is like." 16— 2 "I don't want to forget it; it's the most comfortable crib as ever I was in. I wish I'd a got three months 'stead of three weeks. I'll do summut wot'll make it hot for me next time, no fear."

"It is very shocking to hear a child like you talking so."

"Child! That'll do, mister. Don't you make no bother about me. I shall be all right when I find somebody to pal in with. That's the wust on it. I don't know nobody, like another cove."

"Have you no father?"

"Dead."

"No mother?"

"Oh, how do I know? Don't you make no bother about me, I tell you."

"What has become of your companions?" I asked at a venture.

"Inside here," he replied, with an envious glance towards the prison; "all three on 'em got four months, and I got six weeks; and I was the wust. Never mind; don't you make no bother about me, I'm all right."

"Do you mean to say that you have resolved to remain a thief?"

"I mean to say that I ain't a-goin' without grub." "But why not work for it honestly? You are compelled to work in prison."

"I ain't got no trade."

"Would you like to learn a trade? If I were to endeavour to get you admittance to a reformatory, would you"

"No, I wouldn't," he interrupted, with an emphatic wag of his head; "no reformatories for me, thanky! Four 'ear 'ard labour to learn to be a snob! Don't you make no bother about me, *I'm* all right. " And to show it he dexterously threw a summerset over the post chains.

"How are you going to get a dinner?" I asked him.

"Sell these yer boots," he answered readily. They were coarse new boots, provided, as I suppose, by the prison authors ties.

"Don't do so. I will give you half-a-crown on one condition—that you will promise to think of what I have told you and keep your hands free from dishonesty until you have spent it fairly in lodging and food-"

"Oh, I'll promise that, mister, and jolly glad to do it. I won't do a wrong thing till the 'arf crown's gone, swelp me Gord I won't; there. Give us hold."

"And you'll be off at once away from the men in the publichouse there?"

"Yes; I'll do that too."

I gave him the half-crown, and he received it with such hearty thanks that I was quite hopeful of him. Moreover, he walked away with a manner as determined as though nothing short of violence would induce him to return but when I had proceeded a quarter of a mile on my way, happening to look back, there I saw him hanging about the door of the publichouse, where I have no doubt my half-crown secured him a welcome at the hands of the carrotyhaired one and his friends.

AN EVENING WITH FORTY THIEVES. i—TT is a singular and startling fact that at the present writing there are thousands of young gentlemen varying in years from ten to eighteen, and born and bred in and about the most enlightened city in the world, who in the secrecy of their hearts hold it to be true that Jack Sheppard, house-breaker, prisonbreaker, thief, and murderer, was the most splendid fellow the sun ever shone on, and who find their *beau ideal* of a hero, not in Lord Nelson or the Duke of Wellington, but in "Blueskin," Claude Duval, or some similar ruffian, whose brilliant career was in due course extinguished by the common hangman before the debtors' door at Newgate.

What is the depth of their admiration for their darlings may be gauged by the amount of pecuniary sacrifice they are constantly prepared to make for their sakes. They may buy that large, well-conducted, and at least harmless periodical, the *Family Herald,* for a penny; or, if their literary palates are tough, and require more vigorous tickling, there is the *Metropolitan Journal,* with Piercy Gander the Younger, and raw-head and bloody bones held well in leash; or there is the *Londo7i Feeler,* only a penny, and large enough to cover the floor of a room, and occasionally unclean enough to stain the floor-boards indelibly. Besides, there is an unclean and abominable class of weekly prints, for such as like their mental food extremely high-flavoured, to be procured at the rate of two sheets a penny; but the real admirer of Blueskin will have nothing to do with any of these. Blueskin's is the shrine at which he worships (he worshipped "Bludjon the Burglar," whose shrine was erected at the same temple through one hundred and eighty-four weeks and at a cost of fifteen-and-fourpence), and thither he carries his hard-earned penny and receives in exchange a half-sheet of rubbishing paper impressed with eight small and dirty pages of battered print descriptive of his hero's delectable history—of how he set the old woman on the fire, how he cut the miser's throat to possess himself of several hundred-weights of his gold, but happening just as he was packing up the booty to catch sight of and fall madly in love with the miser's beautiful daughter, is overwhelmed with remorse, and gallantly offers to settle a fair half of the miser's ill-gotten hoard on her if she will consent to fly with him; of how she shrieked, and he implored, expostulated, and finally smote her on the head with the end of his loaded riding-whip; of how he carried her through the garden to where his horse was waiting, and, vaulting into the saddle with the insensible damsel still pressed in his arms, rode away with the speed of the wind towards Wimbledon, pursued by eleven Bow Street officers; of how, hotly pressed, he shot the leading officer through the head, and the noise rousing the miser's daughter, she at once espouses Blueskin's cause, and plucking a couple of spare pistols from the robber's belt, turns about, and while the horse is still pursuing its mad career, steadies herself by resting her lovely rounded chin on her lover's shoulder, and lets fly at the two foremost mounted police, bowling them over; of how—*to be continued in our next.*

I know all about it, you see, ye patrons of gallows literature. What is more, I know Blueskin personally. I met him only last Saturday in Fleet Street, coming out of the shop of the news-vending vampire in whose employ he is. Had you met him after leaving him last week only in a velvet coat and lace ruffles, flinging about his gold like a lord, and drinking mulled claret with his two sweethearts, you certainly would not have recognized him. Mr. Haddick is the name of the vampire who keeps Blueskin's pen wagging, and when I met Blueskin, although his shabby hat was pulled well down over his eyes, an alarming length of visage remained uncovered. He appeared so deeply absorbed in thought that I at once made up my mind not to disturb him; but he saw me, and, coming after me, laid a shaky hand on my shoulder. "Hallo, how do you do?" I asked him. "Well," said he, "a man that is done can hardly be said to be doing at all; I'm done. I've been working like a horse to get two numbers of 'Skin done this week for the sake of the couple of pounds, and now Haddick's out, and I'm booked till Monday. I'm dying for a drop of rum—that's a fact; haven't had a drop since I got out of bed. Lend me a shilling, that's a good fellow, and soon as I get that tin on Monday I'll remit the amount in postage-stamps, 'pon honour." It was impossible to resist the poor beggar's appeal. He was pale, he was haggard, and his eyes were the dull eyes of a dead man. He had better have been a dead man than have emitted from his mouth (I found it out when he approached his face to mine to whisper) such a rum-bred pestilence of breath. His faded thread-bare coat was buttoned high at the throat, either to conceal the dirtiness of his linen or the naked fact that his solitary possession in that material was at that moment undergoing the process of washing; the knees of his trousers shone, as did not his boots, which were patched at the sides and aslant at the heels. This is Blueskin. He is a worthy young man at bottom, I'll be bound, and would be still if he had abstained from scavengering for Haddick and Co., and indulged less in rum. But I've heard Blueskin say that he can't get on without rum—that all his inspiration arises from that and the bowl of a dirty pipe; and really I see no reason to doubt his assertion.

To return, however, to the thieves. The tavern where on the evening in question the youthful aspirants to hempen honours assembled for their orgie is situated in a narrow back street in the neighbourhood of Kingsland Road. Half a glance at the Ram and Teazle should be enough, if not to enlighten the passer-by as to the real character of the house, at least to warn him to keep on the street side of its threshold, It is a dingy-looking little "public," with a narrow doorway, and down a step to the bar. If the legend inscribed on the greasy door-posts may be relied on, there is a good dry skittle-ground in the rear. Nor, as a peep in at the bar discloses, are skittles the only amusement provided by the Ram and Teazle for its patrons. It is an old-fashioned little bar, with a wooden counter, and its interior is plentifully decorated with stuffed and celebrated dogs, from the tiny three pounds weight toy terrier to " Mr. Snape's bull-bitch Hagnail, who died in giving birth to her eleventh litter," as a neat blackbordered card tied about the hideous monster's neck declares. There are bills stuck about the bar relating to the pugilistic interest, and the pedestrian interest. Likewise there is a notification that a "free and easy" takes place every Monday and Saturday at the Ram and Teazle, with Billy Rafhbone in the chair, which notification taken by itself is to a person versed in vulgar jargon intelligible enough, as meaning a convivial gathering of persons of either sex, and at which every one present is expected to contribute a song, or at least to join in the chorus; but the "free and easy" at which Billy Rathbone took the chair must have been somewhat different from this, for written on a card which was pinned at the bottom of the free-and-easy placard was an intimation that "rats for the pit" might be had on application to the potman. I almost wished that it had been either a Saturday or Monday, that I might have seen in what manner "rats in a pit" could be brought to enhance the ease and freedom of a party bent on merry-making. The attraction for the evening when I went there, however, was of a nature so private and select that nobody but those who had "the office" (which in honest English means private information) was the least aware of it. I had "the office." I cannot disclose who gave it me, but I may say that I got it at the Brick Lane Dog Show, together with a ticket, and paid for the price of three pots of ale. The ticket had inscribed on it:—

"A raffle will take place at the Ram and Teazle, for a silk handkerchief, for the benefit of Plummy Jukes, who was trotted in on the 2nd of this month, and needs your kind assistance. Many can help one when one can't help himself. Tickets, one shilling."

I further ascertained that the crime for which Plummy Jukes was "trotted in" (committed for trial and taken to the House of Detention in the police-van) was picking pockets in an omnibus, and that as he had already been twice imprisoned for the same offence, it was thought that it would go hard with him unless Plummy was provided with a legal adviser, and it was to meet this expense that Mr. Jukes's brother had got up the raffle.

It was fixed to take place at nine o'clock, and a quarter before that hour I was standing before the Ram and Teazle's wooden bar in company of thieves, Nobody had gone upstairs yet, and the landlady, who was a strong-framed person, of bony aspect, and deficient of three of her front teeth, was evidently out of temper at the tardy arrival of the raffiers. "Cuss such raffles as this; if she'd ha' known it she'd ha' seen them before she'd ha' had the fire lit," and when any thief that stood there asked in the civillest manner to be served with a pint or a quartern, it was thrown down before him, and his money snatched up with a scowl instead of a thanky. "Give us a light, please, Mrs. Pratt." "What the devil next? How long have I been your slavey? Help yourself, or go without." The young fellow sniggered in a conciliatory manner, and picking up the fag of a match from the dirty floor, lit his pipe at the gas-light. Alas! my young friends, how matters in this respect must have altered since those oldfashioned thieves and cut-throats—Richard Turpin and Thomas King—caroused in the Red Lion in Drury Lane!" ' What ho there, drawer! hand me a light, you villain, or I'll slice thee to mincemeat!' exclaimed Dick, at the same time flinging at the unlucky menial about a pint of the burgundy that remained in his flagon by way of attracting his attention. With teeth chattering and shaking knees the trembling varlet obliged, quaking out an apology for not paying stricter attention to the wants of his customers. ''Tis well,' exclaimed the generousminded Dick, 'since I have given thee a wet jerkin, here is a guinea to get thee something to wet thy inner man as well.' "—*Vide* "The Knights of the Road," chap, ccclviii.)

There were but five thieves at the bar when I went in, but in the course of ten minutes the number was increased to eleven, all young men, two mere lads of fourteen or thereabout. But where was the dash, the reckless, devil-may-care deportment that should distinguish these pinks of a fraternity whose well-known motto is, "Light come, light go!" Where the insolent cock of the hat, the boisterous mirth, and the ribald bragging talk? Not here, certainly. A more downcast, spiritless company of young men it would be hard to find, seek London through. What conversation there was was ca.ried on in whispers, and that with much restlessness and anxiety and evident mistrust one of another. Had Plummy Jukes been their dear brother, and they had come to his funeral, tey couldn't have appeared more melancholy. "They will revive when they get upstairs, perhaps," I thought; "they don't care to give way to hilarity and free speech before that shrewishlooking landlady," and, just as I thought so, four other thieves came in in a gang, which swelled our number to fifteen—on observing which the landlady grew more gracious, and suggested that we had better go up, and not stick there blocking the gangway; so up we went.

She need not have made so much fuss about lighting the fire, for even after this lapse of time it was but a smoky, halfkindled affair, and the "club-room," with its low, black ceiling, its grimy and tattered wall-paper, and the table-tops festooned with sticky, dusty rings and patches, the results of last night's "free and easy," looked cheerless and dismal enough as we entered it. It remained dismal. The fire was roused, and the naked gas jets set at their extremest brilliance, but the company remained dull and dumpish as ever. They called for gin and rum, and it was drunk as freely as water, and water it might have been for all the effect it had on their spirits. There they sat in twos and threes, whispering their business, ever with a keen glance of suspicion for their neighbours, and evincing no more disposition for revelry than though they were a coroner's jury. I was pleased to find that I was not the only individual who sat and smoked his pipe alone; by the time twenty of the fellows had assembled there were at least four of them in that predicament.

By half-past nine the number of thieves increased to thirty, and it was then suggested that the raffle might begin, and the dice were brought in along with the handkerchief, which, amid a faint attempt at cheering, was tied by the corners to the gaspipe overhead. Plummy's brother, a rat-eyed, slim-limbed thief, about eighteen years old, took scores as the dice were thrown, and collected the shillings from such as had not already paid them. To save time each raffler took but one cast of the dice, and, to my great satisfaction, I threw seven, putting my chance of winning the handkerchief out of the question.

Sixteen won it, and then the company, by this time forty strong, showed symptoms of greater cheerfulness. Two pounds thirteen was the sum announced by Plummy's brother as the proceeds of the raffle, which left a deficiency of only seven shillings to fee a lawyer on Plummy's behalf, and this latter sum was instantly "whipped round" for and obtained. Mr. Jukes's case was, as I understood it, desperate. It appeared that he had been caught in the act of cutting out a lady's pocket in an omnibus, and attempted to bolt out of the vehicle while it was still in motion, and that when the conductor attempted to collar him, Plummy turned round and stabbed the conductor in the face with his scissors, which unluckily he had not had time to replace in his pocket. With two previous convictions against him, the universal opinion appeared to be that Plummy would get five years.

After a comparatively animated discussion as to Mr. Jukes's chances, it was proposed that we should have a song. Now again there seemed a likelihood that the spirit of lawlessness and bravado which must of necessity possess every robber by trade would exhibit itself. In all probability the staves of the evening would include "Nix my dolly, pals," "The Taplow Tinker," "Hurrah for the road," &c. Plummy's brother took the chair, and he was just the fellow of a cut to chant a Newgate ditty. Again, however, I was disappointed. Plummy's brother, throwing sublimity into his razor-like visage, rose to his legs, and in very fair style sang the pathetic ballad of " Why chime those bells so merrily?" which was ferociously encored, and he then obliged with "Beautiful starwhich, of the two, seemed to take better with the audience than the first song. Then a gentleman sang "Poor old Jeff!" a ballad descriptive of the trials and sufferings of an aged negro, with a touching account of his last earthly moments and his heavenly prospects. Then followed the "Ship on fire," " Mary Blane," "The Wolf," and "Take back those gems"—the last by Plummy's brother, who evidently was the crack vocalist of the party. What other songs were sung I don't remember, but I can positively say that not a single comic one was amongst them, or one in the least degree laudatory of the practice of misappropriating your neighbour's goods. For all the immorality there was in the songs sung by my forty thieves, they might have been forty worthy young members of some newly-invented religious sect vocalising in their place of worship.

Of course it would be quite ridiculous to suppose that this abstinence from boisterous and rude amusement arises from any lingering remnant of good originally planted in the breasts of this band of ruffians. Take any one of the forty, and, if he could meet "poor old Jeff" carrying his passport to Paradise, he would not for a moment scruple to deprive him of it, if it could be sold for half-a-crown, and as for taking back "those gems" in real life, Plummy Jukes's brother would find himself laughed at as an idiot by his thirty-nine companions, if he even hinted at such a weakness. Why, then, are not the rogues merry in seasons of relaxation from the toils and hazards of business? For the simple reason that it is impossible to them. They are never released from business or a dread of its consequences. The sword suspended and only held back by a hair is constantly over their heads quivering, and each moment threatening to fall. They dare not indulge in pleasures that wait on honesty. Take five hundred professional thieves, and you won't find ten per cent, of them married to the mistresses of their home. "Where's the use," say they, "when I'm here to-day and gone to-morrow?" The thief by trade can have no real friendships; and to set his heart on any person or thing is but to lay a rod in pickle for his unfortunate shoulders, for at any hour—any minute—he may be "wanted;" and then the solitary cell and the long, long days of bitterness.

So it always was, my young friends. It was the same in Dick Turpin's time, and the same in Claude Duval's. The thief always was and always will be the hardest worked and most miserable of all labourers.

THE SOUTH COAST FISHERMAN.
T T was not at all a pleasant evening that on which I set out, according to previous arrangement, to join my friend William Fludyer, and embark with him on the trawler Happy Return on a night's fishing venture. The fine dry weather that had prevailed through several days had given way before a shifting of the wind, the clouds were gloomy and threatening, and a penetrating fine misty rain was descending. Our craft was already launched, and stood about a quarter of a mile from the shore, and so spying her I must confess to indulging the cowardly hope that Mr. Fludyer considered the weather too unpromising to make my companionship desirable, and had, therefore, gone off without me. In this, however, I was disappointed. All unexpectedly I was hailed by a nautical friend of Mr. Fludyer, who lay in wait for me in his row boat, and in ten minutes I was welcomed aboard the trawler.

I thought that I had, by means of a stout overcoat and a cap with ear lappets attached, made tolerably good provision against rough weather; but, as a glance convinced me, my rig was almost tropical in its scantiness compared with that which en. veloped the captain and his crew of two. The way in which these fellows take care of themselves in the matter of clothing quite unsets one's preconceived notions of the "hardy fisherman." It may be necessary to their health—nay, the fact of so many hale and hearty men amongst them of three score years and ten sufficiently proves that they are not over-careful; but truly no rheumatic old landswoman that ever lived pinned her faith to flannel more confidently than do these brawny ocean harvesters. Here was an autumn night—not a favourable night to be sure, but still the time of year was August; nevertheless Mr. Fludyer was encased as follows according to his own confession. Next his skin he wore a substantial shirt of gray flannel; over that a shirt of striped cotton; over that a woollen guernsey; over that a cloth jacket; over that a tanned smock that reached to his knees; over that an oilskin "coverall" reaching high as his ears and low as his ankles. So much for his body comfort, but of his legs he was even more careful. First he wore socks of wool, then "pants" of wool that descended just below the knee and were there secured; then a pair of blanket breeches; then an enormous pair of woollen hose high as his thighs; and over all these various wrappings a pair of sea-boots that left nothing of the last-mentioned hose visible. On his head Mr. Fludyer wore a tarpaulin sou'-wester quilted within with some fleecy material, and on his hands knitted mittens. "And do all fishermen on this coast wrap themselves up in the same manner?'' I inquired. "All except chaps that coddle themselves; they wear a waistcoat as well, and sometimes a neck-wrap," Mr. Fludyer replied; "but for my part I think that sweltering is bad for a man."

From stem to stern our trawler measured perhaps five-and-twenty feet, the centre of the vessel being put to no better account than to serve as a receptacle for her ballast, which was the shingle of the shore loosely shovelled in. The mackerel smacks adopt the more convenient and certainly tidier method of confining the ballast they carry in little sacks holding each about half a hundredweight. Divided from what may be called the hold, where the ballast is, and situate between that and the cabin at the head of the ship, is a square well or tank, into which, as it is caught, the fish is thrown; but decidedly the most marvellous feature of a trawler's economy is the cabin before mentioned.

It is no exaggeration to say that before the secret was disclosed to me I never so much as suspected its existence. To be sure I saw adjacent to the fish-well a square dark hole that might have been covered by an ordinary domestic copper-lid, and half concealed by a coil of ropes, but this I supposed to be merely a receptacle for fishing gear and odds and ends; that, however, was at a time when the Happy Return was stranded and off duty. The "hole" in question, as I now saw it, was no longer a black one. Jutting out by the side of it was a stumpy tin spout, from which smoke was issuing, and down below was a lively glow that bespoke a fire. "You had better come down and dry yourself a bit, and put on a ile-skin," kindly suggested Mr. Fludyer, and with that he laid hands on the edges of the square hole in the floor, and lowered himself, as it seemed to me, atop of the stove where the fire was glowing. "Put in your legs, and I'll guide 'em," he presently called up, perceiving that I hesitated in my descent. "That's it—steady; there you are."

There I was. How shall I describe the place? First as to its size. From the floor to the ceiling it measured less than four feet. Standing upright was quite out of the question—there was nothing left for it but to crouch or sit down. Its length may have been eight feet, perhaps nine, certainly not more, and its breadth at the widest part seven feet, and at the narrowest, where the bows of the vessel rounded, not more than four feet. This, however, was the fisherman's kitchen, and parlour, and bedroom, and larder, and scullery. By a series of ingenious contrivances which I will not attempt to explain, within the narrow limits of this small apartment he contrives two sleeping bunks, and to plant a cooking stove, and to provide a coal-hole and a crockery cupboard. Stowage also is there for a tea-kettle (made square so as to accommodate it to the shape of the stove), a frying-pan, and a candle-box, and a bread-pan, and a water-keg and much combustible matter in shape of spare sail and tarred rope, and a can of turpentine, the use of which will presently appear. Considered in relation to the contiguous fireplace, the sight of these latter articles occasioned me some uneasiness, for there was enough sea to cause the boat to pitch fore and aft, and there was absolutely nothing to prevent the blazing coals from tumbling out about the floor. At the back of the stove the timbers were covered with lead, and the stove itself was well secured; but that was all the precaution considered necessary. Fishingboats had caught fire, Mr. Fludyer admitted, but not frequently. All cabin stoves were fixed so; he had never been in a boat where there were different arrangements, or where more care was observed. If this is so, it is nothing less than miraculous how to large a number escape conflagration. With a rough sea pitching the vessel about, and a stiff breeze blowing, a firework factory would seem a safer asylum than the cabin of a fishing smack when the cooking fire is at full blast. I remarked to Mr. Fludyer that, in my opinion, the peril of keeping a fire going in such a crowded little place exceeded the advantages to be derived from it. "Indeed," said I, "if you will pardon me for saying as much, well wrapped as you are, I find it hard to believe that the entire abolition of your stove would cause you much inconvenience. To be sure, toiling all night, it is necessary that you should have refreshment; but would not a bit of cold meat and a draught of beer from a bottle meet all such requirements?"

But Mr. Fludyer good-naturedly shook his head. "You don't understand matters," said he; "how should you, when belike you never had on a wetter shirt than you caught in a shower of rain, nor were forced to fish for your supper? Part of our wages is our lot of victuals aboard. I don't speak for myself, but take the case of my chaps. More likely than not, since dinner-time they haven't eaten a bit. Well, we bring aboard food for the night, and enough of it, you may be sure, since the price of it is taken out of the bag before the taking is shared. We aren't allowed meat, but we are allowed bread ar.d butter and coffee and sugar. I dare say we might have the value of coffee in beer, but how far would that go? Besides, the men like the hot coffee—and so will *you,* I'll lay a farden cake, come about one in the morning. Well, as I said before, we aren't allowed meat, but of our fish we have the pick. Did you ever eat a sole cooked wet out of the sea? No! Well, maybe we'll give you that treat too. Talk about doing away with our bit of fire, why, what should we do without it in the winter time, when we are far out fishing for herrings? We aren't like sailors aboard big ships with their snug berths to turn into; we might as well be on a raft as on that deck of ours, and we are right in the teeth of the weather constantly. Come to face it hour after hour, in a pelting snow perhaps, with a slippery floor and sails hard and brittle as glass to the touch, and ropes that cut your hands as you haul 'em in, *that's* when you love the bit of fire and the snug shelter it stands in!" And Mr. Fludyer, unconscious of the gratitude that was illuminating his countenance, affectionately stirred the glowing coals with the toe of one of his monstrous sea-boots.

By eleven o'clock we were about eight miles from land, and coming on deck we found that the nets were put out. It was very dark now, so that it was necessary for the men to work by lantern-light. By-the-way, it was curious to observe, as regards this same lantern, that modern improvement in candle-making is recognized and appreciated even amongst these slow folk; and, instead of the red-nosed, dim, old-fashioned "dip," a slender mould graced its socket. Such candles, Mr. Fludyer assured me, were now universally used on board the various craft, and were found to be cheaper in the long run.

The recovery from the sea of the fishing net, and the hauling of it up on to the deck, is managed by means of a long iron shod pole, called a trawl, and a small windlass fixed at the bows of the vessel, the net rope encircling the barrel as the handle is turned. In about an hour Mr. Fludyer gave the signal for "hauling in," and, all-expectant, I stood by with him as he held the lantern, eager to see what luck Neptune had sent us. The length of time occupied in winding in the ropes was significant of the depth of water beneath us. Clink, clink, clink. It seemed that the net would never be wound up, when, all unexpected, an end of it appeared in sight, and was promptly taken in hand, and lugged in by great armsful. But there was no sign of fish. Brown net, brown net, brown net, until quite a great heap of it was accumulated ; but not so much as a dab or a flounder. I thought it time, and only an act of friendliness, to condole with Mr. Fludyer. "No luck this time," 1 remarked. "That's more than you can tell," replied the fisherman blithely, "we won't holler before we're hurt," and just as he spoke in came the catch.

It never occurred to me that the fish that were taken would naturally retreat to the extremity of the net—to the remotest corner of it—and the last to be drawn in. Such was the case, however. I was astonished at the quantity of what Mr. Fludyer called " muck" that was brought up with the haul of mixed fish, and amongst which they flapped and wriggled. All manner of strange coarse sea-weed, and slimy green vegetable growth from the ocean floor the "ground rope" had dragged, with stones, and mud, and the broken skeleton of some long fish picked bare by aqueous monsters that had not spared even the eyes in the pearly white skull—all these came up with the catch, which to a man, the fountain-head of whose piscine knowledge had been hitherto a fishmonger's shop, was a curious spectacle to contemplate. I never dreamt that fish—common fish, such as one is in the daily habit of seeing dished at table —were so splendid as regards brilliance and variety of colour. There were struggling in the net's meshes three great jolterheaded fish of the species known as salmon bream. They were at their last gasp, poor fellows, and their wide-open, goggle eyes and enormous puckered mouths sufficiently expressed the horror and astonishment that filled them; but what might suitably be called their plumage was gorgeous beyond description. Burnished gold was but as lead compared with the dazzling shades of chrome and orange that went towards the embellishment of the fishes' scaly armour, all spangled with glowing specks of emerald and ruby turquoise. These, however, were secrets of the ocean with which dull-eyed men may not grow familiar. Even as the bream drew their last breath, and waved a glittering farewell to life with their eloquent tails, their jewels paled in the lantern-light and became mere fish-scales. Even the plainest of fish look curiously handsome taken alive from the sea—all except the skate tribe. The gentle reader, although he may never have eaten of this poor man's fish, may have seen it exposed for sale—a grotesque creature, with the body of a huge plaice and several whip-like tails, and a face like—well, I scarcely know how to describe the face, and will only remark that rude fishermen have another name for the skate—" old maids." There are a pair of eyes to the face of the skate, and the semblance of a human nose, and a sourly-curved lipped mouth set with spiky teeth; and it is not a pretty sight to see the fish, which seems very tenacious of life, curl and wriggle its many tails, and gnash its spiky teeth, and wink its eyes.

Thirteen soles, a small turbot, three salmon bream, two skate, and about a dozen and a half of "dabs," comprised Mr. Fludyer's first haul, and with it he appeared to be contented. The nets were clear of the rubbish with which they were fouled and cast in anew, and the fish thrown into the well. "Now we will have a bit of something to eat," suggested Mr. Fludyer, and selecting a couple of pairs of the finest soles he disappeared below, telling me that he would call me when supper was ready. He did so, and sitting down on the cabin floor, with one of the bunks before mentioned for a table, with no table-cloth, with a small yellow pie-dish in lieu of a plate, and a two-pronged iron fork to feed myself with, I sat down to the most delicious fish supper it was ever my good fortune to be present at. The fried fish lying in the yellow crockery looked not a bit like soles, being still enveloped in their tan-coloured skin, and rolled up as one may roll up a sheet of paper. They were, moreover, cooked in bacon-fat, which Mr. Fludyer declared was better than anything else for the purpose, and far superior to lard, or even fresh butter. I inquired how he had contrived to roll up the fish, and he replied that he had had no hand in that—that they had rolled themselves up, and that they always did so if put in the pan as soon as they were dead, but before they "grew cold." Anyhow, I never tasted such soles—indeed, I doubt if such are to be tasted, except in a fishing-boat at night, ten miles out at sea, with an appetising breeze blowing.

Going on deck we made another haul in, but with no great amount of success, all the fish that came to land consisting of seven soles and a brill, and about half a peck of flounders. There was another fish, a splendid-looking fellow, larger than a salmon bream; but soon as Mr. Fludyer caught sight of it, he seized it dexterously beyond the gills, and with a most vengeful expression of countenance rammed its head against the side of the vessel, very effectually breaking its neck, after which he flung it back into the sea.

"Why did you do that?" I asked. "Isn't he good to eat?"

"He's good to eat other fish, blarm him, and to tear the net, too; that was a dog-fish," explained the fisherman.

Once more the nets were cast in, all in the pitchy dark, and barely was this accomplished when startlingly close at hand came the sound of a human voice singing out "Ahoy!" and right in our path a bigger vessel than ours appeared distinctly visible. Quick as thought one of the men skipped down into the cabin and re-appeared bearing in his hand the turpentine can before mentioned. There was a bung in the can, and a stick running through it; and when the bung was withdrawn, it appeared that some substance like tow was wound round the end of the stick that lay saturating in the fiery liquid. To the tow the man applied a match, and in an instant there was a great white glare at the end of the stick, which was held over the side, plainly denoting our position to the approaching ship.

Next haul we had better luck, and yet better still in our sixth and seventh, which was the last, and by 5 a.m. we were back to our starting point, Within half an hour of that time our catch was landed in bushels, and, partitioned into lots, was turned out on to the beach, where the fish-buyers were eagerly assembled. It was knocked down by the auctioneer to the various bidders, the whole realizing the not immense sum of one pound seventeen shillings.

AT A SUGAR BAKING. TO EGARDING the mild and innocent-looking sugar-lump,--so pure, and bright, and sparkling, it is by no means easy to believe how its production can involve any prodigious amount of hard labour and man-sweating; so it is, however. Accidentally it came to my knowledge just recently that the manufacture of the saccharine luxury—a branch of trade of considerable importance, and providing with employment several thousand men at the east-end of London alone—was looked on, on account of its excessive hardship, with such dislike, that even that pattern of patient drudgery, the Irish labourer, could by no sort of persuasion be brought to undertake it. I was credibly informed that the bribe offered had taken even the seductive form of beer unlimited; but that still, marvellous to relate, the Emerald Islander remained obdurate, and the sugarbakers were compelled, as has ever been the case, to resort for "hands" to the German labour market. There appeared to me something so unaccountable about this last feature of the business, that I resolved to go and find how it came about.

I cannot give the name of the bakery selected, as I have clean forgotten it; but the reader will be at no loss on that score, since I was given to understand that one system regulates the business, and that one bakery is as much like another as peas of a pod. It is by no means a hole-and-corner business, as one might be led to imagine it was, judging from the rare occasions of its being brought under public notice. In the neighbourhood of Back-church-Lane, in Whitechapel, there are dozens of these baking, or, as they would more properly be called, boiling-houses. They are buildings enormous in size, usually occupying the whole of a street side, and so high that the massy "mats" of sugar craned up to the topmost story, and there dangling from its chains, looks no bigger or more substantial than a fishmonger's rush-basket that the wind might blow away.

A kind-hearted German missionary was my companion, and soon as I put my head in at the door of the bakery, the nature of the manufacture in progress was at once made apparent to my senses. Just as unmeasured indulgence in sugar is nauseating to the palate, so was the reek of it palling to one's sense of smell. You could taste its clammy sweetness on the lips just as the salt of the sea may be so discovered while the ocean is yet a mile away.

It was a sort of handy outer warehouse, that to which we were first introduced—a low-roofed, dismal place with grated windows, and here and there a foggy little gas-jet burning blear-eyed against the wall. The walls were black—not painted black. As far as one might judge they were bare brick, but "basted" unceasingly by the luscious steam that enveloped the place, they had become coated with a thick preserve of sugar and grime. The floor was black, and all corrugated and hard, like a public thoroughfare after a shower and then a frost. The roof was black, and pendent from the great supporting posts and balks of timber were sooty, glistening icicles and exudings like those of the gum-tree. "Sugar, sugar everywhere, but not a bit to eat." Exactly the Bogeydom to which should be consigned for a term, according to the degree of their iniquity, the owners of larcenous little fingers so persistent in their attacks on the domestic sugar-basin. At the extremity of this gloomy cave, and glowing duskily at the mouth of a narrow passage, was dimly visible a gigantic globular structure in bright copper, and hovering about it a creature with bare arms and chest all grizzly-haired, with a long bright rod of iron in his grasp, which incessantly he waved about the mighty caldron; this was doubtless the Sugar Ogre himself, in waiting for juvenile delinquents.

Being in no dread of the ogre, however, we approached him, and discovered him to be a very civil fellow, quietly minding his business. The copper structure above-mentioned proved to be nothing more necromantic than a gigantic pan, in which were, gently seething, ten tons of liquid sugar. The vessel was all covered in, and looked as compact as an orange, the shape of which fruit it resembles; but in the side of it there was a small disc of glass, and looking through it one could get a glimpse of the bubbling straw-coloured mass within. The iron rod the guardian of the pan called a "key," if I rightly remember, and his sole occupation appeared to consist in dipping it in at a little hole in the vessel's side, and withdrawing it again, along with a little blob of melted sugar, which he took between his finger and thumb, and drew out and examined by the light of the gas.

From this we were conducted to the factory where the manufacturers of moist sugar were working. It may appear strange to the reader that the term "manufacture" should be applied to what every schoolboy knows to be a natural production, but it is by no means an incorrect term notwithstanding. Some sugars are prepared at the place of their growth, and sent here ready for immediate use; but the great bulk of it is exported in a very rough state, dense, strong smelling, and of the colour of mahogany, and before it can be brought to assume the bright and inviting appearance it bears when ticketed in the grocer's window it has to undergo much torture by fire and machinery.

It was not a nice-looking place that to which we were introduced. It was not a pleasant way that led to it, inasmuch as it was in an underground direction, and through passages gloomy, low-roofed, and narrow, and lit with gas just enough to show all manner of wriggling and revolving machinery overhead and threading the walls. Down we went, however—our conductor kindly making the passage safer by illumining it by means of an old newspaper hastily twisted into a torch, and there we were in full view of the makers of moist sugar.

The fullest possible view under the circumstances it should have been written, for a clear view was impossible; which, as we presently discovered, was a matter to be thankful for rather than to regret; horrors bursting suddenly on the unprepared vision have a bad effect sometimes. The place was nothing but a vast cellar underground, and lit from without only by a window here and there high up where the street pavement was, and as closely grated as though it were an object to keep flies 'out of the factory. The heat was sickening and oppressive, and an unctuous steam, thick and foggy, filled the cellar from end to end. Presently, however, when one's eyes grew somewhat accustomed to the gloom, a spectacle of a novel and startling character was presented. Seeming, as it were, to grow out of the dense haze, busy figures appeared. Black and white figures running about, and flitting and skipping in the most extraordinary manner. Watching the figures, however, they were presently discovered to be men in a condition of at least semi-nudity. On one side of the cellar were two gigantic pans of sugar, melted and hot and smoking, and out of these the labourers, naked but for a covering for their legs and some sort of apron, and their bodies bathed in sweat, and their fair hair reeking and hanging lank about their wan faces, scooped up the liquor into the pails, that would contain half a hundredweight, and hurried across the cellar to deposit it in vast revolving basins set in motion at lightning speed by machinery, and where the brown sugar was bleached and dried, to be presently shovelled out and added to the great heap that reached high nearly as the ceiling. Regarding the close, reeking, stifling place, the disgusting atmosphere, the incessant toil (machinery will not wait), and the disgusting conditions of it, the validity of the Irish labourer's objection became manifest; better a hod of bricks with a sixty-round ladder to mount out in the open air than such mean, enervating drudgery as this. "They'd be dead without their beer unlimited," remarked our guide. "And does it not hurt them?" "Well, it helps to knock them off, I dare say." So that it amounts to the same thing, only that the unlimited beer-drinker of the sugar bakery has the advantage of lengthy dying.

Out of this cellar and through others similarly occupied, and then upstairs, and here to be sure was another strange sight. This was a branch of the loaf-sugar department. It was an extensive floor, a hundred feet by seventy probably, and covering the whole of it were packed loaf-sugar moulds as closely as the cells of a beehive are arranged. The moulds were stuck point downwards into earthen jars that at once upheld them and served as receptacles for their "drainings." I do not understand the process that was then operating, but what was to be seen was a dozen men of the semi-naked sort like those below crawling like frogs over the surface of the sugar moulds, getting foot and hand hold on the edges, some with a sort of engine hose squirting a transparent liquor into the moulds, and others stirring the thick stuff constantly in the latter with their hands. "I should imagine that you were not mucfi addicted to the consumption of sugar," I remarked to our guide. "I can never taste it; it has no taste, no more has nothing for me," he answered; and one could easily understand how that happened.

Upstairs, again, up crystallized stairs, with "toffee" for a handrail and hardbake to knock your head against if you were not aware of impending beams, to a room likewise full of moulds (they turn out twelve thousand loaves a week at this establishment), but where the greatest novelty to the eye of the uninitiated are many heaps of what in appearance is the exact counterpart of mud off the public roads. It was not so, however, as the guide explained it; it was merely the scrapings of beams and the shovellings of floors, and gangways, and workshops, and it was intended for filtration through charcoal, after which it would be deemed worthy to take its place as a marketable commodity.

Upstairs again—the place seemed to grow hotter the higher we climbed; and here was the "filling" department—the place where the moulds were filled with liquid sugar, that flowed out of great taps. This, it seemed, was the hardest part of the sugar-baking business. Like every hand in the establishment, with the exception of the foreman and overlookers, the labourers here were midway nude (the disgusting practice is evidently one of habit rather than necessity amongst German sugarbakers; we saw in one room—a comparatively cool room—half a dozen fellows squatted down engaged in the not over-heating occupation of painting moulds, but they were as naked as the rest). The moulds, as we were informed, when filled with the melted sugar, weigh a hundredweight and a half, and the liquid, as it runs, is hot. The task to be performed is to fill the moulds at the taps and carry them across the great warehouses and arrange them close together for "setting," each in its own jar in the manner already described. A gang of a dozen or so are so employed, and as the work is piece work, hurry is the order of the day. But hurry is not easy with a hundredweight and a half of sloppy hot sugar to carry in an inconvenient vessel, and the result is that as they shuffle off in line with their loads there are many lurches, and stumblings, and elbowings, and the contents of the moulds hugged to the chest slop over the naked bodies of the carriers, and then harden and crust to a coat, doubtless as inconvenient to wear as it is disgusting to behold.

No wonder that the poor wretches so employed drink much beer. With no more exertion than leisurely walking about demanded, before I had been in the factory a quarter of an hour, I was drenched with perspiration, and was not a moment free from a trickling down my face. To be sure, since indulgence in beer assists the sugar-baker in his work it is commendable in the master to provide it. But, as I am informed, it is in his power to carry his kindness a step further—he can abridge the sugar-baker's labouring hours. The poor fellow's wages are quite as low as those of the Irish hodman, but, unlike the last-mentioned, he knows nothing of a "nine hours" law. The sugar-baker works all hours. What he calls a fair day's work is twelve hours, but it is not rare for him to be kept at the slavery above described for sixteen, and even eighteen hours—from three o'clock in the morning till eight at night—without a penny of overtime or extra, pay. He cannot help himself. If he leaves one factory he must enter another exactly similar. It is a sight, I am told, to meet a group of the poor fellows just hurried from their beds, and making haste to their work at three o'clock of a winter's morning. Unrested, shivering, pale, and agueish, they are eager to get back to the heat and the beer; they need "warming up," as they say, and that object effected, they manage to potter through the weary day somehow, and then they shuffle home to bed, and so on between Sunday and Saturday. The only time, my good missionary friend informed me—and he should know—when you can catch sight of a sugar-baker neither abed nor at work is on a Sunday afternoon, when he enjoys the luxury of idleness and a pipe at his own door or window, AT THE "TURNSPIT," QUAKER'S ALLEY. HE ticket read as follows:— RATS! RATS! RATS!

On Monday, the, the Canine Fancy may make sure of a treat by dropping in at Billy Skunko's, The Turnspit, Quaker's Alley, Somers Town. Rats in the pit at Half-past Eight precisely. Previous to the above entertainment, Mr. Chitley will sing his (inch Peeler against Edward the Topyob's celebrated bird, for a pound a side. Cages uncovered at Eight. Plenty of rats on this occasion, with squeakers for youngsters and shy 'uns. After the sports a harmonic meeting, with The Renowned Billy Himself In The Chair.

The gentleman who kindly furnished me.with the above document (which was at once a programme of the entertainments and an order of admission) being doubtless of opinion that a person of my evident ratty tendencies would experience no difficulty in the matter, simply informed rne that "the 'Spit was somewhere nigh the Brill," and that Quaker's Alley was in the same delectable neighbourhood. I had previously heard of the "Brill"—indeed, knew my way to that imposing palace of gin and bitters tolerably well. So thitherward, in the first place, I inclined my steps, and then came to a halt, that I might inquire of some likely-looking wayfarer whereabouts was the "'Spit."

Advancing at a hurried pace from a dark and dirty little street immediately before me, came an individual whose oily locks and neckerchief stamped him as of the "fancy;" and if further confirmation were required, there it was in shape of a square little parcel neatly tied in a cloth, and carefully tucked under his arm.

"Which is Quaker's Alley, my friend?"

"On a-'ead, and the fift to the left. I'm a goin' there."

"So am I."

"Wuth your while. Wuth anybody's while. Got anythink?" "How do you mean?"

"What are you going to Billy's for?—to kill or sing, or only to look on and do a bit of tebbing if you sees a openin'?"

I certainly was not going to Billy's to "kill," nor to sing unless on compulsion, and not having the least idea what "tebbing" was, I was likely to miss my chance of making a bit at it, though the opening that revealed it was never so large. So I replied to my friend that until I saw how matters went at Skunko's, I wasn't sure what I should do.

"I'll tell you what you *mustn't* do, or you'll blue all the stuff (lose all the money) you've got with you," remarked my friend confidentially—"you mustn't lay as much as a oat on Chitley's finch."

"What makes you think so?"

"What makes me? AVhy, common sense makes me. Havin' eyes in my 'ead makes me. He's a cur, that's what Chitley's finch is. He'll keep it going like steam when there's nothing great brought agin him; but show him a out-and-out battler like the Topyob's, and he's down on the knuckle bone before you've chalked five to him."

"That's one side of the question," I replied, deeming it prudent, even at a trifling pecuniary sacrifice, to affect some acquaintance with the subject. "What's the odds against Chitley's finch?"

"'Taint odds at all; it's evens. What I'm a tellin' you is on the quiet. How-somever, I'll go you a half-dollar level if you're a-mind."

Of course I was a-mind, and we shook hands on the wager. 'My name's Chick," said he proudly, "don't you make no mistake. I'm good for half-a-dollar or a fiver either." After this Mr. Chick, who evidently regarded my half crown as already bagged, became more chatty than ever. The conversation turned on chaffinches, and he gave me the history of the one imprisoned in his pocket-handkerchief. It was good at "pegging," he informed me, but had no heart for match singing. As I gleaned from Mr. Chick, pegging is a rural pas-time, and one not without attractive fea-tures to persons eager in the pursuit and capture of wild creatures. First of all, you require a pegging finch, which sim-ply means a chaffinch that has been trained to preserve his equanimity and disposition to sing under the most for-eign and singular circumstances. "A good pegger," said Mr. Chick, "should be able to make hisself at home any-where, and pipe up at word of command as well when carried in the jacket pock-et as when hanging quiet agin the wall. Dark or light should make no difference to him, nor carrying about, nor nothink. " When your chaffinch is educated to this pitch of perfection, he is fit for the pegging business. When you set out, however, on a bird-catching expedition, you will require besides (your "pegger" in his little cage being enveloped in a thick handkerchief) a stuffed bird of the same species mounted on a stick, at one end of which there is a spike and some slips of whalebone somewhat thinner than a pipe-stem, and each with a spike at the end; and some good bird-lime in a tin box.

So equipped, you take to the country, and stroll through the pleasant lanes un-til you hear the peculiar note of a chaffinch in a neighbouring tree. Your pegger in his prison hears as quickly as you do—more, quickly, probably—and at once opens his pipes and lets out a loud-sounding challenge. It was only the love-call (as Mr. Chick expressed it) that the bird in the tree previously had uttered, but, hearing the strange clarion, at once replied as a bold bird should—as a jealous, loving husband should,'who, after no end of fighting and fierce contention, has secured to his spouse a poplar tree all to herself, and suddenly is made aware of some sweet-throated rival approaching its sacred precincts. There is an exchange of vol-leys, and then the bird-catcher makes his little arrangements. His experienced eye discovers the tree in which the terri-ble little Blue Beard, or rather blue-beak is, and in the trunk of it he sticks the pointed end of the stick the stuffed bird is mounted on, so that it stands out fair in view. Then he anoints his whalebone slips plentifully with bird-lime, and fix-es them likewise in the tree's trunk, two just above and two just below the stuffed bird. Then he places his pegging finch, in its enveloped cage at the foot of the tree, strewing a handful of grass over it. Now he can retire from the spot and leave the dispute to be settled be-tween the two live finches and the stuffed one.

The contest is of short duration. Banging their musical artillery at each other, each moment faster and more fu-rious, the free bird flies about and darts from tree to tree and from bough to bough, bent on discovering the insolent invader of his domestic peace and tak-ing signal vengeance on him. Presently he spies him, or rather he imagines that he does; but, instead of the aggressor, it is only the innocent dummy. Jealousy, however, is blind as love itself, and swift as an arrow the brave chaffinch swoops down, alas! to find himself en-tangled amongst the whalebone slips, the treacherous smearing on which holds him fast, or, if he is strong enough to bring them down, it is only to run screaming along hampered by the cruel skewers, until the bird-catcher comes and makes the capture sure. As many as twenty prime singing chaffinches (of course it is only the males who are thus lured) may be thus captured in a single morning.

By the time that Mr. Chick finished his interesting disserta tion on the art of chaffinch snaring, we arrived at the Turnspit" an ill-looking little beershop, smelling villanously of dogs and birds and stale tobacco and beer-slopped-sawdust. The bar was a small one, but the parlour behind, where the Skunko family lived and ate (and slept, too, if the presence of a press bedstead might be taken as evidence), was opened to it and appropriate to its ordinary use. Un-der a table was a heap of pots and cans awaiting the necessary process of scrub-bing, and on the table were bottles and measures, and other implements of the beer-retailer's tra,de. Round the walls were ranged stuffed birds, and stuffed dogs, and pictures of fighting men in every imaginable attitude of difficulty, and a picture effectively coloured of the "man-mungoose," who, with his hands tied behind him, fought fifty rats in a pit by biting them to death. Dog collars and leashes and muzzles and bird-cages made up the remainder of the decora-tions. Mr. Skunko and his wife and el-dest daughter were at tea in the parlour, and on the rug before the fire were sev-eral canine treasures, including a long-suffering looking shaven French poo-dle, the ears of which a Skunko baby was viciously gnawing as it sprawled on the ground.

Not knowing exactly to what part of the premises my order gave me admis-sion, I pushed open the first door I came to. A glance convinced me that this was neither the ratting nor finch-singing de-partment; but it was worth a peep, as showing to what degrading shifts and inconveniences men will submit rather than forego their hobbies. The room in question was a nasty little place fitted as a taproom, but it also served as a washhouse for dogs, and the washing at that moment was in progress. One animal, an enormous fellow of the retriever cross-breed, had undergone the ordeal of the suds, and now was reclining on a long board before the fire, while a dog-barber combed and curled its hair. Another dog, however, was at present in hot water, and whining and shivering on a table, while the potman rubbed and scrubbed him, splashing and slopping, and filling the evil little den with unwholesome steam; there, however, dimly visible through the mist, sat half-a-dozen gentlemen of the fancy, calmly smoking their pipes and sipping beer, and discoursing of birds and dogs and rats.

It was in an apartment adjoining that the singing match was to take place, and preparations were being made for it as I entered. Since I have something besides to tell of, and space is precious, I may not enter at length into the particulars of the chaffinch conflict. The room, which was capable of accommodating about sixty persons, was full, and at least half of those present were smoking; nevertheless, the rival songsters hung facing each other on opposite walls, gave their notes with full throats, answering each other just as Mr. Chick described the caged bird and the free one answering each other at a pegging bout; while a well-trusted authority sat at a table and made a chalk mark on it whenever Mr. Chitley's bird or the Topyob's (the mysterious cognomen of this last-mentioned personage, to my disgust, I afterwards discovered was merely "potboy" disguised in what is known in certain circles as "backslang") uttered a note; and finally, as Mr. Chick had predicted, Mr. Chitley lost.

"Now, gentlemen," exclaimed Mr. Skunko, "the preserves is open and the game laws is suspended for this night only." At which little pleasantry everybody laughed, and in a mob followed their host to the rear of the premises.

Out at the back door, across the yard, and into another horrible-smelling building, which, soon as Mr. Skunko lit a glaring gas jet, was revealed the skittle ground of the establishment. Likewise it was the storehouse of Mr. Skunko's canine stock-in-trade. Round about the walls were tubs and kennels and railed boxes, and, startled by the incoming of so many strangers, instantly there was a clanking of dog chains and such a chorus of dog music as I had not heard since my visit to the Home at Battersea. With mastiffs and yard dogs and terriers and bandy, blear-eyed bulldogs grinning in malice, and madly struggling against their collars to get at the legs of Mr. Skunko's guests, I was delighted to hear his cheerful assurance, as he went first with the light, that there was no danger "if we didn't get a joshlin' and scrouging within their reach."

The rat pit was on the frame of the skittle-alley, with boards placed round about breast high. Here we were out of reach of the dogs, and at the end was a sort of raised platform for the more favoured of the company. On a great bunk at hand were several iron-wire cages of rats smelling their doom, and squeaking and scratching to get out; and over these Mr. Skunko presided. Round about the pit were the fanciers who meant to test the killing powers of their dogs, and who carried the pets hugged in their arms.

"Let me have half a dozen, Billy," exclaimed a customer; and at once Billy opened the stocking-leg mouth of a rat cage, and fearlessly plunging his hand into the vermin nest plucked out by their long tails, one after another, six rats, flinging them, as it seemed to me, with unnecessary force into the pit. Instantly the customer dropped his dog over the barricade, and the work of slaughter began, the spectators yelling encouragement to the plucky little terrier, and banging the boards of the pit with their hands and feet to startle back any maddening wretch of a rat that sought so to escape from the inexorable jaws of "Wix," which, as I understood, was a handy abbreviation of "Wixen." In three minutes there remained in the pit six still rats, a few waifs of bloody fur, and a dog licking his lips.

Then came another customer and six more rats. Then a gentleman well known in the pigeon-flying interest, with a new dog he was mighty proud of, and ordered a dozen rats for him all at once. But the pride of the pigeon-fancier was doomed to suffer; the dog was even more afraid than were the rats, and ran away from them, whereat the spectators banged the boards in derision, and made such ridicule of the poor dog and its owner that the latter presently grew furious, and vaulting into the pit snatched up the rats and shook them in the dog's face, at the same time calling it all manner of horrible names for its cowardice. But the dog wouldn't bite, and being enjoined by Mr. Skunko that he was "cuttin' time to waste," the pigeonflyer stamped on all the rats, and, fetching his dog a kick, sent it howling over the heads of the audience into the middle of the skittle-ground.

The next customer had a very young dog that he wasn't sure of, so he ordered for it a rat with the " teeth drawed." Except from the mouth of a mad dog it is difficult to imagine a more ticklish bit of dentistry than that of extracting the incisors of a full-grown rat. But, to my astonishment, Mr. Skunko made light of the job. Catching the creature somehow by the throat, he forced open its mouth, and, as far as I could see, with no other implement than his strong thumb-nail, wrenched out as many teeth as he pleased, and then flung the poor mutilated rat into the pit to be mumbled and worried by the savage puppy—the result so pleasing the puppyowner, that the toothdrawing process was repeated again and again..

So the "sports" proceeded until the floor of the pit was stained red, and as many dead rats as would fill a bushel basket were heaped up by the cages. The best of the customers served, came those of the humbler sort—hard-up and out-o'work men, who had stinted themselves of beer even all the evening that they might reserve fourpence to buy a rat to show their dog off. It was very curious to hear these customers begging for a " whacker, one what'll want facing," for their fourpence, and watch their eager faces craning over the pit's edge as they joyously clapped their hands and laughed aloud to see their beauty pin the "warmint". Equally curious was it to see the utterly penniless fancier, with his cur under his arm, excited by the sport till he had lost his shame of beggary, going about inquiring imploringly, " Who'll give my dawg a rat? who'll be a penny to'rds my dawg havin' a rat?" and all the while his hungry stomach would be grateful for a pen'orth of bread.

By ten o'clock I had seen so much of the "Renowned Billy" at the pit, that I had no heart left for viewing him in the harmonic "cheer" he was presently to fill, and so I came away.

THE MISCALLED "HORSE" MARKET.

P to a very recent period it was my settled opinion that the individual taken in over the purchase of a horse was, of all victims to barter and bargaining, least to be pitied.

Again and still again, for the hundredth time, do such cases figure in the newspapers police reports, showing how that "in answer to an advertisement" or " in consequence of the representations of the prisoner, of whom he had no previous knowledge," the credulous prosecutor was induced to part with his money, receiving as its equivalent what to all appearance is a sound, serviceable quadruped, perfect in wind and limb, but which, soon as the vamping has worn off, appears a wretched imposition wrapped in horse hide: spavined, ring-boned, and a roarer, and afflicted with aches and incurable afflictions, numerous almost as the matchless qualities it was warranted the possessor of. Nevertheless, rascally as may be the Jeremy Diddler who swindles the poor man, the behaviour of the latter through the transaction of which he complains is so inconceivably stupid—(it is marvellous what an assistance towards detecting the short-sightedness of others is the spectacles of fact revealed astride our own acute organ of scent!)—as almost to provoke one to exclaim, "Serve him right." Serve him right, in the first place, for being so weak as to swallow the horse" coper's flimsy "reasons" for disposing of the animal at such a ridiculously low price; and in the second, for affecting a holeand-corner method of dealing in the affair without the least excuse. Supposing that he wanted to buy a bullock instead of a horse, would he go hunting about in obscure places for one? would he listen to the rigmarole of a drover as to a bullock "he knew the property of a grazier, who had no further use for it," or of a cattle dealer recently married and about to discontinue the keeping of it, his wife having objections? Not he. He would go straight to the public market where all is open and above-board, and he would select from a thousand in broad daylight, and bid and pay his money in confidence and security. And why not adopt the same plain plan as regards a horse? Is there not a public horse market as old established and wellknown as the market for sheep and horned cattle—subject, indeed, to similar regulations, tolled by the same toll-takers, officered by the same officers, who are constantly on the alert (assisted by the officers of the Society for the Prevention of Cruelty to Animals) to see that order and decorum are preserved, and that unsound and diseased horses are not smuggled in for sale?

Until recently such was my belief; and had I grown rich enough to buy ahorse at the market in Copenhagen Fields, thither I should have gone straight, uch, however, is my belief no longer. I have been to see, and I have no hesitation in declaring that a horse market—that is, a market where sound and capable horses of every degree are brought together for sale, as sheep and cattle are—has no existence. It is altogether a mistake to suppose that a man may go to the market at Islington on a Friday, which is called market day, and so that he has money enough in his pocket experience no more difficulty in the buying of a good horse than he would in the purchase of a heifer for killing. In a public horse mart it would not be astonishing to find rough customers as well as polite, just as there must of necessity be low as well as high-bred brutes on sale. It would be manifestly wrong to debar the hawker of turnip-tops and carrots from the privilege of buying or selling a quadruped, but why the costermongerly element should prevail to the total exclusion of every other is a mystery altogether incomprehensible to an ordinary mind. Old Smithfield had a bad name. When people talked about its reform—about mitigating the ruffianism, rampant there twice a week—other people replied, "It is of no use laying clean straw in a filthy sty. Smithfield *is* Smithfield, and never can be made better. Stay until we are enabled to erect a genteel market in the suburbs—everything handsome and spick and span, commodious enough to make jostling, let alone crushing and higgledy-piggledy uproar, inexcusable, well lit with gas, and with experienced officers in livery to enforce order and regularity. Then you shall see a difference."

And there are folks—folks high in office at corporation councils, and who really should know what they are talking aboutdeclaring that there is a difference. You may read their speeches on the subject, and gather from them that they regard the new market as a triumph and as a success beyond their fondest anticipations. According to recent testimony certain police magistrates share this opinion, and endeavour, by their tender dealings with hasty-handed drovers who happen in the heat of business to break a sheep's leg or gouge a refractory cow's eye out, to let meddling officials understand that the present condition of the market is all that can be desired, and that it would be better to wink at such trifling errors of judgment than drag them before a public tribunal.

This much, at least, may be said, that if the condition of Old Smithfield was worse than that of the present market—(I am speaking of the character of its Friday market)—it is a wonder that the citizens did not combine and drive the abomination from their midst years and years before they did so. As before observed, it is not a horse market in the broad and proper sense of the term at all. Creatures of the genus *equus* figure in it, it is true, but only of such sorts as are to be seen in the shafts of the vehicle that contains the stock of the small coal man, or of the night cab, or of the barrows and "shallows" and." half-carts" of hawkers of fish and green stuff. That nobody expects to find in the market animals superior to these is sufficiently proved by the fact that nobody but costermongers and other gentry of the hairy cap and belch er-neckerchief school finds attraction there.

Such a melancholy show do they— the ponies and horses— make, poor creatures, that it is satisfactory to observe such a scant gathering of them. It may arise from my partiality for the animal in question, but to my mind there is something peculiarly distressing in the fact of an old horse tied up for sale. Tethered to the boundary bar of the alley, he hangs his head till his ancient rounded nose touches it; and you may easily enough fancy his thick-lipped, bit-fretted mouth puckered, and his eyes half closed in dismal cogitation. A penny for his thoughts, poor old fellow, would be a good investment. Is it the first time he has been here? It is doubtful. His back is saddle-galled, and it is plain where the ill-fitting collar has wrung his shoulder, in spite of the cunning brown ointment with which the wound is plastered. His legs are thick and clumsy at the hocks, he is pot-bellied, and "worn out, worn out," is uttered from those cavernous jaws and hollow flanks. His mane is as thin and as painfully sleeked and plaited as that of a vain old woman, and it is a mercy that the respectable creature cannot see its tail, with its few remaining hairs ridiculously eked out with straw, so that the bald stump may not stare an intending customer out of countenance. "Woa, Merzepper I" exclaims a ruffian, fetching the old horse a clout with his whipstock. "I should ha' thought as how you'd ha' married a poleaxe afore this, Merzepper. Who brought him to the market this time, Jack?"

"Blest if I think that anybody brought him," replies Jack. "He comes here so reg'lar that if he found his stable-door open of a Friday, it's just as likely as not that he'd find his way here of hisself."

And that Mazeppa might not lose his share of the joke, Jack made a scientific cut at the old horse's flanks with his stinging whipthong, causing it to rouse suddenly out of its reverie with a clatter of its feet upon the stones. "Woa, blood!" laughs Jack, and passes on with his friend.

A little farther along was another animal of a totally different kind from the last-mentioned. The remnant of a high-bred creature this, with a small head and a nose so accurately set in a long and direct line of good breeding that Time itself cannot bow it. But it is deaf, as its still ears indicate, and its nearly closed eyelashes reveal two dull white lines. But the sense of smell remains constant to the veteran, and its red nostrils quiver as expressively almost as a plebeian horse's living optics. But it is old, wofully old. A well-bred horse makes the most unfortunate of old horses, for his hide will bear as much "doing up" and polishing and dressing as a poor old lady's satin gown, and until its fiery blood chills in death, a goad or the lash of a whip will rouse it instantly. This is the sort of horse that is always "as good as coin," as Jack's friend expresses it, as he pauses before it, and as I was glad to see, doing homage to a more respectable animal than himself by abstaining from giving it a cut. "What'll it fetch?" asked Jack's friend. "Under the 'ammer!" replied Jack, showing by a ticket tied to the high-mettled one's tail that it was to be disposed of at auction. "Why, under the 'ammer it'll fetch three quid (sovereigns)." "What's it good for?" "Well, it ain't the season, else I know what it 'ud do clipping for; it 'ud do for 'Ampstead 'Eath. He'd be as good as half a quid a day to a cove to let at a bob a 'our." Thank thy lucky stars, O "Lot 17—a brown gelding, faulty," that it is *not* the 'Ampstead 'Eath season, and that no uglier a customer than a man with a badge and a caped coat cries " three-pun'-flve " just before the auctioneer's hammer falls.

For be it known, the horses, and donkeys, and carts, and barrows are sold by auction as well as by private treaty, in the new market. The auctioneer's rostrum is a convenient canopied affair, with room within for the man of the hammer and his clerk. He is not a stuck-up, stiff-starched auctioneer, like many of his brethren, but is on familiar terms with the sinister brood that surrounds his pulpit, and he addresses as "Bill," the strong young man that runs, or rather drags, the poor unwilling brutes up and down that they may show their paces. "What! twenty-seven and six for a strong and useful horse! run him up again, Bill." "It's only got three legs, mister," exclaims one of his audience. "Quite enough, too, if he can run like that on 'em, Charley; put it at three, and give ten shillings a leg for him. Going for twenty-seven six! Why, it isn't twopence a pound! Going for twenty-seven six! Just the horse for a little greengrocer, and twenty-seven six only! Thirty shillings! going for thirty shillings, for the last time!" After this I saw four other horses sold, and the highest price realised was four pounds fifteen, from which fact the reader may derive some sort of idea as to the quality of the steeds submitted for sale at the London horse market.

It is a marvel that the owners of the wretched animals find it worth while to bring them there and pay market dues for their disposal—especially as, according to the beautifully bemuddled regulations, there is not the least occasion for their doing so—as, indeed, a considerable number of costermongers and barrow-men have been shrewd enough to discover. The broad road and pavement that surround the vast market place are to all intents and purposes as eligible ground for bargaindriving as within the gates, and there is nothing to pay for the privilege. There you may see them in long strings: horses, and donkeys, and ponies, and mules, with their heads and shoulders projecting over the public footpath, which is further impeded by the proprietors of the mangy row, each raising his ungentle voice in the praise of his own goods and in depreciation of his neighbours', which, together with the slashing of whips and the trampling of great boots out of the kennel on to the path—the roaring rage of unsuccessful negotiators, and the malicious laughter at and mockery of the rage—the yelling and shouting and mad

" hi-hi-ing " of the rabble in the road by way of " encouragement" towards any unlucky quadruped who is being run up and down in behalf of a may-be purchaser, all conduce to make the outside of the market much more lively and business-like than the inside.

But since the public take so unkindly to the horse market, it is a wonder that the authorities do not close it; they must be money out of pocket.

Quite so, gentle reader; but you do the corporation of the city of London less than justice if you suppose that they are so blind to their pecuniary interest as to let so much as a penny rust for want of turning. It is not the horse that pays; it is the rag business, and the old iron business, that bring in the money. It is not a horse market that is held every Friday at Copenhagen Fields; it is but a " marine store" market, and it would be only fitting if on that day the emblematic heads of bulls and calves were taken down from the gate, and black dolls hung in their place. Petticoat Lane, Rag Fair, the New Cut, and Great St. Andrew Street, are invited to bring their various wares, and they accept the invitation. Whether more questionable characters find encouragement, and are granted space on payment, I would not like to venture to say. Anyhow, there were two of the gentry known to policemen as "duffers," each mounted on a stand, and plying his trade of humbugging the shillings out of the pockets of the milksops about him by sleight-of-hand trickery, in the open market, and in full view of the market officials, who took not the slightest notice.

It is hard to say what may not be bought at this vast ragshop, facetiously called a horse market. Old harness, and stable utensils of every sort, with old wheels, and springs, and axletrees, and lengths of chain, and bars and bolts, one might expect to find; but beside these one may buy a blanket, or a bedquilt, or a bar of fancy soap, or a cock linnet, or a tinker's barrow (there were two of these), or a pair of second-hand boots or shoes, or a bed-wrench, or a pair of trousers, or " six white mice in a cage for a tanner!" or an entire suit of left-off volunteer uniform, or a goat, or a bull-dog, or an accordion. If ones wants were of so extraordinary a nature as to lead to an inquiry after an admiral's cocked hat, here it may be found, or a second suit of livery, or a cowl for a chimney-pot, or a dozen of staylaces, or a smutty pot or kettle.

AT A PENNY WEDDING. HPHE ancient parish church of St. Mildred-in-the-Marsh is situate in about as mean and miserable a neighbourhood as can be imagined. It lies.back but a little way from the shops and hucksters' stalls of a cheap and nasty market-place, and a shoeblack and a sweetstuff-seller have their unmolested stations on the steps of it. Out o' workers and hulkers lean their lazy shoulders against its pillars and smoke short pipes. If any one were to put to you the question at which of the London churches would you least like to be married, supposing you to be acquainted with the edifice in question, you would without hesitation reply "St. Mildred's-in-the-Marsh."

Yet, strange to relate, the number of marriages there celebrated are as ten to one compared with any other church for miles round. At most other churches a wedding is an uncommon event happening on a week-day—a spectacle calculated to cause an obstruction of the Queen's highway, and to excite much curiosity and commotion. Likewise, in most poor neighbourhoods there appears to exist considerable doubt and uncertainty as to whether the solemnization of marriage is a sight to which the public are admitted. Half the number of persons who hang about the gates and jostle and elbow to catch a glimpse of the bride, would enter the sacred edifice if they were clear as to their right to do so, but what with the church being only partially open, and the proud and haughty bearing of the bridegroom, who mounts the steps for all the world as if they were those of his own private mansion, and he was about to take up his blissful residence there for ever and ever, and the inhospitable and resentful countenance of the beadle, who scowls on the curious looker-on, and conducts himself generally as though he were the haughty one's footman, they are overawed, and meekly keep their places; only the more juvenile portion of the assemblage venturing to " take it out" of the bridegroom when he reappears, looking not unfrequently as though he had somehow mislaid his title to the family mansion, and would have given something considerable had he been permitted to escape, sheepish and perspiring, by a back way.

There is none of this nonsense of affectation about the majority of the customers of St. Mildred-in-the-Marsh, however. Neither going in or coming out can they be justly accused of sheepishness; indeed, they are, as a rule, cool and businesslike, as though, having paid a deposit on the purchase of a donkey or a handsome barrow, they were just going in with their witnesses to settle the bargain. It is no doubt a very shocking thing to say, but there can be no doubt that many of them enter on the solemn contract with no more elevated thought or feeling or consciousness of the tremendous responsibility they are about to undertake, than would accompany a transaction of the kind mentioned; and, as may easily be imagined, the most disastrous consequences may ensue. Overzeal is seriously to blame in this matter, of which the system pursued in the parish of St. Mildred furnishes an apt illustration.

The court and alley dwellers of St. Mildred may be reckoned in thousands, and amongst them the standard of morality as regards the institution of matrimony is of exactly the height of a broomstick, and no higher. Not that they despise the cere, mony, or are unwilling to engage in it, indeed—and as I have had occasion ere now to point out, once consummated they are curiously proud of it, and go to the expense of buying a frame in which to display the certificate which vouches for the fact, hanging it against the most conspicuous part 01 the chamber—under the clock being the spot preferred; but the marriage fee daunts them. There are two shillings for the banns, and ten or twelve for the parson, and a shilling for the pew-opener, and another for the beadle—(it is curious how the class of persons alluded to reckon on these two shillings as part and parcel of the marriage fees), fourteen or sixteen shillings in all, and for what? The costermonger has never money to waste on what in his heathenish eyes appear as luxuries. At the best of times, which of course is in the fruit season, he never has a pound to " chuck away," as he expresses it. He is too business-like and speculative for such a thing to happen— too fond of investing and laying out his money to the best advantage. If his pinnacle of joy could not be attained without the intervention of the "gentleman who puts the banns up," and the parson and his clerk, the operations would be submitted to with manly resignation; but since the lady is of a business-like turn of mind, and economical too, and with very little persuasion can be brought to see that sixteen shillings invested in four bushels of damsons will of a certainty yield a more ready profit than the same amount laid out in a bit of paper no bigger than your hand, why, no more can be said about it—except, of course, that it discovers a frightful depravity of morals which cannot be too persistently preached against.

Towards altering this detestable condition of affairs, certain good men of St. Mildred's have taken prompt and determined measures. They give the court and alley dwellers distinctly to understand that so far as they are concerned marriage fees are abolished, and that any Jack and Jill taking it into their heads have only to step round the corner, and give notice of banns— without a penny to pay—and three weeks afterwards they may march into church, and be made man and wife, and no one, not even the beadle or the pew-opener, will ask them for a farthing! And on the face of it, it would seem that such a scheme could not work otherwise than well, but in so serious a matter it is worth while to inquire somewhat deeper. Bad as the old system, "if you'll take me, why I'll take you," may be, there was this security about it: since the pair concerned had no other after-hold on each other, it was scarcely likely that they would come together until the woman was tolerably well assured of the ability of the man of her choice to maintain her in something like comfort, while he, unless, as is scarcely likely, he exercised less discrimination over the transaction than he would over the purchase of a sieve of gooseberries, would take care to acquaint himself with some particulars of the lady's character and temper. As a rule, of the two contracting parties she would be found to observe the greatest amount of shrewdness and caution, since the law, having no sympathy with such illegitimate business, leaves her pretty much to her own devices, and after their left-handed marriage is consummated, however obstinate and brutal her left-handed husband may prove, she has no other weapons wherewith to control and keep him in order—always supposing her to be the weaker vessel in a physical sense, which possibly in this case is a rule subject to very many exceptions—but kindly influences and persuasion. Breaking in on this condition of things comes the house-tohouse preacher, backed by the minister of the parish, offering to make any number of them who may feel inclined man and wife in the regular orthodox and legal fashion, without fee or reward, and no questions asked. "Don't say 'I am too shabby to appear at church to be married' "—(this I know to be the language of a well-intentioned City missionary, while urging the matter to a shilly-shallying pair who, as I believe my friend had grounds for suspecting, meditated coming together after the old and iniquitous method—" don't say 'How can Polly get married in her old print frock and with boots wanting soling and heeling; let her come as she is, and you come in your flannel jacket, you will be as welcome as if you came in silk and broadcloth." This may perhaps be no great temptation to hold out to the man, but since it without doubt is a temptation, it is as broad as it is long—and broader, as the Irish saying is. In Polly's case, while flash Jack, with his great throat encircled by a bird's-eye "Kingsman" of irresistible pattern, and the latest and most "nobby " invention in smoked pearl buttons adorning his fustian jacket, is urging his suit, Polly may be thinking, "Ah! it's all very well just now, Master Jackey; you're all a nice cove, and one as I should be proud on— if it lasted; but I've heard about your sort, and it ain't a lastin' sort. Bilin' hot love is werry well, only it has a way of bilin' over and puttin' the fire out, and then, my lad, it's no better than cold coffee for a gal so long as she likes to stay with you, and stand to the drinkin' of it." Or on the other hand, Jack may be a spooney big boy—(they mate at a frightfully early age in these parts)— all promise and bad prospects; in which case Polly, although she may like him very well, will certainly refuse to take up with him—at present, at least; she will wait awhile, until he has shown himself capable of earning as much money as his fellows. "If you're of the same mind then as now," says Polly, "why, I don't care if I do."

As before remarked, at this juncture in comes the offer to splice them creditably and legally at no expense whatever, and it furnishes sufficient reason for Polly to give her instant consent, whether Flash Jack or Spooney Jack be her suitor. "If he takes me for better or worse," she argues as regards F. J. , "why, he'll have to stick to me; it'll grow natural for him to stick to me if he's my reglar husband, and I'll have more hold on him to manage him f or, in the case of S. J., she will reason, "He ain't much now, poor fellow, but if I have him all square and 'spectable and with the 'lines' to show for it, it'll make him look sharp; anyhow, it's nobody's business but our own, and we'll rub along somehow, I'll warrant." And, to the delight of the good-natured conspirators who are the marriage-fees out of pocket, the bargain is struck and the banns published forthwith.

And Polly and Jack, provided she is not too prone on most trivial occasions to shake in his face, with scornful spite, the "lines" that bind him, may get along tolerably well. If it were proper at all that the balance should be turned in his favour, no better weight could effect the purpose than that embodied in the Seventh Commandment. It is in cases where this urging to get married in a decent and Christian manner is directed at a pack of scarce-grown boys and girls where the great mischief is to be feared. Everybody knows how mightily anxious young folk are to embark on the matrimonial ocean, without a thought as to the necessary outfit in the vicissitudes of the voyage, or its aim even: in such cases this offer of a free passage is peculiarly attractive. It is possible that they may accept it in much the same spirit as they would a present of a ticket for the play or a trip to Hampton Court, availing themselves of it at least quite as much out of love of pleasure and novelty as love of one another. If this be so, then the mischief sown is incalculable. "But," I think I hear my well-meaning friend the City missionary exclaim, "you are arguing in the dark; you have no idea of the profligacy which exists amongst these young folk, as you term them; but indeed they are shockingly old in vice. It is not to the single and absolutely free that we appeal, but to those, old or young, who should be married and are not. Surely you can confer no greater act of charity on such people than to bring them together and tie them by honest and Christians means?" No doubt this is for the most part true, and probably a great deal more might be urged on the one side; but as regards the other side I would be permitted to suggest that marriage is not invariably a cure for profligacy, and that before now it has been found inexpedient to couple together creatures of a kind simply on the broad principle that creatures of a kind should be coupled together, irrespective of their various vices and foibles; and further, although to hurry people hot from their beds of sin to engage in an experimental moral journey may be excusable—even though slightly injudicious—the holy altar of God's Church is scarcely an appropriate starting-post. And further still, in bringing about a marriage between the young people such as Polly and Jack, who, youthful as they are, are steeped as high as their necks in those vices which usually pertain to their elders, is it not possible that you are forging and rivetting Jack or Polly, as the case may be, to that very staple of iniquity by which he or she first fell, and from which either might presently have happily slipped away but for your interference? You may by your mistaken kindness have harmed both for that matter, since each in the first instance must have furnished ingredients that brought about the consummation you so deplore—ingredients which of themselves may be comparatively harmless, but which blended work wreck and ruin as surely as gunpowder. It is not unlikely that by-and-by, being free to do so, they might have parted company and returned to their original condition; but what if you weld them irrevocably?

A HOLIDAY WITH THE SEA-FISHERS. MESSRS. TINKER, TAILOR, and CANDLESTICKMAKER, respected brother toilers and gainers of bread by the sweat of your manly brow, to as many of you who, on a fair and sunshiny Saturday afternoon, standing in the proud and enviable position of men who have just concluded another of many satisfactory weeks' work, and have got the wages snugly buttoned in your breeches pocket to prove it, and who having deliberately argued the matter, have arrived at the sensible conclusion that a bit of a holiday is now your due, and that you mean "going in for it," this paper is in all good fellowship dedicated.

About the holiday! What is to be the extent of it, and where are you going to enjoy it? Is it your intention to join the party that has chartered the green-grocer's pleasure-van with the blue silk curtains and the pair of grays and piebald leader, which starts to-morrow (Sunday) morning at eleven o'clock precisely, from the "Three Cows," its destination being Epping Forest? Are you for boating it on the Lea, or for steaming to Greenwich, to disport in the park there and invest ninepence in tea with shrimps on the summit of One-Tree Hill? Are you bent on a day's jaunt with the missus in Wiggins' shaycart, along with Mr. and Mrs. W.? or shall Citizen Z. and a Putney tea-gardens partake of your patronage? Maybe there are many worse ways than either of those mentioned of spending a holiday; certainly there is at least one way that is both better and cheaper.

It must be observed, however, that this better and cheaper way demands the sacrifice of Monday as well as Sunday. "Then *that;'* I think I hear Mr. Candlestickmaker exclaim, "that settles the business. It is pull enough out of a man's bit of savings to spend a dozen or fifteen shillings on a Sunday, and it can't be done cheaper, if you only take the missus and the baby, go the cheapest way to work; but when it comes to wasting Monday, to say nothing of the extra spending, why, it can't be done. It may be all very well for chaps that can afford it—single chaps who carry all their cares and responsibilities under their hat, or for snobs who never on any account work on Monday; but with a respectable mechanic like myself it is different. I'm a sober man, and stick to my work, and if I for once in a while let the rope fall slack on a Sunday, I'll bet a penny that you find me hauling at it precious soon next morning towards fetching it all right and taut again. I'm bound to do it; I should very soon find my affairs in a tangle if I did not."

All very nice and proper, Mr. C, a very noble sentiment, and one in which Betsy your wife coincides. But did you never find—this between ourselves, of course—did you never find in footing it along the rigid line which, in your bumptious self-reliance, you chalk out for yourself, that you have obliterated the chalk mark to such an extent as to make it difficult to recover your way, when having gone the length of your before-hand measured tether you turn about for your starting-point? Did it never happen to you that when Wiggins, who is a fat and good-humoured man, and never such jolly company as when he is mellow, observed, " Come, let us have another sixpen'orth round before the ostler puts the mare in the shay; we don't kill a pig every day, Mr. Candlestickmaker "—did it never happen, I ask, that you have been led to consent solely out of your excellent opinion of yourself as a man utterly incapable of porcine slaughter for as many even as two days consecutively, and who consequently for the time being can afford to act generously towards himself, and that you have had that other glass of grog—ay, and another after that, just to keep the cold out, for by this time it is late in the evening, and chilly driving through the green lanes? Don't be ashamed to own to the weakness, Mr. C.; there is really very little sin in it. It is one of common perpetration. I can answer for myself, at all events. I am not of your guild, but I, as well as yourself, know a Wiggins, and have yielded to the pleasant villain's seduction many a time, and am still on the friendliest terms with him.

But there is this difference between us, Mr. Candlestickmaker. After an evening with Wiggins, for the life of me I cannot rise with the lark next morning. I am full of yawns and gapes, and have an ache in my head, and an unpleasant sensation at the pit of my stomach, and want of all things to lie still yet a while. But you are all right, Mr. C, or rather you would be, only that those detestable shrimps you had yesterday at tea at Greenwich, or the nasty smell of the river as you were coming home from Putney, or the disgusting indisposition of Mrs. Swigger in the greengrocer's pleasure-van during the homeward journey; or the damp grass on which you injudiciously sat down in Epping Forest, has quite upset you; and on waking at half-past five a.m., very little reflection convinces you that rather than carry such a sorry-looking face amongst your shopmates you had better lose a "quarter" and "pull yourself together a bit." And very much refreshed are you for that extra hour's sleep and that cup of tea of extra strength, and quite chirp and cheerful you set out for the shop after breakfast. But as ill-luck has it, just as you are turning the corner—thinking of nothing in the world but the day's work before you—whom do you run against but Mr. Tinker and Mr. Tailor, who were your companions of yesterday, and who strangely enough find themselves unaccountably "upset" as you were, so much so indeed that they began to grow alarmed, and when you encountered them they were on the way to your house to inquire if you likewise were a sufferer. Such tender solicitude must not pass unrecognized, especially as the "Three Crows," the house from which the van started, is close at hand, and the best beer in the neighbourhood is drawn at the "Three Crows," and at the rear of that hostel there is a good dry skittle-ground. And there goes your Monday, Mr. C, and there go several more shillings than you would care to tell Betsy of, when, still a little unsteady from the effect of those pernicious Greenwich shrimps, you return home at n p.m. with a peace-offering in a little bottle in your pocket.

I won't inquire the number of shillings invested at the "Crows" or the gross amount of them and the twelve or fifteen shillings spent on Sunday. I will guarantee that together they will make a sum sufficient, or very nearly, to defray the expenses of the holiday that I recommend. So put the money in your pocket and follow me, and I will show you such value for it as shall satisfy you, or you are indeed hard to please.

You shall start from London Bridge, Betsy, and the baby, and yourself, while it is yet early in the fair and sunny Saturday afternoon—(you knock off at two o'clock, please to recollect); and taking train, shall enjoy, through two hours and a quarter, a swift and healthful journey through a lovely country of pasture, and hops, and growing grain, finally alighting in one of the prettiest and quaintest, and cleanest sea towns in the kingdom. Whilst yet in the railway carriage, and distant a mile of your destination, you shall know that you are approaching the sea by reason of its soft breezes coming out to welcome you, and leaving the flavour of their kisses on your lips; and stepping out at the station you will be at once for rushing down to the beach. This, however, would not be fair towards Betsy, who finds baby a tremendous drag at ordinary times, and now that its infantine appetite has been invigorated by the keen country air, its mother's distress must be something considerable. Besides, you have a lodging as well as a tea to seek. And with little or no trouble you shall find both—a tea ten times nicer and quite as cheap as can be procured at a close unclean London coffeeshop, and a bed the hangings and sheeting of which, on account of their snowiness, make Betsy hold her breath in awe and admiration.

After tea there yet remain to Saturday three fair hours of daylight. Then you shall fill your pipe and accompanied by your wife, go down to one of the most wonderful beaches to be found round the British coasts. This if the tide is out. If it is not you shall find delightful seats so close to the ocean that you may kick a stone into it, and there you may sit with the evening sun sparkling on the watery wilderness before you and on the few-and-far-between white sails of the yachts and black sails of the fishing-boats, and on the waves looking like white sea horses with their ample snowy manes all blown a-tangle racing for the shore; meanwhile you calmly smoke your pipe, and discourse to Betsy of the azure main and as many of its wonders as you are cognizant of.

Let us hope that the tide is out, however—far out, for then you shall see something that shall astonish you. You shall see protruding through the brown, fast-set sand, gnarled roots and mighty boles of treesJsnapped off short as you could snap a tobacco-pipe, and when you see this you see all that remains of what was once a great green forest skirting the sea; but one night, three hundred years ago and more, there arose a mighty tempest, and the sea put out its giant arms, and bursting its old boundary, captured the land on which the forest stood, and dredged it of its trees and shaped it to suit its will, and from that time to this would never let it go.

And you shall walk a little farther along the brown sands soft as any carpet, and presently you shall come on a broad space of heaped-up stones, each of a ton weight at least, and skirting the stones short butts of timber worn sharp as needles through constant wave-washing. And when you see this you see all that remains of a magnificent pier (the second or third) constructed at a vast expense by good Queen Elizabeth, and great was the pride and rejoicing of the townsmen. "But behold! when men were most secure, and thought the worke to be perpetual, on All Saints' Day, in 1597, appeared the mighty force of God, who with the finger of His hand, at one great and exceeding high spring tyde, with a south-east wind, overthrew the huge worke in less than an hower to the great terror and abasement of all beholders."

Walk still farther along this wonderful beach for the distance of about a mile, and you shall come on another marvel. Bedded in the brown sand there is a ship that foundered there a hundred years ago. You may count her ribs jutting out here and there like old teeth, and thereby tell her shape and length. It is only her upper works that have gone to decay; locked in the sea bed her under decks and her hold are sound enough, as was proved scarce forty years since, when aparty of adventurers, taking advantage of an uncommonly low tide, set manfully to work to dig the sand out of her. They dug down as far as the old ship's bows and fished out a barrel of knives and some other trifles, but the sea would stand no further trifling with her lawful treasure, and rising up with a will drove the daring landsmen off, and somehow since that time the experiment has not been renewed. There is a fortune for you, Mr. C, if you can hit on a means of raising that old Dutch ship; her hold is known to be full of sheet copper!

By the time you have explored this last wonder, and smoked out a pipe sitting on one of the buried ship's ribs, the tide will be rising, and you had better turn your face lodging-ward, or you will find no time to play " ducks and drakes," to which sport of your boyhood you will be irresistibly enticed by the thousands of handy little flat stones lying about the shore. The windows of the house where you are to lodge shall overlook the sea, and until deep dusk, in happier chat with Betsy than you recollect for many a day, and with a brown jug of simple ale, you shall there sit. Now you shall discover another odd fact in connection with this holiday. Dusk shall find you sleepy and inclined for bed. It is Saturday night, and were you in London bed would be out of the question for two hours to come at least, but here you shall have retired and be soundly and healthily asleep long before half-past ten of the clock. Your artificial Cockneyfied habits will not avail you in these parts. Nature has the great sea to look after, and cannot waste time pottering over you, and making as regards roosting, one law for you and another for cocks and hens.

You shall rise early next morning, which is Sunday morning, and while Betsy is busy over her own and baby's toilet, if you take my advice you will stroll down to the beach, and at the price of a couple of pots of beer avail yourself of one of the greatest luxuries in life— a sea bath. Then back to the enjoyment of a jolly country breakfast. Then for as delightful a walk as can be imagined— field, forest,-flowers, fruit, and sea all combining to make the scenery perfect. Then, if you have a mind., to church; to a lovely old church, tiny as a barn, and shapeless under its ivy mantle. Or if you choose you shall instead climb a huge cliff 400 feet high, and ramble over the ruins of one of the very oldest of English castles, so old that nobody knows who built it. It is a poor old tottering wreck now, and looks as though it was under considerable obligation to the green climbers whose tough limbs bind about its gray stones; but once, a thousand years ago about, it was a tremendous place, with a great army within its walls to resist the landing of any of Britain's foes that might design to attack us by way of the sea. Times are altered since then. Admission to the castle cost William Rufus the flower of his army; now you may get in for 3d., and in place of the whiz of cross-bolts the invader hears nothing more harmful than the popping of the corks of gingerbeer, which potent beverage is retailed by the old lady who keeps the gate at the rate of 2d. per bottle. Home to dinner, afterwards sauntering on the beach. Home to tea, afterwards sauntering on the beach, sitting about, lying about, picking up shells, hunting for star fish, for mussels, for whelks—anything till bed-time.

"And up in the morning, once more to walk, sit, and lounge upon the beach, I suppose/' says Mr. Candlestickmaker, with the least bit of a sneer disfiguring his manly countenance. Not exactly, Mr. C. If that were all I had to offer you I should not have been so pressing in my invitation for you to prolong your holiday till Monday. No; the best part of all is in store for you. Be up betimes, and you shall see the fishermen come home in their black boats and be witness to the sale of their night's catch. It is a strange sight for a Cockney who never saw fish except in a dish at home, or at the fishmonger's, or any other sort of fisherman but he of the rod and line at the New River's brink expending fourpen'orth of bait for a ha'porth of gudgeon.

Our fisherman himself is a being worth the journey to behold. He is a brown being—rusty, ruddy brown. His smock is of that colour, as are his heavy, baggy blanket trousers, and his great hairy hands and his long, odd-looking, weather-beaten face; his very hair is rusty, and his brown tarpaulin sou'-wester seems to have ripened in the sun like a pear. He is a slow man—slow of gait, slow of speech and deliberate, and meditative in his puffing out of tobacco smoke. His eyes have a solemn look about them as those of a man grown used to constantly impending peril and past fear of it.

But he can be brisk enough when briskness is required, as you shall witness, if you rise betimes and watch him manoeuvring his boat to the beach to get the first of the market. By his boat I mean the row boat that attends his smack. There are twenty such smacks standing off the shore, and the business of each is to land its catch with all speed, so as to secure a good sale. Frorn the smacks the fish is brought to the beach in baskets in the row boats, and then turned out in heaps—plaice, flounders, mackerel, eels, anything the sea may have yielded. The buyers for the town and for the London markets gather round the heaps, and the auctioneer is present. He is not a spruce, black-coated auctioneer like his brother of London, but a brown man like a fisherman, and dressed as such. He does not go about his business like a London auctioneer, but backwards. There are no biddings. Standing by a heap of fish on the shingle, cries the auctioneer, "Who'll give ten shillin' for this lot of plaice? Who'll give nine shillin'? Eight and six? Eight? Seven and six?" "Snaps!" somebody shouts, and that somebody is the buyer. (" Snaps" is the magic word that clinches every bargain.) And so with, all the heaps, one after another, and in an hour's time you may meet the fish-wives, and even the fishers themselves, in all parts of the town bawling their dabs, and their soles and their mackerel; which they carry in tubs or baskets, slung to a yoke, after the fashion of London milkmen.

You, however, must not go home empty handed to breakfast, Mr. C.— you must buy of the catchers a brace of fine mackerel bright from the briny, and have them instantly split and grilled with a little butter and pepper and salt. The worst of the treat is that your appetite for London mackerel is spoilt for ever afterwards.'

After breakfast

But exigency and space forbid. After breakfast you must find your way about without my guidance, Mr. Candlestick-maker. I am allowed but one more line, and that I will devote to giving you the name of the wonderful place in question—it is Hastings.

AN "ANTI-IDIOTIC-ENTERTAINMENT COMPANY."

COME time ago it was my melancholy duty to set before the reader an account of a visit paid to a metropolitan musichall. I gave specimens of the songs that were sung, and, to the best of my ability, portraits of the talented gentlemen who sang them. Since that time the working man, weary of hewing wood for his betters (and with no better prospect than six feet of elm planking as his final share), and of drawing water (going thirsty the while), has courageously demanded a reform of his estate, and with no small degree of success. It is his laudable resolve to have a finger in pies of his construction, an active finger for syrup and plums; the time has passed when he was content to sit patiently in the scullery, waiting for dish scrapings and broken bread from Dives' table. "We will have you to know," says the working man, "that we are intelligent creatures as yourselves, and insist on being treated as such."

And quite proper too. No one was more delighted than myself to hear the working man express this noble sentiment, and bearing it in mind the other evening as I chanced to be passing that same Grampian Music-hall visited last April, it occurred to me to drop in and see what degree of reform the working man had worked for himself in the way of his means of recreation. The result was that I came away more than ever impressed with the idea that of all companies of modem scheming, few would have a better chance of success than an Anti-Idiotic-Entertainment Company.

And I will tell you why, John Jones. I, too, am a working man—working away with my tiny steel tool and ink-bottle often and often when you are comfortably abed and asleep, John—and therefore I claim the privilege of speaking with you plainly as a brother toiler may. I would advocate an AntiIdiotic-Entertainment Company as a means of freeing you—us —from the tyranny of ignorant men who monopolise the control of your chief place of amusement, and the evil example of the snobs who make these places their nightly haunt, and who by their empty-pated applause of what is there to be heard and witnessed, delude you into the notion that it is all very fine and desirable. And let me beg of you not to misconstrue my meaning. You are fully able to judge for yourself what suits youj and are little likely to mistake French polish for real mahogany, or Cheap Jack ware for true Sheffield cutlery. But you are shy of speaking out your mind individually. You don't go to a music-hall to make a row; you go to enjoy yourself, to take the good with the bad, and float easily with the stream. "What suits one man's taste may not suit another," say you, out of your good nature, "and though I may dislike suclvand-such, why, it's quite evident that there are many about me that enjoy it very much. Just listen how they stamp and clap, and jingle their glasses! Why, I should be set down as a meddlesome jackass if I gave vent to what my feelings are on the subject; and after all, what do / know about music?"

It is just because that you and I, John, know little about music—because we place ourselves, as we are invited to, in the hands of the knowing ones who assume to cater for us—that we should be better treated. As for the glass-jingling and hand-clapping, don't you believe in it. Nine times out of ten it emanates not from your fellows, John, but from the meerschaumpipe-smoking, brandy-and-water-drinking numskulls, who toady the chairman, and crave the notice of Piping Jerry Sullivan, whose mail-phaeton, with the silver lamps, now awaits the pleasure of that Horizontal Hyena of Laughter for whose services all the music-hall keepers in London are outbidding each other.

You have a sound head on your shoulders, John, and allow me to tell you that in your heart of hearts you despise the contemptible fare commonly set before us at the music-hall as thoroughly do I. It is impossible that you can do otherwise. Let us together discuss a few choice morsels from the dainty dish.

Here comes funny Fred Molloy. At present he is one of the stars of the Grampian company, and you may read his name as such on fifty red and yellow placards in a walk of a mile. In the midst of an uproar of applause, Freddy approaches the footlights in the attire of a Bedlamite, with a set grin on his expressive countenance, and a dab of red paint on his nose, and makes his bow to the audience. All these celebrities have their "points," of which they are extremely jealous. Freddy's "point" is contained in a little bit of dirty rag with holes in it, and which he makes believe is a pocket-handkerchief, and withdraws from its receptacle with a flourish to blow his nose before he begins to sing. By mistake, however, he thrusts a thumb and fore finger through two holes in the rag, and applying them to his nose, blows on them—a disgusting trick, and one that would earn for him a kick in private society, but which sends the numskulls into hysterical laughter.

Then he commences to sing. He has no voice—none of these "Hyenas of Laughter" have; so his sole dependence is on the fun contained in the words of his song, and his droll manner of rendering it. Listen! His ditty is of a servant discovered at the enchantingly ludicrous occupation of chopping mince meat by the individual Freddy-represents. Freddy whistles her down the area, and the mince-meat chopper replies, "Don't be a fool, you fool; go away." But he will not go away, and annoys the young woman until she promises to meet him next Sunday. And she doesn't meet him, and then he discovers that she is in love with somebody else. That is the whole of the legend, and be sure there is not much in it, and, despite the irresistible way in which Freddy thrusts his tongue out, and bangs his hat about, the song would possibly fall flat were it not for its miraculously funny chorus:

"And her mince-meat knife went chop, chop, chop,
Chop, chop, choppetty chop—chop!"
in which the audience are invited and expected to join, Freddy giving them encouragement by a "Now, then—all together," and a stamp of his foot. And join in it they do, the imbeciles, as you may hear, John, with the frantic and approved emphasis on the final "chop" as Freddy demands. Just fancy, my friends, a company of rational beings being led by the nose to such idiocy by Funny Freddy Molloy.

Encore! encore! encore! Here he is again! This time he wears a white apron and sleeves, and announces in Catnach rhyme that his name is Sam and that he keeps a ham and beef shop, and that he used to be in love with a young woman, the daughter of a coal-dealer, but that unfortunately her parent got into difficulties and shut the shop up, and went abroad with his daughter. This was all, and set to a tune such as might be played on a Jew's harp; but the chorus! By Jove! it was better than the mince-meat knife:

"But now she is gone and left her Sam,
She has gone to Seringa-patam-atam-atam!"

What would you think of your eldest son, John, if at Christmas, or any other festive season, when called on, he should favour the company with this sort of thing? Why, he would be laughed out of countenance before he had got through with the second verse.

Encore! encore! and at least three rummers smashed by the enthusiastic numskulls, and once more Freddy appears. This time in private attire, and without the paint on this nose. He is no longer funny; he is moral and instructive, and no longer wipes his nose on a bit of rag, but on the whitest of white handkerchiefs. Pray do not mistake the benign expression of his countenance for a comic expression, and titter, or he will at once frown you down so low that you will remain prostrate through the remainder of the evening.

His theme is edifying as it is original. Of course, John, you were never before warned against despising a man because of his ragged coat; or enjoined to "love your neighbour as yourself;" or " to do a good turn when you can;" or "to return good for evil." Never since your grandmother's death, or before, were you made aware that "a friend in need is a friend indeed;" or that "wilful waste makes woful want;" or "that a stitch in time saves nine." It was left to Funny Freddy Molloy, with his nose still streaky of red paint, to raise the eyebrows of his comic-singing visage and smirk cantishly while he impresses you with his teaching. Eugh! Drive us mad with your "Patam-atam-atam," excruciate our feelings with your "Mince-meat knife," trundle over our common-sense like Juggernaut in your "Ugly Donkey Cart;" but for the sake of the time when you must—if you have enough of some sort of luck ——become an old man, probably used-up and forgotten, and with no more palatable butter for your crusts than your bitter reflections, don't trespass on the beat Mr. Chadband long since made his own.

Shall we stay any longer, Mr. Jones? We must, just a little while, for the stage is once more occupied. Not by Mr. Molloy this time, thank heaven! but by quite an undistinguished person, and his greeting is not overwhelmingly hearty. But listen to what he is singing, and in a sweet voice too. You are glad we stayed; and so am I, John; it is a treat at any time to hear f Sally in our Alley " well sung. Why don't that fellow leave off tinkling his glass? Why, because he's one of the numskulls, I suppose, John; and would much prefer "Slap Bang" to the touching old ballad now being sung. Ah! now you can clap your hands, Mr. Jones, and so can I, and so can all our fellows. You don't know much about music, you say; why, you've shown that you do. "Ay, ay, but *that* sort of song everybody relishes, you know."

"Encore! encore!" But the numskulls are silent, and Mr. Chairman announces,

"Billy Whiggles will sing the next song, ladies and gentlemen!"

"Come away, John. Billy Whiggles is as like Freddy Molloy as peas in a pod."

The fact is, John Jones, you have been so entirely giving your attention to what is your due as a working man, that you have quite neglected what are the rights of your leisure. Well, you know the power of your voice now, my friend. All you have to do is to cry " off," and Billy Whiggles is annihilated in a twinkling.

GUIDES TO THE TURF
T T cannot be too generally known that at the present season an alarming and shocking epidemic is threatening the metropolis. It is not a new affliction, being familiar to the public as "the betting nuisance." Fifteen years since it raged to such a terrible extent that the law was roused to action, and made desperate endeavours to mitigate, if it was not possible to eradicate, the evil by clearing out the hot-beds of the contagion known as "betting shops," and curing

their foul promoters and proprietors by sweating them on the treadmill and sousing them in prison baths, and holding them fast even after that until they provided substantial security that they would for the future shun their old ways of abomination.

For a time the snake was scotched, but by-and-by it crept out again—shyly, however, and not as a householder; being content to lurk about likely street-corners seeking whom it might devour—always with a watchful eye for the policeman on his beat. Finding that its resuscitation was either unheeded or observed and winked at, the nuisance grew bolder, and emerging from the slums of its birth, marched into the City, and boldly took its stand. The Fleet Street end of Farringdon Street appeared a promising spot. Passing to work in the morning or home in the evening, or going to or returning from This paper was written at the time when betting in the streets had be" come such a nuisance that it was found necessary to take prompt measures for the suppression of the vice, dinner, troops of rash and stupid young fellows—clerks, warehousemen and factory lads—came that way, and there can be little doubt that for some considerable time the betting man had a good time of it. It speedily became apparent that he did. On his first reappearance after his long seclusion, his presence was scarcely calculated to inspire confidence in the breast of his clients, and only the most insane infatuation for gambling on the part of the dupes that he angled for stood his friend. His clothes were lamentably shabby, his hat black and seedy and battered, but well brushed invariably, while his last week's shirt modestly retreated from view under the protecting lappet of his waistcoat, and the consolation of the blacking-brush was unequal to the task of inspiring his down-trodden high-lows with smartness. But lo! tended by kind fortune, these trifling infirmities were speedily remedied. The seedy black hat gave place to the jauntiest of white ones, the inconsolable boots to a pair all shiny leather and drab cloth, while a sportsmanlike pin sprouted out of the betting man's flashy neckscarf, and his watch chain was an article not to be weighed in the puny scales of a gold smith. His sudden good fortune intoxicated him, and he took to swagger and insolence. It was nothing to him that honest men required the pavement that he and his choice companions impeded by mobbing on it that they might the more conveniently compare and regulate the baits proper to catch flats with, and if by accident he was elbowed, he resented in bullying and bluster, and not unfrequently by threatening pugilistic consequences. This was his ruin; a repetition of this objectionable behaviour attracted the attention of the police, and the fiat went forth that the betting man was to move on. If he did not move on fast enough, he was shoved into the gutter, and if this did not expedite his movements, he was helped along to the station-house.

As may be readily imagined, such unceremonious treatment c aused not a little excitement amongst the fraternity of the little book and pencil. The British householder who reads this has probably had opportunity of observing how a horde of blackbeetles will scuttle away if in the night-time a light is suddenly brought to them. Just such a panic affected these human creatures. Deserting the corner of Farringdon Street, they fled across the road—the main body into Bride Court, and a few stragglers into the alleys leading to by-way taverns, from whence they emerged timorously, and snatched crumbs from the highway when the backs of the policemen were towards them. After a little while, however, the bull's-eye again flashed among them, and they emigrated in a body once more across the road and down Farringdon Street, until they came to a piece of waste land in the select neighbourhood of Field Lane and Saffron Hill, and this field they held for a year or more, until one fine morning, on coming to their hunting-ground, they discovered erected on it a board bearing the simple intimation that trespassers would be prosecuted; and there being no more waste land in the neighbourhood, to all appearance they "moved on " as the police directed, and congregated no more.

Only to appearance, however, as I recently discovered—the fact being that whereas the public at large has deemed these sharks and man-catchers defunct a year and more, they have all the time been alive and active, increasing as vermin will, and plying a roaring trade, with the full cognizance and under the eyes almost of the police.

In Farringdon Street there is a narrow, old-fashioned way known as Fleet Lane, and at the end of this, extending towards Snow Hill, is a public thoroughfare, flanked on one side by the arches of the Metropolitan Railway, and on the other by a hoarding that shuts in part of the ground on which the Fleet Prison formerly stood. It is not a capacious thoroughfare, being, if I may trust my memory, about twenty feet wide and a hundred and fifty yards long. It was about one o'clock in the day when I visited the pretty place, and that I may make no mistake as to the number of people there assembled, I will say simply that the said thoroughfare was crammed full, chiefly of gulls making bets and kites taking them. Regarding the motley mob from one end of the street, the spectacle was a curious one. On the paling side of the way, and extending the street's entire length, in a straight line almost, was a show of what at first sight appeared to be picture boards of the kind that in old-fashioned times were borne by catchpenny chanters of horrible domestic tragedies, the pictures being illustrative of such of the horrors as were most effective when depicted in vivid colours. A closer inspection, however, disclosed that these boards were only a handy means of publishing to the mob the terms on which the betting-men were willing to deal. To give the reader some idea of the extent of the betting business carried on in this alley, I may state that I counted these boards—each one having announcements of at least half a dozen races, with the names of the favourite horses and the odds that might be obtained against them—and they amounted to *sixty-three*. Every betting-man stood by his standard, and every standard had its bearer, generally a thin, ragged wretch, eager to earn twopence anyhow, and contrasting strangely with that tremendous swell, his master, with his flashy clothes and his golden ornaments, and his brazen face pitted all over with "rogue " as indelibly as though he had been afflicted with that disease in place of smallpox in his early boyhood, and had suffered a very bad attack indeed.

Whatever might be the difference in the published odds, one rule was universal, and appeared on the face of each rogue's bill of fare, and that was, "Under no circumstance whatever will a bet be booked unless the money is paid." Let not the innocent reader suppose, however, that this little arrangement involved the staking of any money by the betting-man. If he laid four to one that a horse did not win, he insisted on having the sovereign to hold until the race was decided, and all he gave in exchange was a ticket with a number on it, and the terms of the wager. Under any circumstances, therefore, he is sure of *your* money. You are quite at his mercy. If he finds it convenient to adhere to the conditions of his contract he will do so; if not, he will not, and there is no law in England that can compel him.

Nevertheless, he does a brisk trade. You see, his views as a man of business are not lofty. It is true that on many of the boards appears the intimation that no less a sum than two-andsixpence will be dealt with, but it is only reasonable to infer, therefore, that there are noble sportsmen of the alley who are more accommodating, and who will do eighteenpenny and even shilling business. And doubtless there is wisdom in fixing the scale so low, not a small trade being done with shop-boys, as one was bound to observe. It must be a poor boy indeed who, inclined to betting, has not eighteenpence; or who, having it not, cannot—somehow—raise it; especially when the odds are twenty to one, and that knowing prophet "Kestrel" of the *Penny Turf,* declares that that one must win. What *is* eighteenpence, or even half-a-crown? It isn't like a sum that one would miss—that *any one* would miss. One's master, for instance. Besides, it is not like stealing; it is only borrowing just for a few hours, and it can be put back, and no one the wiser. Of course, the flashy gentleman who so ostentatiously rattles the wealth contained in the natty wallet strapped to his side would be very much shocked if the bare possibility of a half-crown so obtained finding its way to him were suggested. They are all honest young fellows that deal with him; they must be, how otherwise could they be such constant customers? If he occasionally misses a familiar face, that is not surprising. The lads were lads of spirit, and have very likely made a fortune and retired.

Considering the number of persons engaged in the betting lane, the quiet that is preserved is somewhat astonishing. In this respect the betting men here found differ from their brethren of the Epsom and Ascot rings. There is no roaring and bawling out of the extraordinary odds that the self-sacrificing professional is willing to lay; no bewildering Babel of the names of a whole stampede of horses cried at the same time. The betting men of Fleet Lane have a more settled and steady business to pursue than your great race-roarers: their customers are of a different stamp. That may be perceived at a glance. There is no pell-mell rushing to "get on," as the racing cant goes; the great care is—and it is visible on the faces of nine-tenths of the shabby throng—how to invest the trifle so shamefully perverted from its proper use, how to lay out this crown or pound that shall be the last--the very last— if this run of infernal luck continues. Never was seen such a poverty-stricken, haggard lot of gamblers. Of course there were exceptions. Well-dressed men with more money than brains; slop-dressed swells of the barrow-driving order, who, through some lucky (!) stroke of betting, had placed themselves for a month or so above corduroy, and beer and bread and cheese; and not a few infatuated young men, evidently shopkeepers, and who, because they had proved their aptitude for making money by plain dealings in cheese and bacon, had grown to regard their good-fortune as invincible, and to be trusted to any extent, no matter how apparently daring. But the great majority of the Fleet Lane company was a miserablelooking crew enough. Journeymen printers and bakers and butchers (an astonishing number of butchers), and factory hands with cap and apron just as they hurried from the shop in their dinner hour to see whether the first favourite was still firm, or whether The Rake had advanced a point, or was it really true that The Hermit was scratched. Finding their fears dispelled, or perhaps their previous anticipations more than justified, then came the question, should they "put on" a little more—just a crown say? To be sure, they had not the money to spare, but the matter might be accommodated by the pledging of a watchchain, or that greatcoat that will lie useless till the winter. And there he stands in a maze of indecision staring hard at Mr. Marks's betting board until somebody comes bustling up, inquiring "What's the odds on Dragon?" "Ten to one." "I'll go a pound on it." "Phew! everybody is winning money on that horse!" says the dubious cabinetmaker, who has been pondering whether the watch-chain or the overcoat can be best spared to pawn. "Here goes for another crown anyhow." And straightway he pays down his money for an additional burden of anxiety and worry that, win or lose, must be bis for a week at least.

No doubt that amongst the shabby ones there are scores of unlucky wretches who have wagered themselves out of their shops and situations, out of their good coats and sound shoes —out of their minds almost. You may know them at a glance. Gaunt, hungry-eyed, wistful creatures without so much as a sixpence in their pockets, who come here day after day to wander over the treacherous marsh where six months ago they stumbled and sank in the betting bog, for ever beggared and stained by the disgraceful mire that sticks to them. It is hard to understand what they do here, or what satisfaction they, without as many halfpence as will make a jingle in their pockets, can find in listening to long odds and short odds, or in seeing gold and silver pass from Bob to Bill. But there was a stranger sight even than these poor bankrupts to be seen amongst the. betting mob—at least so it appeared to me. In the midst of the journeyman wagerers and the shop-boy wagerers, and the general tag-rag and bobtail, were two old ladies, decently dressed in black, both of them of sixty years old at least. There they were with a card of Bath Races between them, scanning the horses' names and the odds against them, with their wrinkled old brows contracted, and their toothless mouths pursed up as though their lives hung on some event there set forth. Despite these 'evidences that the old ladies were "horsey," I could hardly have believed it, until, being close enough, presently I heard the oldest of them exclaim, turning to a "knight of the standard," " I'll take the odds against Stewpan for the Nursery Stakes, Mr. Fiddler," and the bet being clinched, they went off hobnobbing and grinning, as though of opinion that they had the best of Mr. Fiddler this time, if they never had before.

THE LATEST DERBY PROPHECY.

Y dear unfortunate brother Jack-of-all-work-and-no-play, to-morrow morning we shall read in the newspapers that yesterday (to-day that is), the scene of the great national horse race was more than ever numerously attended—that all London and a greater part of the provinces assembled to grace and do honour to the joyous occasion. This is what the newspapers say invariably on the morning following Derby day; but you and I, Jack, as business men (alas!), know that this, if not all fudge, is so to the extent of seven-tenths at least. The stayat-homes may be counted in thousands and hundreds of thousands, hapless ones whom "all the Queen's horses and all the Queen's men" would be unequal to the task of tearing from the hum-drum wheel to which they are eternally bound. The next best thing to going to the fair is to listen to the wondrous account of some privileged being who has sniffed the aroma of lamp oil, whose blest ears have drank in the dulcet music of the gong, and whose favoured feet have tripped it amongst booth sawdust. I may therefore be doing not amiss if I endeavour to bring to the labour-fettered Turk the mountain that he may make no pilgrimage to.

My gossip shall take the form of a prophecy, and I will wager even money (not being of that greedy and grasping nature that hankers after odds) against any man's that in the main I am correct. There is no secret in it. I have no private information from the clerk of the course, nor have I the ear of "the stable mouse," or any other treacherous listener, fourlegged or two. Seeing the Derby is like seeing the Lord Mayor's show or a wedding—especially a wedding, that being a ceremony the terms of the performance of which are immutable, except as regards the names of the competitors about to start in the race of life. So is a Derby a Derby, last year, this year, next year, any year.

The first *bond fide* Derby arrivals from London make their appearance about the dusk of evening. They emerge in twos and threes from the road that leads to the metropolis—poor, limping, lame, and ragged ones, wearied nigh to fainting with their long tramp, and dusty, and oh! so hungry and thirsty. These are the hangers-on and pickers-up of crumbs that fall from the field of the cloth of gold, the humble servants and willing slaves of the rollicking well-to-do host that to-morrow will camp on the Downs. They, the tired and famished ones, bring with them their stock-in-trade, their cigar fuzees, their boot blackers and shiners, and their humble single brushes with which to "brush you down, sir," for a penny. They enter a flourishing town, these poor down-at-heel beggars; the shops are aglare with gas, and everybody is preparing something that may be sold to eat to-morrow. When you get past the town clock from the London end, it is like putting your head in at a kitchen door where a feast is preparing. The confectioners' windows are piled with buns as though a whole week of Good Fridays was before them; the interior of the regular eating-house-keepers' shops are invisible beyond mounds of boiled and'roast and pyramids of handy-sized pies; and even the humble wayside cottages are bold in their announcements of "hot water for tea parties," and the window boards, where customarily the sweet-smelling flower-pots stand, are now laden with loaves of bread and unpicturesque saveloys. The famished ones from London rejoice to see such abundance of cheap fare, and hurry to buy a supper with that painfully-reserved twopence halfpenny. But alas for them, poor beggars, racing prices have already begun; penny loaves have passed out of the knowledge of men, and saveloys are quoted at a hundred premium. But they must deal in the town as best they may; they have to go farther and may fare worse even. They have to go the length of that dreary, steep, chalky lane, that more than any other that ever was planned is like to that oft-quoted lane destitute of turning, and smuggle a bed under the hucksters' carts, or, failing this, stretch their travel-strained limbs on that sacred plain that to-morrow shall sprout guineas thick as buttercups. If any gentleman has his doubts about this all taking place, I will back my prophecy against his opinion for a "pony," or a whole horse, or a whole hog, or anything else he may fancy.

Likewise I will bet level that last night, long after the betting men lodging in the town had gone to their feverish beds, there emerged from a white house just outside the town—a pretty innocent-looking house—a carriage drawn by stout horses, and driven by a sturdy coachman. Within the vehicle are two able men at least, as had they need to be who guard a treasure. If anything happened to that chariot in its passage up the hill —and it is not impossible, for there are many thieves abroad in and about Epsom lo-night—to-morrow's Derby will be recorded as an imperfect Derby, by reason of its lacking the indispensable "c'rect card." The types from which the "c'rect cards" are printed are arranged in a secret chamber of the pretty white house, and are carried up to the Grand Stand, where there is a printing machine, and where, before four o'clock in the morning, cards by the thousand will be struck off, all ready for the ragged speculators who come at that early hour clamouring to buy them.

Again, I prophesy that at an early hour this morning, the theatre of what by-and-by will be all so rich, and gay, and sparkling, was as much like Bartlemy fair as bereft of its gangs and roaring showmen is possible. None of the "company" have as yet arrived—no, not one; but if you counted the multitude swarming in the vicinity of the race-course, you would find that they number a thousand at least—servants all of the legion by-and-by to arrive with lots of money to spend. There are the proprietors of refreshment booths and sparring booths, and booths for fiddling and dancing; there are the thimble-rig men and the Aunt Sally men, and the men who have tramped from London with a couple of pails, and who mean to drive a roaring trade as water vendors; and there are the "niggers," dozens and dozens of them, poor wretches, with yesterday's blacking mottling their sad faces, the straw in their towzled hair revealing the secret of their last night's bed; there are the clothes brushers, and the shoe blackers, and the hopeful merchants whose heart and hope is in the bundle they carry, enveloped in a dirty pocket-handkerchief, and comprising "noses and hair" for the wear of idiots, and absurd little dolls to stick in hat-band or button-hole, and gay garlands of coloured paper for the decoration of the brows of tipsy costermongers and their women. All these and many, many more, unwashed and shivering and hungry, throng about the jolly bright cans where the coffee was steaming, and where bread and butter might be purchased at a halfpenny a slice. I will wager, too, that, bustling in the throng—the busiest of the busy—there was a red-nosed old barber, with the tools of his craft stuck in his belt, and his hot-water pot mounted atop of a sort of tinker's brazier swinging in his hand, crying out, "Who'll be scraped! who'll be scraped for a brown!"

Neither do I find it more difficult to predicate that as the morning grows towards noon there will emerge from that long lane extending from the town to the Downs the vanguard, the prudent few who eschew uproar, and have an eye to a choice of situation from which to view the race—of the mighty host presently to follow. Then will the "Grand Stand," all spick and span, and showing white as a mushroom sprouting out of the green, wake to life the rapidly-filling galleries, dispelling the idea founded on a view of its gigantic emptiness that never by any possibility could it be completely occupied. There will be Mammon's acre, commonly known as the betting-ring, but which is no ring at all, but merely a straight slip railed in in front of the Grand Stand and abutting on to the course, show signs of animation that each succeeding" minute increases. They are not all members of the aristocracy who seek and gain admission to Mammon's acre, but, as a rule, vulgar journeymen bettors, who come to Epsom in the same business spirit that moves the grazier and the butcher to visit the cattle market. If you are in pursuit of gaiety and frivolity, seek it not on Mammon's acre; it is no more a holiday feature than the maggot that gnaws at the core of an apple is part of that fruit. No laughter, no mirthsome joking, nothing but grim and sour-mouthed chaffering, buy, buy—buying and bartering, and bargain-driving. Regard these throngers of the ring, and learn that " making a book" is no more a pastime than is balancing a ledger at a grocery store. It is hard work—work fitter to be performed in shirt sleeves than in dandy coats, as is evident from the copious perspiration that bedews the brow of every votary of the pencil and little book as he goes to and fro, elbowing and crushing his way through the mob, roaring out what he will bet and what he won't bet, and seeking whom he may devour. My dear brother, Jack-of-all-work, depend on it that you are safer at home. There is contagion in the breath of these roarers, the flourishing of the little book; the sheen of the leather satchell slung at the roarer's side is as fatal to the unwary one as the bird trapper's daze is to the lark, and nothing but having no money in your pocket can save you from falling to his lure. See now how the poor pigeons, excluded from the hawk's cage by that inexorable half-guinea entrance fee, swarm about the bars, and thrust between their little bets fast as the pretty birds within can gather them! But they are never satisfied; they take, take, take, and still, like young ravens, their beaks are agape, and they go on crying, "More! more! more!"

They will go on crying while the long lane extending to the town disgorges its troopers, and the vast hill over against the Stand grows thicker of men than corn stalks in a field; and all round about, and extending in a long, long line far as Tattenham Corner, which is a full quarter of a mile from the winningpost, are barouches, and drags, and coaches, and 'busses, and wagons, and carts, and costermongers' barrows in so compact a mass that it would not be a very severe acrobatic feat to skip from one to the other the whole length without once touching the ground. They will continue to roar, and cry, these men of. the ring, until the ringing of a bell. This signifies "clear the course." Up to this time, the sacred way has not been strictly guarded against intrusion. It is railed in on either side, but many have crept beneath the rails, and lie sprawling on the turf, happy to rest their wooden heads where the mighty hoofs of Vauban or the Marksman may presently tread. But now they must clear out, for at the ringing of the bell suddenly appears from the police barracks within the Grand Stand an army of policemen, who spread themselves across the course, and sweep all before them, wasting no words with trespassers, but hustling and squeezing them beyond the rails, head first or heels first, until the way is clear.

Then the roarers of the ring will cease their hubbub, for the first race is about to be decided. There will not be much excitement over this amongst the multitude. As a body it has but a rude appetite for horse racing, and views these little affairs as merely the fish and soup that precede the more substantial— the Derby, at which each and every one of its items intend to carve a stake, be it never so small a one; so, during this minor affair, the melody of the niggers is scarcely hushed, and may be distinctly heard the cracking of the bullets against the iron targets, there sped by daring riflemen, who shoot through a length of tin tubing, "for fear of hacksidents," as the prudent proprietor of the butts remarks. -The two preliminary and minor races disposed of, then approaches the Great Event. There will be a considerable lapse of time between the race for the Burgh Stakes and the Derby race, which will be made the most of by the men of the "ring." Since the last race they have remained for a few minutes quiet; but now they will begin again, gradually raising their voices until the Babel is deafening, but it will not be remarkable since the infection has spread all abroad through the line of carriages, and coaches, and 'busses, and barrows, and right away over the hill, and everybody is at the delirium of betting fever, and there is a universal shaking of hands that is worthy of a better cause. This amongst the novices, however; there is no shaking of hands with the betting men of business, black and white and a deposit on the nail being a system much preferred.

Then once more will the bell toll, louder and bolder this time, as if conscious of the tremendous affair it heralds; and again will the doughty A's charge the trespassers, and drive them back beyond the boundary. Then will be seen emerging from the neighbouring paddock, where the equine champions have been saddled, a long string of horses, gaily mounted by their jockies in butterfly suits. But although they enter the course it is not to race, but merely that their various patrons may see their paces as they perform a preliminary canter by way of warming to the work before them. There will be a general hum of admiration, and no wonder; for surely, as a grand sight, that of a troop of splendid horses, in the glory of their youth and strength, can scarcely be surpassed. Then they will be off and away to the other side of the hill, where a severe old gentleman, in a scarlet coat, awaits them to marshal them in proper order and give the momentous signal for the start; and all this time the roarers of the ring are hard at it, anxious to gobble up a few more verdant ones while there is yet time.

Time flies. Clang! clang! clang goes the bell as merrily as though it had a sure bet on the race, and ten thousand voices will exclaim " Now they're off!" and then there will be a silence. It will even seem that the tolling of the bell betokened the departed lives of the roarers, they will be so still. But lo! they revive again. On the dizzy summit of the Grand Stand an eager scout, spying through a glass, has caught sight of the striving team turning the bend of the horse-shoe course, and gives instant word of which is foremost, and the precious name will be caught and spread quick as ignited gunpowder. "It's Marksman! He walks in!" "No, no! It's Vauban! Ha, ha! Vauban, Vauban!" "Palmer! It's Palmer! by jingo, it's Palmer!" "No, no, Vauban!" "Marksman!" Van Amburgh!" "Vauban!" "Marksman! Ha, ha." "No, no!" "Yes, yes!" "Palmer!—Vau—Vauban"

Who on earth is to complete a prophecy in a satisfactory manner in the midst of such a clamour!

THE SOUTH COAST FISHERMAN.

S a nation it is not to be denied that the flesh-pot has for us Englishmen attractions superior to those of the fishkettle. Indeed, if we make item of the number of shops in London devoted to the sale of the finny tribe, and compare the result with the figures that go to show the number of establishments given over to the retailing of beeves and muttons, it will be found that our relative liking for fish and flesh is as nearly as possible on a par with that of Jack Falstaff for sack and bread. It would be a long way from fair, however, to measure the matter by this standard, and declare it settled. It is not the upper nor the middle classes who are the chief fish eaters amongst us. So to speak, it is not one fish in twenty that, as an article of diet, is promoted above the bottom round of the social ladder. Of course there are exceptions. The lofty salmon or the aristocratic turbot may disdain as their agent a person less respectable than a West-end Groves or a City Sweeting; but the honest plaice and the generous mackerel have no such absurd scruples. They are the fish of the poor—their meat, their bread; and as such are blest in their mighty increase. Nobody out of their own circle (except diligent inquirers, whose business it is) can form anything like an adequate idea of the tremendous importance of a plentiful supply of Billingsgate produce amongst the wretchedly poor. Let any person feeling an interest in the matter station himself as early as five o'clock in the morning in the neighbourhood of the Monument in Thames Street, and note who are the Billingsgatebound traders that come that way. For one tradesman's cart he will be able to count ten hand-barrows, piled with empty fish baskets and spangled with glittering fish-scales, propelled by lusty costermongers eager to secure good marketing. If there are fifty tons of fish in the market, not more than a fifth of that quantity will find purchasers amongst fishmongers of the shop-keeping class, the great bulk will be bought by the fishhawkers and street stall-keepers. It has always seemed to me that the subject offish in plenty does not meet with the consideration it demands, there always appearing an inclination to regard the produce of the sea rather as supplementary on our estimated food supply than as one of its prime pillars. The newspapers furnish us daily with the market price of butter, and bacon, and corn, and bread, and pork, and butchers' meat. We are enlightened as to how wool and tallow sells, and should jute or indigo grow dull, we are promptly apprized of the melancholy fact; but beyond some rare and brief notification to the effect that salmon is plentiful and lobsters scarce, the town is kept in utter ignorance of the doings of its busiest market of all.

Fish abounding at Billingsgate means for that day food, cheap, wholesome, and plentiful, for tens of thousands, who otherwise would go hungry or sparsely fed on what for their health's sake were better left untouched. The worst of it is that the market supply of fish is so very uncertain—as uncertain as the wind, in fact. No thrifty housekeeper of Poverty's regions dare say, " To-morrow we will have soles or plaice at dinner." With the scores of industrious hawkers of the commodity who wheel their barrows Billingsgate-ward, "Will there be fish to buy" is a riddle that may not be solved until the market is reached. There may be a "glut" as it is termed, or there may be a "clean market," leaving the disappointed barrow-man no alternative but to fag home again with his unladen vehicle. We who have a choice of flesh or fish can have but an inadequate idea of what this return of empty barrows portends. Over Cow Cross, and Bethnal Green, and St. Luke's, and Lower Lambeth, is spread a gloom that the brightest sun is impotent to dissipate, nor can it be wondered at when it is known that empty barrows is a term synonymous with "empty bellies." With sixpence in her hand, the mother of half-a dozen growing boys and girls— some of them out at work, and with a steadfast eye to that pivot of their round of labour, dinner-time—may purchase three or four, and not unfrequently five pounds of thoroughly fresh and wholesome fish, albeit a little coarse, and which with a few vegetables furnishes a nutritious meal, hot and comforting; but of how much use is poor mother's sixpence when dearth of fish compels her steps towards the butchers' or the "cag-mag" shops *(i.e.,* shops where heads, tripes, and such-like shamble offal is retailed) of Poverty Market? Not that she will be affrighted by the tremendously high prices that the butchers will demand for his goods. It is a fact, seemingly curious, but not at all so when the matter is fairly considered, that the causes which operate to double the price of butchers' meat in decent neighbourhoods have no effect on the dealings of the men of flesh whose odious shops crowd Brick Lane or Whitecross Street, except perhaps that it enables them to ticket their limp and bloodless joints and flinders of meat at a somewhat lower figure than in ordinary. They can afford so to do. Murrain among sheep flocks and plague amongst cattle mean fat fields for the harvesting of this class of butcher; but, alas! it means no better than death in the pot to poor mother above mentioned and her famished brood. Truly it would be a most excellent thing if something could be done to promote the catch of fish! Perhaps if the fish consumer and the fisherman were brought to have a more intimate knowledge of each other the matter would have a better chance of being considered.

"What does the fish-eater know of the fish-catcher?" As I ask myself the question I am indulging in a pipe of Bristol birdseye, and reclining on the deck of the fishing-smack "Happy Return," William Fludyer master. I am a privileged person. I have known William through calm and storm now approaching three weeks. I have put off to sea with him as the sun went down, and through the night watched the outcasting and indrawing of his nets; with him at midnight far out on the ocean I have drank tea out of a pint basin of yellow delf, and eaten of fish that may be said to have leapt from their briny home into Mr. Fludyer's frying-pan. I am quite at home on board the " Happy Return," and my host so little regards my presence, that he does not allow it in the least to interfere with his afternoon's employment of reseating a pair of heavy blanket trousers, his needle being a sail-needle, and his thread tarred twine.

"What does the fish-eater know of the fish-catcher?" I repeat to myself, regarding honest William Fludyer, with his brown-tanned suit and his brown-tanned face and hands, and his weather-worn sou'-wester slouched at an easy incline on the back of his gray head. "Here's better luck to-morrow," exclaims Joe Sprouts, condoling over a pot of beer with a brother barrow-man on a dearth of fish; but neither has a thought beyond Billingsgate. Just so with the poor fish consumer. With the bakehouse drudge he is quite familiar. He has drank with him, talked with him of the hardships of the trade to which he is bound. It is no news to him that the baker is toiling in his dusty den when other folks are abed and asleep. In all probability his circle of acquaintance embraces butchers' men, and brewers' and grocers' men; but concerning the man on whose energy and perseverance he is dependent for the very next comforting meal he shall eat, he is as ignorant as of the manners and customs of the Fans and Ashebas of savage Africa. And this despite that grand essential of modern civilization and advancement the railway, which makes of the hundred miles that parts our fishing town from Whitecross-street but a matter of three hours' journey. The consumer and the fish are brought closer together, but the consumer and the fisherman are as strange as they were a hundred years ago, which shows, if there were need to show it, that human skill and ingenuity are matters totally distinct from human kindness and sympathy, and that it is possible to attain high perfection as locomotive engineers, and yet remain but indifferent Christians—to transport from this port to that our precious carcasses and our worldly goods at the rate of fifty miles an hour, without advancing so much as a step towards that goal which, as no right-minded man for a moment doubts, should be the sole aim and desire of our existence.

The spectacle of William Fludyer (who by this time has set the finishing stitch in the stern of his unmentionables) leisurely busying himself about his little ship as she lies high and dry on the beach, is wonderfully refreshing to a London-worried, work-jaded mind. Not pungently refreshing, but soothingly so, as healthful sleep is. Marvellously alike are the individuals of the tribe of which William is a type. Similarity in breeding, feeding, and occupation may account for this peculiar family likeness in a considerable degree, but not entirely. Lying at rest in the shadow of the great cliffs, and at anchor off the shore, may be counted at least a hundred sail of fishing craft, little and big, and men of the Fludyer mould man them all. In height, in bulk, in the roundness and enormous breadth of shoulders, are the fishermen alike; in slow and solemn gait— even in the practice of walking, when ashore, with their hands closely locked behind them. Deliberate in speech and cautious in answering a question, one is a counterpart of the other, as well as in the childishly reliant expression of their eyes—oh! so very different from the painfully shrewd, suspicious eyes of poor men who battle for their bread in great cities. As a shore animal the fisherman is awkward, not to say clumsy. He is quite behind the times, and his distaste for modern fashion and social usage is unmistakable. He sticks to his own end of the town, which is known as the "fishing" end, and rarely ventures towards the quarters of the genteel inhabitants. When he does it is in company of a friend invariably (the voluminous nether garments of gray blanketing, and the berry-brown smocks of the slow pair, contrasting oddly with the spruce and dapper genteel ones), and they appear to wear a bewildered aspect, and to advance with hesitation and uncertainty, and with nervous glances to the right and left, as though but recently stranded on that foreign shore, and, being as yet not well assured of the pacific disposition of the inhabitants, prepared to take to their heels at the first alarming symptoms. He no more fits the town than the town fits him, but he is not a dolt for all that. In his own sphere he is a most excellent and worthy fellow, and with an amount of real virtue and manliness in him that we keen and polished blades of the town would do not amiss to emulate. One must know these fishermen to discover their many inestimable qualities—most commendable of all is their utter unselfishness. As they are alike in shape and build and feature, so might they be brothers of one family from the cheerful help they afford each other. It is good to see them at the getting off of a vessel in a rough sea such as prevailed just lately. For a week and more a sou'-west wind had blown, and such a surf beat the beach as made it perilous to attempt the launch of any one of the long line of craft that lay in shelter. At last, starved out, the crew of a mackerel smack resolved to run the risk, relying on the co-operation of their friends to set the smack afloat. Nor did their friends fail

them. Turning out of their huts, they swarmed down on to the strand in the heavy pelting rain, and tackling the craft with a will, opposed their united strength against the fiercely-breaking waves that over and over again carried her back. The men conquered at last, but not until half their number at least were drenched through and through, nor could they be otherwise when without hesitation they walked into the sea high as their waist and shoulders. I am glad to be able to mention that success crowned the efforts of the bold mackerel fishers. By dawn of next morning their smack was seen off the shore, and row-boats putting off to her (the sea was raging still, and she dare not approach the beach), mackerel to the number of *three thousand* vvere brought into the market as her catch. This astonishing instance of luck at once fired several other smack masters previously "of half a mind," and with the same amount of hazard and labour, and neighbourly help, they too were launched as their fortunate sister of the previous day had been; but, alas for the uncertainty of ventures by sea! All night the mackerel getters toiled, but come the morning the best news they had for the boatmen who put off eager to relieve them of their freight was that two of the boats had taken each but three score ten of fish, and the others none at all; the result of which was that the luckiest of the venturers received about ninepence a head for their pains.

My present purpose, however, is not to gossip of individual acts of daring and enterprise engaged in by my berry-brown friends, but to endeavour to give the reader some idea of the habits, ways, and means of the little-known fisherman, the faraway individual on whose pluck and perseverance Billingsgate Market depends for its daily replenishing, and tens of thousands of our London poor for their only meal of wholesome food.

Passing a cheap print-shop the other day, I there saw, amongst other pictorial fictions, one apropos of our present subject—to wit, a representation of "The Fisherman's Return." Therein was de-

picted a neat little cottage on the brow of a sloping beach, with roses and honeysuckle twining and climbing to the chimney pots, and a trim little garden in front containing every known and several unknown flowers, in full bloom; and at the end of the garden a bower. Standing on the beautifully hearth-stoned steps of the cottage was the handsomest of damsels, with her black hair in ringlets and a rose at her bosom; with winning smiles and outstretched arms she was welcoming her approaching fisherman husband, who, with curly whiskers and rosy cheeks, was seen gaily entering at the garden gate with a crimson net over his shoulder containing several very fine gold-fish—doubtless the catch of the preceding night, and intended for immediate cooking, that they might serve as a morning repast for the fisherman and his bride in the cosy bower before mentioned.

Truth compels me to declare, although with regret, that the said picture slightly exaggerates the domestic felicity of the common fisherman, who has no more idea of neatness and comfort as a house-dweller than a merman might have. Such as they are, the cottages and the huts are crowded higgledypiggledy amongst the tall black wooden edifices that serve as store-houses for sails and cordage, and the various craft that are there drawn up high and dry for repair. They are by no means sightly specimens of architecture. Some are shabby little hovels, as much under as above ground, and with three steps down into them; others are more imposing in their hideousness, being three stories high—one story piled above the other in the most reckless and tumble-down fashion, with a street door for the basement lodgers, and a ladder with a rope rail for the convenience of those who live above. All the huts and hovels are of wood, which, as a rule, is pitched over, but occasionally painted red or blue, while as much as may be seen of the interior of the fisherman's home is scarcely calculated favourably to impress the observer as regards the thrift and tidiness of fishermen's wives. The prevailing odour of fish is rank and abominable, and is in some degree accounted for by the fact that, decorating almost every window and doorway, are suspended from threads, as London children at play may be seen to suspend pea-shells, various tiny fish of the "dab " and flounder breed. So dried they serve as a cheap relish with bread or potatoes, or are sold in the streets by the children at the rate of a penny a score. Ill-drained, ill-ventilated, and smoky, the fisher's village is not a pretty place, and it is a relief to thread one's way through the alleys the stranded craft make and return to the clear broad beach, and the pleasant spectacle of the fishermen overhauling their seemingly endless nets, piling them in great brown heaps, or spreading them to dry, or busy as bees squatting in a ring mending rents and tears, and "taking up " dropped meshes.

The fishing craft affecting this coast mainly consists of two kinds—mackerel boats and " trawlers," the latter being much more numerous than the former. The mackerel smacks are neater-looking vessels than the trawlers, and larger, their tonnage varying from fourteen to twenty tons, while the carrying powers of the trawler average about ten tons. The difference between a mackerel smack and a trawler is that the one plies only for the particular fish from which it derives its name, and the other accepts all fish that approaches its nets, which, in their capacity, are vastly inferior to those of the mackerel getters. Plaice and soles form the staple of the trawler's catch; but not unfrequently in the mixed collection that is shot down on to the beach before the "auctioneer" may be seen gurnet, and whiting, and sea bream, and all manner of flat fish, from dabs to mighty turbot. The mackerel boats seldom commence operations until they are ten or twelve miles from the shore, deep water making no difference with them, since their nets, "paid out" over the vessel's side, are held suspended at a proper depth by a sufficient number of cork floats about the size of a breakfast saucer; the trawler is compelled to fish in shallower water, since he drags the floor of the ocean for his game. Forming a sort of collar, at the mouth of the net is a heavy cable called the ground cable, and this drags the oozy bottom and rouses the flat fish there reposing and drives them into the meshes of the great bag-like net. Moon light nights are unfavourable for fishing; a clear, dark night, with a moderate breeze blowing, is the best time.

A trawler carries usually three men and a boy, and a mackerel smack from four to six men, according to her tonnage and the season of the year. The magnitude of the nets of the latter, however, and the serious pecuniary loss involved in their miscarriage, forbid a mackerel boat putting to sea shorthanded. Considering the constant peril that attaches to fishing and the moderate gains of its not invariably successful pursuit, it is astonishing how much is hazarded in the tools of the craft. An ordinary mackerel boat carries net measuring twelve hundred fathoms, or over a *mile and a quarter* in length, and about sixteen feet in width—sufficient to shroud the shop windows on one side of the way from Charing Cross to Temple Bar. Such a net would be worth at least a hundred pounds, and besides this the rope and cordage necessary to its proper management cannot be bought for less than fifty pounds more.

Every fishing vessel, with few exceptions, is worked on the "share" system. Say it is a mackerel boat. The master or captain is seldom the proprietor, that person being generally some chandler or retired shipper, residing in the town. He provides the smack and fishing gear, *minus* the nets, and for that he charges one share. Say there are a thousand fathoms of net aboard, and the owner provides five hundred; for these he claims five more shares—a contribution of each hundred fathoms of net entitling the lender to one share. As a rule the captain has nets of his own to lend the boat, and if the complement cannot so be made up, there are always outsiders willing to loan nets on the recognized terms. Let us say that the boat carries a thousand fathoms of net of somebody's; there go ten shares, and the owner's share makes eleven. Then the master and his crew are entitled each to a share for their services, which probably brings up the number of shares against the ship's earnings to sixteen. Let us suppose, then, that after a night's fishing the smack returns to land with a catch of five hundred mackerel—which may be set down as rather over than under the average take—and that the auction price realized for the same when the fish are turned out on the beach is thirteen shillings per hundred. This shows three pounds five for the night's work; but this sum will be further reduced by fully fifteen shillings when the cost of the men's food, &c., and the boat's insurance is settled for, leaving fifty shillings to be divided into sixteen parts, which will give three and threepence per share; and every working fisherman having but one share allotted to him as an equivalent for his services in the venture, three and threepence is all his wages for a long night's labour out at sea. The master, with two hundred fathoms of net to lend, takes ten shillings for his night's work, and the owner gets the lion's share. Property in fishing vessels cannot be so bad a speculation in these hard times. Should the smack be lost, the " club" into which the insurance money is paid reimburses the owner to the extent of one-half his loss —the insurance money, as has already been shown, being paid, not out of the owner's individual profits, but out of the gross stock before a division takes place. Moreover, the crew get nothing for keeping the owner's nets in repair, and it is seldom that in overhauling a mile and a quarter of the tender meshes a few ugly rents are not discovered, providing ample afternoon employment for the crew after they have, in a few hours, slept off the fatigue of the previous night. It must be borne in mind, moreover, that about three and threepence per venture is the average earnings of the mackerel fisherman *when he is at work,* but sometimes he lies idle, owing to rough winds, or, what is to him equally disastrous, no winds at all for days together, and at these times he earns nothing. As an example of this, I may quote the case of my friend William Fludyer, a sea captain in a small way. "Now, what do you reckon your weekly earnings to be, take the year through?" I inquired of him one day, Mrs. Fludyer being present. "Hey! all the year through? or'nary times and other? Well, I should say—mind ye, I don't know 'zactly—but I should say not much over a pound, hey, old lass?" Mrs. Fludyer deigned no verbal response, but looking up from her occupation of flaying whiting, she gave her William a look that plainly expressed her distrust of his arithmetic.

"But that to me seems very little," I remarked.

"It wouldn't be as much as he says if it wasn't for the bit o' net, sir," observed Mrs. Fludyer; "there's lots of the chaps hereabout that don't earn much more'n half."

"Ah, and with four or five youngsters," put in Mr. Fludyer, who had none.

"But how do they contrive to live?"

"Lor' a mussy knows, master," returned William Fludyer, radiant, and as though he derived immense satisfaction from his inability to explain away the seeming mystery. "Lor" a mussy knows; they *do* live, and grow up to strapping chaps and wenches. It's the sea air, I s'pose."

"Don't be a heathen, William," remonstratively exclaimed Mrs. Fludyer, who possessed a pair of arms brawnier than, though perhaps of not so stringy a texture as her husband's; "he don't mean it, only he's sort o' shamed to say."

"Well, it's summat as upholds 'em, or else they wouldn't be upheld; thou'st no 'casion to pick me up'so sha-arp, old lass," returned William, looking an apology at his "missus."

And it may be here remarked that, untaught as they are, the fishermen as a body, as regards abstinence from swearing and all improper language, as well as in observance of the Sabbath day, furnish an example that might be advantageously followed by dwellers in cities. Perfect is the repose that reigns at the fishing end of the town on the seventh day. It must be confessed that the last-mentioned excellent practice has superstition for one of its pillars. "We do no manner of work on Sundays," said Mr. Fludyer, "if we can possibly help it. It ain't found to answer, besides not being right. It's just what the Bible says—everything wants a rest o' Sundays. We do, the sea do, the fishes do. You go a-stirring up the water Sundays and week-days alike, and you'll pretty soon find what it will come to. The nets want a rest, and they'll have it, else they'll go rotten." It may have been my duty to have pointed out to the benighted fisherman that his belief was altogether monstrous and absurd, and exerted myself to convince him that he had mistaken his Bible, or misconstrued somebody else's reading of it; but where would have been the profit? Already he was possessed of the grain, albeit in the husk, and all that I might have preached would not have enriched him, while it might have made him uncomfortable.

I discovered to my satisfaction that the sea has more terrors for those who live a hundred miles away from it than for the men who pass the greater part of their lives on it and fish their daily bread out of it. "It's safer than the shore, that's *my* opinion," pronounced Mr. Fludyer, when questioned on the subject, "though, mind you, I never downright liked it, or, rather, as I may say, it don't like me. I was fourteen when I was 'prenticed to it, and you'd hardly believe, sir, that through eight years I never once put to sea without being sick; hey, arn't that true, missus T "Ay, sir, that it is," responded Mrs. Fludyer; "many and many's the time I've seen him retch and shudder at smell of his great boots as he was pulling 'em on before he went down to boat." "Well, well, I'm not the only one, I'll go bail," said Mr. Fludyer, seemingly not best pleased by the fulness of his wife's revelation; "what I was going to say is this, that though I never took what one might call kind to the sea, I thought then, and now I'm downright sure, that it's safer being there than ashore." "I'd be glad to hear how you make that out," I remarked. "I'll tell you how I make it out, sir. I have been a fisherman now three-andthirty years, and never got a hurt; and how many landsmen of my age can say as much?" "Never got a scar, you mean, William," interposed Mrs. Fludyer; "bless the man, he's had hurts enough." "How?" Mr. Fludyer asked, innocently. "Why, how many times have you been washed overboard?" "Pooh! how many times have you washed up plates and dishes, old lass?" returned Mr. Fludyer, impatient that his good lady should think such trifles worth mentioning. "And twice you was run into and foundered!" pursued Mrs. Fludyer. "That hurt the owner a blarmed sight more'n it hurt me," chuckled he. "And once the lightning struck you, sure-/y you don't forget *that,* William!" "And didn't it strike the markethouse ashore here same night?" retorted William; "didn't it rive the big pollard same night up here on old Wheeler's land? Didn't it kill the miller's horse same night as it stood in its stable? Don't tell me, old lass. It's three to one more dangerous ashore than at sea. I wonder you like to talk the other way after t'other night."-" That was accident." "Accident! yes! one of your shore accidents that was. Never had such a fright, sir, all the years I've been at sea. Tell you how it was. I'd been out three nights, and was glad to get ashore and lay me down abed for an hour or so. Old lass she goes to market. 'Don't you touch they things a-drying round the fire,' says she; 'they won't hurt till I come back.' I just heerd her say it, and that was all, I was so dead set. Well, I falls off, and presently got a kind of dream into my head that I was being drowned, and had to fight for my life if I wanted to save it, and so I woke choking and throwing up my arms, and there was the room full of smoke, and a blarmed old flannel petticoat hanging before the fire, all a-glowing red, and the chair smouldering down to its stumps. Wasn't that a 'scape? Pooh! Don't talk to me about the perils o' the sea." *THE DAY AFTER THE FAIR.* TT was the very last thing expected. The two acres of land, parted from the respectable and orderly highway only by a low fence, was bounded on three sides of its square by the garden walls of certain villa residences, in the occupancy chiefly of the families of men of City business, away from home during the greater part of the day. They are dwarf walls these. A tall man might rest his elbows on the top of any one of them, and any man or boy so evilly disposed might scale them in a twinkling. But nobody went in fear of anything of the sort happening. The piece of land before mentioned, ordinarily used as pasture for dairy cattle, was the property of old Mr. Wiggins, whose detestation for tramps and trespassers was well known, and who had set up on his land a notice that was no make-believe, to the effect that any one caught invading the privacy of his premises would forthwith be handed over to the police, and treated with the utmost severity of the law. It was a pleasant look-out from the back windows across the garden and over the meadow, and such was the sense of security that grew out of long immunity from persecution, that peaches were planted to flower and bear fruit against the walls, and not unfrequently the family linen was left out through a summer night to bleach on the grass plot.

One day a short time since, however, poor old Wiggins went mad. It is rumoured that he has been seen about since, look ing and acting as sanely as ever, but it is to be feared that this is but a treacherous retiring of his malady, and that presently he will break out worse than ever. At all events, if he is sane now, he was mad last Wednesday three weeks; and this according to his own showing. On the day in question a fiend in corduroy and brown leather gaiters, and wearing a closefitting hairy cap upon his head, made bold to wait on Wiggins as on his own land he was peacefully slicing mangold wurzel for the cows, and without preamble demanded to be informed of the sum that Mr. Wiggins would take to grant permission for a horse circus to be erected for the space of one month on this his meadow. It has been suggested that the fiend disguised in corduroy must have been a mesmerist, or a man who had extensive dealings in serpents of fascinating gaze; how else could it have transpired that Wiggins, instead of at once warning the tempter off his ground listened to him, and named the modest sum of twelve pounds as that which would induce him to concede what the fiend required.

Anyhow, he did concede, and straightway the little meadow, instead of being an advantage and a refreshing sight for the wives and the maid-servants and the little children of the surrounding houses with the low walls, became a theatre compared with which a bear garden is paradise. Within five-and-twenty yards of where good mothers and innocent children lived and slept, uproar and blackguardism, and all manner of sin and nastiness, held high revelry during one whole week. Gongs banged, drums beat, trumpets brayed, showmen roared and incessantly shouted "Hi! hi!" ruffians "larked" with any females they met, and shrieks of alarm or obscene laughter was the result; the steam-engines that propelled the gigantic merry-gorounds snorted and yelled through their steam whistles all in the stench and glare of the fierce naphtha lights, which were only eclipsed by sudden and frequent bursts of blue fire, and yellow and red and green, that now and again lit up the infernal scene. Woe for the low walls and the neat gardens where the choice flowers grew! Woe for any and everything portable, even down to so small a thing as a shoescraper, or a houseflannel, or a clothes-prop, or a hank of line left without the locked and bolted doors of the pretty villa garden! There is no class of ruffians so unscrupulous as that which attends fairs. The gipsy unadulterated is bad enough, but when he goes to a Whitechapel school, and on his ingrain cunning and foxiness grafts the sneakiness and meanness of the depraved Cockney, he becomes a delightful creature indeed.

However, the fair is now at an end, and the peaceful occupiers of the pretty houses with the low garden walls may recover from their fright and repair the damage they have suffered.

Quick march is not now the rule of the day amongst fair folks. In the old time, if a three days' fair commenced on the Monday, by Thursday morning not a vestige of it would remain; nay, hours before daylight the long string of caravans might be met on the road bound for new hunting-grounds. But now there is no demand for such expedition. At least a third of the ancient chartered fairs have been struck off the roll, while the laws regulating the letting of land for the temporary purpose of showmen and travelling theatricals have been made, if not stringent enough, at least sufficiently so to render it a matter of no little difficulty to secure an eligible "pitch," as it is called. The consequence is that when they do secure a pitch they make the most of it, working early and late, and exerting themselves to the utmost to keep the game alive, and not scrupling to resort for that purpose to manoeuvres that in the old times of legitimacy would have been regarded even by these worthies as undignified. The fair being brought to an end, however, there ensues a period of relaxation and rest, lasting nearly the whole of the day following, an example of which was here to be witnessed.

It is one of the oddest sights imaginable this "day after" on a modern fairground, and quite enough to cool the ardour of the most enthusiastic fair-goer, and to prove a terrible shock to the juvenile believer in wizards, and learned pigs, and Indian chiefs, and giantesses. No more of make-believe, and screens, and mystery; no more of masks, and tinsel, and romance. Here is the Cherokee savage, who last night appeared before a horror-stricken audience with his wrists manacled for safety's sake, showing his man-eating teeth, and rolling his terrible eyes as though nothing would afford him greater pleasure than to seize that blood-stained tomahawk with which, as his keeper declares, he has slaughtered "'ole tribes of his enemies out on the distant praries of his natif country," and exercise his sanguinary propensities on the multitude. Here he squats, a man of peace, on an upturned tub, smoking a short pipe, and driving hob-nails into the heels of his old boots. Here, too, is the giantess, that wonderful female who, if there is any truth in the painted canvas that yesterday hung before the wooden house on wheels that she inhabits, has been presented to the crowned heads of Europe, the Prince of Wales being so smitten by her charms that as he gazes on her he is compelled to still the beating of his bounding heart by resolutely plunging his hand in at the bosom of his waistcoat; while the more sceptica Emperor of the French, doubting if so much loveliness can be real, is depicted indenting the thick part of her arm with the tip of his forefinger—here is the giantess, nothing more than an inordinately fat and dirty middle-aged draggle-tail, frying bacon over a fire made in a hole in the ground, while her husband, the cockshy man, is busy, with a pot of colour and a house-painter's brush, "touching up" her fair portrait, the blaze of the naphtha lamp having the night before scorched her splendid waist.

Here, too, is Signor Diabolo, the wizard. Since Monday last, and up to the preceding evening, he was invisible to mortal gaze, under a fee of threepence—an awful person, in a black velvet cap, with a funereal plume, and a blood-coloured tunic spangled with jewels to such an extent that he appeared in the dim light as though the fire he was so constantly in the habit of breathing had at last burnt its way through him, and he must presently burst out into violent flames. What could not the wizard accomplish! He could discover gold-fish all leaping alive in any gentleman's hat. He could turn pennies into halfcrowns, and *vice versa,* in the twinkling of an eye; he could take an empty ginger-beer bottle, give it a shake, and, lo! it was instantly filled with sherry wine—at least, so he called it, and no little boy invited to taste it ventured to contradict him. Well, here was the wizard, as vulgar-looking a mortal as ever drove a donkey, in his shirt-sleeves, and a very dirty shirt too, blackguarding his next-door neighbour in anything but supernatural terms, because that the stock-in-trade of the latter—to wit, a learned pig—had surreptitiously entered his dwelling, and stolen and devoured two fresh herrings that the magician had set aside for his dinner.

Here was Fitzrashus Buckingham, the eminent tragedian, and the man who killed live rats with his teeth, and the ventriloquist, forming an harmonious group about the pot-boy with his cans from the nearest public-house, tossing for pints of beer; and here, too, was Mrs. Fitzrashus, desisting from her washing that she might spank the fairy (with whom every small boy in the neighbourhood who had seen her dancing in her gauze frock and diadem and wings had fallen madly in love) because that, being sent on a mission for a pennyworth of treacle, she had generously permitted several of her young friends she had met on the road to dip their fingers into the jar. And, speaking of children, here was one I should like to have kidnapped on the spot, and conveyed straight to my good friends in Great Ormond Street. This was the unlucky little boy whose only claim to be an article suitable for exhibition was that, owing to malformation, or illusage, his poor head had attained a size that was enormous. There was a painting of the "loosus natur," as he was called, outside the caravan, representing the sufferer, his head bearing about the same proportion to his body as a turnipradish to its tail; but, although this was a gross exaggeration, his appearance was monstrous enough to satisfy the craving of the most morbid appetite. There he sat, poor little chap, at the door of the van, with his mites of legs dangling over the steps, and his great head wearily rested against the door panel, and his baby face looking as old and pale and careworn as that of the very poor mother of a very large family. What was he thinking of, I wonder? Perhaps of the dinner he hungered for, and was by no means likely to get. Perhaps of his last beating about that poor head of his. Why not? Dwarfs are plied with gin to make them dwarfish, and the same principle would here apply: the size of the child's head is his master's capital, and is he the sort of man to stick at increasing his capital when it may be effected by a mere rap of his knuckles, as one may say? Poor little victim! one felt it to be nothing short of mean and unmanly to pass on and leave him.

And now let me say a word concerning an especially odious feature of modern fairing. Although a day after the fair proper, as its termination was doubtful a great many sightseers found their way to the spot to wander amongst the dismantled booths and shows, and gaze curiously at the grimy machinery now unmasked that made the hobby horses spin round so wonderfully, and at the horses themselves bereft of their flowing manes and tails, and looking very bald and ashamed, ranged against the wall, ready for packing. Moreover, there was something else to occupy their attention if they were so inclined, and this was the gambling, or, more properly speaking, the swindling and cheating openly indulged in by dozens of rascals whose proper place was a gaol.

It really is incredible how these things go on. There are laws against it. It is as much a part of a policeman's duty to protect the public from the depredations of a card-sharper or other rogue, with a pretty plan for fleecing foolish people of their money, as from those of the common pickpocket. It is known, moreover—and day by day fresh evidence to that effect is brought forward—that the vice of gambling is on the increase, and it is admitted that the most severe means should be adopted to check the abomination; nevertheless, the trade flourishes. It flourishes constantly amongst the betting scamps of Fleet Lane, at races, at processions, at any gathering of the people. It flourished at this little fair of ours to an alarming extent, and that within a dozen yards of the police on duty. Not one of the ancient dodges for swindling a dupe out of half-a-crown was there unrepresented. There was the gentlemen with the "little pea," and "prick the garter," and roulette, and dice, and cards. This last-mentioned phase of the vice was predominant. Without exaggeration there were fully ten of the card rascals down on their knees with the three cards, and loudly proclaiming their willingness to lay any gent "from arf-a-crown to a suvrin that they didn't find the little gentleman." Strange to say every cheat succeeded in drawing a mob of silly young fellows to listen to him, and not at all strange to say every cardsharper was attended by a gang of those detestable scoundrels known by the fraternity as "jollies," fellows who pretend to be strangers and win money, and who incite the unwary to profit by their example. And really, although to cheat as a rule is plain as ABC, now and then the villains work their game with wonderful ingenuity. I was witness to an instance of this. Hovering about the skirts of one of those cardsharping groups was apparently a highly indignant old gentleman, who could not control his impatience at seeing honest people done out of their money. He audibly alluded to the gang as swindlers and daylight robbers, and warned the bystanders to beware of them. So incensed grew one of the jollies presently that after threatening that he would do so, he knocked the old gentleman's hat over his eyes. "I don't care," exclaimed the moral old fellow, " I won't stand by and see people robbed, not if you knock my head off. You've got one half-crown out of him (a green young carpenter), and you shan't get any more if I can help it. " "Any gent arf-a-crown or a suvrin," continued the worker of the cards, shuffling them to and fro. Here the old gentleman hastily elbowed his way to the young carpenter and whispered in his ear, and at the same time holding up his hand and commanding the sharper to let the cards lie as they were. "What for?" asked the sharper. "Because if you do I'll bet you a pound I pick up the Knave of Clubs—he said that he'd lay a pound, didn't he?—(this to the bystanders)—I'll lay you a pound: two if you like. " "One's enough to lose," grumbled the sharper. "Well, one then." "You might let the carpenter go halves," suggested a voice. "So he shall," exclaimed the kind old gentleman generously; "give me your ten shillings, my friend, and win ten by it, and then take my advice and be off, and never bet on cards any more." And the young carpenter straightway eagerly pulled out his ten shillings and gave them to the kind old gentleman, who staked it with ten of his own, and—lost, of course.

I don't know whether the carpenter took the old gentleman's advice, and never bet on cards again, but I am sure that his unfortunate loss did not daunt the old gentleman, for half an hour afterwards I discovered him repeating his act of generosity towards a guileless young butcher.

A WEST-END CHOLERA STRONGHOLD AST Tuesday I looked in at a dirty public-house in Hare Street. There never were such roaring times for a poor neighbourhood publican. He is never the poorer for a cholera visitation, for, although his trade in beer at such periods is lamentably injured, it has always been the fashion to recommend brandy as an anti-choleraic, and under the management of the knowing proprietor of the Pig and Whistle a quartern of brandy sold may be made to yield as much profit as four retailed pots of beer, and so the matter was as nearly as possible equalised. But with this season's visitation of the scourge a new fashion in drinks has been introduced. "The safest and simplest drink during the prevalence of the epidemic is a mild compound of good rum and pure water, taken in moderation," is the formula promulgated by certain well-meaning M.D.s, furnishing a hint not likely to be thrown away, either on the landlord of the Pig and Whistle or his dram-drinking customers, who, so long as they are permitted to guzzle until they are drunk, are quite indifferent as to the means employed. So I found matters at the dirty tavern in Hare Street. An atmosphere foul of reeking sawdust and rank tobacco, and goodness knows what besides, filled the place, and the limited space before the bar was occupied by draggletail women, and shambling, slouching, fishy-eyed men, chiefly of the coarsest labouring and costermonger order, and at least seven-tenths of them were This paper was written during the last visitation of this terrible epidemic. indulging in the "safe and simple" drinks prescribed by the doctors. They were, however, taking the rum neat—a departure from the prescription, excusable, perhaps, on the ground that it was impossible in such a locality to find pure water to mix with it. Likewise, they were taking it immoderately, as the thick cluster of pewter measures and glasses on the counter went to show. But if such a vague term as "moderation" is given for construing to such folks, what better may be expected? I may consider a glass of beer a moderate quantity to be taken at dinner, while the ballast-getter of Radcliffe will take a quart of Tourpenny with his mid-day meal, and another quart afterwards to wet his pipe, and still remain sober enough to refute any allegation that may be made as to his immoderation.

If the maritime superstition that whistling a tune will at certain times provoke the rising of a storm might be applied to all other plagues, it would have been no wonder if the one under discussion had risen and confronted the noisy squalid group there assembled. A puncheon of "fine old vatted rum" was under-labelled in great chalk letters "Cholera mixture!" there was a placard of the Local Board of Health suspended from the same hooks that upheld a flaming show-board concerning somebody's famous " old torn," while another board concerning the advantage of becoming a member of the Hearts of Elm Burial Club was ominously ticketed *"Now'syour time."* Cholera was the one prevailing topic. It was solemnly discussed by the pimplefaced, double-chinned landlady and her barmaid, as the former, with a great dish on her broad lap, was engaged in sorting mulberries for a pie for supper; it was chattered about and wept about by the draggletail women whose relatives very possibly had helped to swell the registrar's last week's terrible "returns;" it was argued by the men with grave sippings of the "mixture" and knowing nods and winks, and noisy talk, and flourishing of dirty pipe-stems, as though it had been a mere Chartist question.

"What I ses is this," exclaimed the noisiest ruffian of the company, as he emptied his half quartern glass and passed the back of his dirty hand across his still dirtier and unshaven mouth; "What I ses is this, we've got it hotter in these parts than anywhere else, and why is it? Why, cos it ain't like a district where nobs and swells lives; we're all factories, and breweries, and manufactories, and the rich uns what belongs to 'em hooks it away at evenings, and goes away to Peckham and them airy parts. What do they care about the smells and that so long as they pulls in the a'pence? We're nothink but a great large muck-bed what they grows their musharooms on— that's what we are. If they had to live here amongst us, with their kids and their missuses it would be werry soon altered. Look at the West-end, *they* ain't had no cholery. Oh dear, no; and what's the reason on it? Ask Belgravy, and Great Wictoria Street, and them slap up parts; *that's* what's the reason on it."

If "that's the reason on it," said I to myself, I am very glad Of it, since it is significant of the fact that all those hideous slums that once disfigured and endangered the district between Westminster Abbey and Pimlico have been routed and destroyed. Peter Street no longer exists there, nor Tufton Street, nor Strutton Ground, nor Old Pye Street, nor that most foul and disgusting of thoroughfares, St. Anne Street. The parochial guardians of the West-end were wise in time. It is gratifying to find at least some few exceptions to the bungling batch. I must go and see these mighty improvements, and how they have covered the old ground. And shortly afterwards I went.;

Alas! it is my melancholy duty to inform you, Mr. Frenchpolisher, or Bird-fancier, or whatever you were, that you are altogether mistaken when you suppose that the immunity from cholera enjoyed by the inhabitants of the West-end is due to the destruction of the old hot-beds of disease above enumerated. I have been there to see. Alighting at Great Smith Street, I found my way to Peter Street, the filthy and thief haunted, and there were Cook's Court, and Leg Court, and Shepherd's Place, and the Laundry Yard, exactly as of old, except that nearly all of them wore a false front of white-wash that would scarcely bear scratching with the nail without betraying the hideousness beneath. The faith of those whose business it is to look to such matters in whitewash is wonderful. I met a man and his labourer emerging from an alley, the one with a ladder and the other with a great empty pail and a brush. "What have you been doing down there*?*" I asked. "Polishing of 'em up a bit, sir," said he with a satisfied air; "limewashed 'em back and front." "But how about the insides?" said I; "how about the rotten floors and the leaky roofs? Pray have you done anything as regards the water-closet accommodation, have you enlarged the little cistern that supplies the vast number of people that live up here with water?" "How could I, sir? You can't do all that with lime-wash." "Put surely you have other remedies for these things besides limewash?" "Oh, yes, sir; there's Condy's fluid, and there's chloride of lime; no fear of anything breaking out while you let us have enough of that sort of thing."

No fear of the mad dog biting while you muzzle him and hold him down by the throat, but you can't be always holding him down; or even if you had the time and the patience how foolish it would be to do so, when by a few vigorous blows the ferocious brute might be put an end to and no more difficulty over the matter. Cholera is this mad dog that periodically makes its appearance amongst us worrying and ravaging; but we don't shoot it or knock it on the head; we pat it and coax it to lie down, and after it has grown weary of running a-muck, and probably bitten to death several kindly hands engaged in its pacification, it consents to curl down to sleep—till dog-days come again.

That the mad dog has not at present extended its ravages to the west-end of the town is little short of miraculous, and would really favour the idea that there is a degree of dirt and nastiness nauseating even to cholera itself. Take Old Pye Street, with its foul kennels, its tumble-down houses, and its swarms of unclean inhabitants teeming at the windows and doorways. It used to be said that, like Fryingpan Alley, Bluegate Fields, and a few other choice parts of the metropolis, Old Pye Street was a place into which after nightfall no single policeman dare venture, and looking in at its mouth at broad noon it would not be astonishing if the same condition of things still existed. There is no mistaking the haunts of thieves and desperadoes. The inhabitants, or rather the male portion of them, never seem *at home.* During the day-time business is naturally fiat with them, and after they have slept off the fatigues of the preceding night they lounge about and amuse themselves till it is time to go to work again; but, though they remain at their own doors, chaffing or horse-playing with their mates and females, it is never in dishabille. Middle-aged thieves, young prigs, and that prevalent specimen of the order, the hulking, lanky big boy thief—they are coated and capped and booted like firemen on duty at a station, never knowing one minute from another when they may be wanted.

Explore crooked, filthy St. Anne Street, and wonder not so much that it is spared as why it should be. Talk of Bethnal Green, talk of Club Row, and Hare Street, and the courts and alleys to be found in these thoroughfares, there is not one so shocking in its dirt and squalor as St. Anne Street—which is within a couple of stones' throw of Westminster Abbey and the Houses of Parliament. What the water supply of this locality is I cannot say, but judging from the terribly dirty condition of the children, I should be inclined to doubt its abundance. To call them "dirty" children, and then to leave the matter, would be to convey a very inadequate idea of their deplorable appearance. You, my dear madam, may have seen children in a state you would properly stigmatise as disgracefully dirty because their hair was dishevelled and their face in a condition of grubbiness, but I question if you can imagine the standard the dirtiest child in St. Anne Street attains. You would scarcely take it to be a child at all. Its hair is thickly matted, and overhangs its weak eyes; it has no more clothing than a ragged little petticoat and frock, which are filthy to look at as its skin, which is saying a great deal. But the most remarkable parts of its person are its feet and legs;

they are blacker than a negro's. For Heaven knows how long a time—since the warm weather set in, probably, and admitted of such a luxury —has it waded in the inky kennels, and the sun has baked on its feet the matter adhering, and it has waded again, and the baking process has been repeated, until its toes are webbed with dried mire, and there it rolls and gambols with half-adozen of its fellows over the muddy stones in front of the houses in a worse plight than a little pig in a sty. In St Anne Street, as though mocking its beastliness, there is a tremendous building, belonging to a baths and wash-house company; but almost opposite to it, by way of balance, there is a dust-yard, with the usual collection of filth and garbage, and old men and women squatting up to their waists in dustbin produce, while they sift and overhaul it; and in the said dust-yard there is a cow-shed, where something like a dozen cows are bred and fed, and supply prime new milk to the hale and ailing of the neighbourhood.

There are many places in the neighbourhood more or less like Old Pye Street and St. Anne Street, not forgetting Leg Court, the Laundry Yard, and Elizabeth Buildings—all containing houses with the same absurdly lime-washed faces, and all in reality foul and stinking as ever. That they have no back yards at all at some of these places is evident, for there were to be seen—it was Saturday, the washing day of the deeply poverty-stricken—several girls and women, with their tubs and pails out in the street, dabbing out their poor rags, to be presently suspended on brooms and props from the windows above for drying.

The worst feature of all, however, and it was to be seen in whatever direction one looked, were the swarms of half-naked, shockingly dirty children. It was the worst feature, and the most painful, because it meant so very, very much. And that I was not the first one to discover this it was my great good fortune presently to be made aware.

In Peter Street, getting towards Tufton Street, there is a quietlooking house in a row with the others. It has a shop, but the windows are now partially whitened, and nothing now is sold there. On the door is a notification that this is the infant nursery, all information concerning which may be obtained on ringing the bell.

I rang the bell, and a decent-looking woman answered, and in reply to my inquiry, civilly informed me that the matron was from home, but that I was very welcome to look over the establishment. The shop and parlour appeared to be used as a sort of office and living rooms in one. The young woman took me upstairs to the first-floor, where one of the oddest sights it was ever my lot to witness immediately met my view. In the front room, which is a large room, there is a space in the middle railed round like a miniature horse circus, the rail being about eighteen inches high, a netting of string extending from it to the floor. Spread within this ring was first a wool mattress, then an indiarubber sheet, and over all a warm woollen rug. This was where the babies, the tiny things from a month old up to toddling size, disported, and there they were disporting—happy and contented, seemingly, as birds in a nest.

Toddling about the room, which was plentifully furnished with comfortable little chairs, were several other little children, all with clean faces and well-brushed hair, and all wearing an ample pink pinafore with the sleeves tied up with a bit of blue ribbon. There were toys to play with, and pictures on the walls, and a swing, and a magnificent rocking-chair, presented by some kind patron; and somehow the decent little women in charge of them had such a capital way of managing them that they were all as merry as grigs, and in the best of humours one towards the other.

Out of this room you came to one even prettier, for here ranged along the walls were tiny iron cots with white sheets and feather pillows; and this is where the youngsters tired of play were laid to rest of afternoons. There was one so resting now, with an elephant out of Noah's Ark in his chubby hand.

The civil young woman took me a little higher in the house, and showed me a lead flat securely railed in, and on one side of which were growing some blooming scarlet-runners. This was the babies' playground.

She took me to another room which was the bath-room, and the water-closets were here too, but without the very faintest evil smell, a fact accounted for, probably, by the existence of a capacious cistern, as large as many in the neighbourhood, that had to do duty for an alley of twenty houses. And when I had seen all that was to be seen the civil young woman told me what it all meant.

Five years ago some kind ladies in the neighbourhood, pitying the shocking condition of the little children such as I have endeavoured to describe, and knowing that the mischief arose chiefly out of the circumstance of their mothers being compelled to be out at work from morning till night, laid their heads together and opened this babies' home. They undertook the charge of little children from a month old and upwards from seven in the morning till eight at night, to feed, tend, nurse, and wash them for the sum of *threepence* per day. And ever since they stuck to the good work, with what blessed result who can tell? The average attendance of children at the nursery I am informed is twenty; they have received as many as thirty; and, without doubt, the greater part of these, had they not been snatched from it, would have been shockheaded, black-legged, gutter grovellers, like the poor little wretches to be seen all round about.

I have reason to believe that the good ladies who started and persevered in this noble work would do more if they had the means, for it need not be told that threepence a day per subject does not pay expenses or nearly. It is not only the food that has to be bought. These pink pinafores, for instance, were provided that the babies might appear uniformly decent; and the feather pillows for the tired little heads were not procured without money. On public grounds this tiny institution has a claim on public charity, especially at this season; for who knows how much its exertions

MR. BUMBLE AND HIS ENEMY "THE CASUAL."

TAKING a tour through the world we live in, bounded eastward by Lombard Street, where our place of business is, and northward by Highgate "Villa, where we reside, and contemplating the manners and customs of the inhabitants— consisting chiefly of the wife of our bosom and our children, and our maid and man servant—we rejoice to find the condition of mankind so fair and promising, and all that certain writers are in the habit of avowing as to our social advancement so beautifully true. To be sure, occasionally our ears are shocked by the noise of complaining, nay, of downright growling and the howling of despair, out in the wilderness that lies beyond the boundaries of our world; but such sounds only betray the existence of unconscionable mortals such as ever did and ever will do their wicked best to disturb us in our child-like confidence in the wisdom and justice of an all-seeing Providence. "No more than others we deserve." We acknowledge our unworthiness, humbly and unreservedly, while, at the same time, we submit with becoming resignation to the enjoyment of our undeservings

It would be a happy change if all manner of people would in this respect do as we do. We would not exclude the beggar who comes tapping at our door, or even the miserable one who lies down at the workhouse gate, and so consigns his manhood and his long-cherished self-respect—long-cherished, but finally starved to death—to the grave. It would be an excellent thing if all such persons would take to heart the teachings of that sweet little hymn, and indulge in the frequent ejaculation of that most comforting line of all, "no more than others I deserve." If they only knew the amount of cheerfulness and content the practice would ensure them, decidedly they would adopt it. Why should they not? Surely if we paying sixty pounds a year rent and taxes have no objection to, nay, find a pleasure in the lowly confession, they should not be so prideful and stubborn as to refuse. If it did them no good it could not possibly do them harm, and, like common politeness, its exercise would cost nothing. No more than others do we deserve a fine coat of broadcloth, and a feather-bed to lie on, and a handsome mahogany table on which to spread our dinner of fish and flesh and fowl—it would be monstrous, and enough to call down a judgment on our head if we asserted otherwise, yet, somehow, we have them. A fact that naturally tends to the increase of our child like confidence in Providence and inclines us to take things, including the fine coat and the roast meat and the rich gravy, as we find them; and moreover, to keep them: for it becomes a grave question, when our blindness to discover what really *are* our deservings is made so manifest to us—it becomes a question we should do well to ponder—whether we are justified, for the sake of gratifying our generous whims—but another term for vanities—in bestowing our goods on outcast wretches plainly branded as beings who deserve, and consequently get so much less than we get.

If these are not our sentiments, the teachings of the British Bumble have been lost on us. Ever since he was installed in office has he regarded with curious dislike certain of the subjects confided to his rule. He has no objection to the "inmates" of his brick palace, the boarders and lodgers in perpetuity. Their government is his pleasurable business, and every hour provides a something to stir anew the proud emotions that naturally belong to a man born to command and with ample opportunity for exercising this privilege. For the regular recipient of his "out-door" bounty Bumble has no great affection, but it is for the casual—the dregs of poverty that come with the Act of Parliament in their hands, as it were, and rap with it authoritatively at his gate for admission. The casual, in Bumble's eyes, is an abominable thing, an irritating nuisance, a sty on the parochial optic. The first law of nature with Bumble is Settlement, and the casual is its exact antithesis, and not content with being so, never so happy as when he can contrive to bring his disturbing influence—confound him!—to bear against what is settled and comfortable. You can no more catch and confine him and pin him down than you can perform the same operation on the foul vapour that comes belching up from a sewer grating. Worse than all, the casual —no matter what shape he assumes—has not the slightest respect for Bumble. The ruffian casual laughs at him, and sings funny and oftentimes libellous songs concerning him as he breaks stones or picks oakum. The to-be-pitied casual, the unfortunate fellow driven to workhouse shelter for the night by a noble desire to keep life and soul together just a little longer, he despises Bumble and regards him wrathfully, as well he may, for the beadle is furiously blind and knows no distinction of casuals, treating them one and all as a pack of lazy, dirty, and unwholesome scoundrels loathsome to the eye and contagious to the touch, and fit only for the treadmill and the hulks.

Now this is the great mistake, a mistake disastrous as it is pig-headed and unreasonable. Without doubt, and as I out of my experience can testify, the scoundrelly element is not wanting in the casual ward.

Take the number of applicants for temporary workhouse shelter at sixty, in all probability at least half of that number will be worthless wretches, cadgers by birth and breeding, and with habits and minds as foul as the rags that hang about their bodies, and possessed of a devilish desire to contaminate and drag to their own bestial level every human creature that mischance throws in their way. Nor is it easy to point out how this may be avoided. If you keep open door for outcasts it is scarcely to be expected that the worser part will, out of tender consideration for the better, consent to stay out all night in the wind and rain. To be idle and dissolute is not to merit death by rheumatism or starvation. There will be sheep—black, white, and gray—in the outcast flock, and it is impossible to stand at the ward door with a stick and thrust back all whose appearance is objectionable. Without doubt the black sheep are excessively tiresome customers for Bumble to cater for; there can be no question that it is annoying in the extreme to have the laws and regulations of the house laughed at and set at defiance by a band of such desperadoes; but if this is bad for Mr. Bumble, what, in heaven's name, is it for the decent outcast, the man whose poverty is none of his own seeking, who would avoid it if it were possible, and who is urged to ask workhouse charity, having no choice between that and lying out on the street pavement? Such a one accepting the asylum offered him is a wronged and outraged man. It is the law of the land, that for the relief of urgent poverty, and as a loophole of escape against such temptation as may beset a hunger-baited man wandering the streets at night, every parish shall provide a place where shelter and a meal may be obtained on application; but what sort of humanity is it to invite a poor benighted wretch out of the highway lest his necessity make him a thief, and then thrust him into worse company than he would encounter if he *had* turned thief, and was caught and sentenced to prison? It is as though, in pretended compassion for a man lame of a limb, you carried him to a hospital and laid him for cure amongst patients stricken with deadly fever. As before remarked, it is difficult to point out a way of amendment for this evil, but since it must be endured it is scarcely too much to expect from Bumble, who fails in his duty, albeit unavoidably, some amount of patience and discrimination.

That he is lamentably deficient of both has been long apparent. Doubtless he means well, poor man. As often as he is taken to task by the public press he responds in some way or other. Either he sulks or he whines, or he bullies or he begs. He is for ever patching and botching and making alterations, and pulling down and building up, so that nobody can say but that he is a busy man. It is as though he flew to muddle to escape from his perplexities and responsibilities as other foolish men fly to strong drink. Previous moves of Mr. Bumble in this line have been magnificent, but the most recent, and that which has provoked this letter, outvies them all. He has gone muddle-mad at last.

He has hit on a grand scheme, the purport of which is nothing less than to abolish workhouse casuals utterly. He has consulted with his brethren, and they have laid their cocked hats together, and declared the scheme feasible, and joined hands and taken solemn oaths to stand or fall by it. The most curious part of the business is, that they have somehow contrived to win over to their cause several metropolitan magistrates, and so aided and abetted they are doing a tremendous stroke of business. The mainspring of Bumble's scheme for casual abolition is extremely simple, and an example of its working will at once make its efficacy apparent.

"At the Thames Police-court fourteen casual paupers were charged with neglecting to perform the task of work assigned to them in return for a supper, night's lodging, and breakfast. The workhouse superintendent explained that three of the prisoners were called on to pick two pounds of oakum each, This paper appeared about four years since. The same "regulations," however, are still in force. —J. G.
and some others to break each two bushels of stones, and they were allowed four hours in which to execute the task; but not one of them did the whole of the work. One man picked eight ounces of oakum and said that he could do no more, and one picked twelve ounces. The others broke only a portion of their bushels of stones. All the persons pleaded that they could not do the work, to which they were not accustomed. *Mr. Benson sentenced them to a fortnight's imprisonment, and to be kept to hard labour*"

Now, let us in the first place consider the terms on which a starved, broken-down, houseless man (for he is the "casual" proper, be it understood) enters the workhouse doors. He is not admitted as a beggar, but as a poor man wanting a job of work so badly that he is willing to accept one of the parish; and no Jew sweater drives a harder bargain than does Mr. Bumble. I have the report of a model workhouse before me, and' I see that the two meals contracted for consist of twelve ounces of bread and one quart of gruel. At the present baker's price the bread should be worth threepence, and any one who has tasted workhouse gruel can have no hesitation in believing that it may be manufactured for a penny a quart at a handsome profit. Twopence is the outside value of the sort of lodging that the casual gets, and there we have the total of the casual's gettings—sixpence! For this *four hours'* labour is exacted. Because the destitute labourer is so very pinched, and needy, and helpless, Mr. Bumble finds him employment at the rate of three-halfpence an hour! It is nothing to the purpose to say that the picking of two pounds of oakum is worth no more than sixpence; possibly it is not, but that is an affair for the consideration of the taskmasters. It is four hours' labour anyhow—hard, tedious, disgraceful labour. Mr. Bumble having advanced to the poor roan goods of the value of sixpence, claims of him the forepart of the next day, and then turns him into the street hungry, and with scarcely the ghost of a chance of picking up a job, for the jobs are all picked up before afternoon.

He is turned out, that is to say, provided he has executed the work demanded of him. He is "allowed" four hours to pick his oakum in, and be he ever so willing a man, should he lose his race against time, no excuse will avail him—he must pack to prison. Can anything be more monstrous or unjust? It is all very well for the taskmaster to tell the magistrate that two pounds of oakum may be easily picked by the most inexperienced person in even so little as three hours (this would make it *twopence* an hour); but this statement I deny. Any prison warder will tell you that the shredding of hard tarred rope is a business of knack, and not of sturdy perseverance—that an experienced prisoner will do more of the work in one hour than a novice in six. The consequence is so palpable that it need hardly be pointed out; it is on the novice at oakum picking, the tender-fingered worn-out tailor, the decayed clerk, or worker at a trade requiring mental rather than muscular exertions, that the full weight of Mr. Bumble's whip falls; these are the men whose only crime is poverty, who are sent to prison, while the Dodger and his friends, to whom oakum picking comes ever so much easier than ABC, complete their task at their leisure, and obtain their liberty in time to pilfer a dinner.

If this course is persisted in, what the ultimate result will be requires no Daniel to foretell. For fear of the pains and penalties impending, the inexperienced oakum-picker will shun the casual ward. Finding himself hungry and in desperate strait, the outcast not as yet criminal may be driven to reflect: "If I seek refuge in the workhouse for a night I shall possibly be unable to perform the task set me, and then I shall be sent to prison; there is no escape for me. But supposing that I do not seek workhouse shelter? Supposing that I make a bold dash and steal the value of a pound? Then there is a chance for me; and if I fail, why it is only the prison after all." In this way Mr. Bumble will possibly be enabled to shirk some of his casual responsibility, but he will not escape scot free. He will not scare away these dexterous-handed ones the Dodger and his friends. They can perform the oakum trick with ease, and without doubt will continue to avail themselves, to the exclusion of all decent and deserving folk, of the accommodation afforded by the casual ward.

Lightning Source UK Ltd.
Milton Keynes UK
UKOW05f0625031215

263953UK00017B/381/P